Understanding How Women Vote

Understanding How Women Vote

Gender Identity and Political Choices

Kelly L. Winfrey

Gender Matters in U.S. Politics
Juliet A. Williams, Series Editor

 PRAEGER™

An Imprint of ABC-CLIO, LLC
Santa Barbara, California • Denver, Colorado

Library of Congress Cataloging in Publication Control Number: 2018028187

ISBN: 978-1-4408-4030-2 (print)
       978-1-4408-4031-9 (ebook)

23 22 21 20 19   1 2 3 4 5

This book is also available as an eBook.

Praeger
An Imprint of ABC-CLIO, LLC

ABC-CLIO, LLC
130 Cremona Drive, P.O. Box 1911
Santa Barbara, California 93116-1911
www.abc-clio.com

This book is printed on acid-free paper ∞
Manufactured in the United States of America

Contents

Series Foreword

From the nearly century-long campaign for women's suffrage to ongoing contestation over reproductive rights, to 2012 presidential candidate Mitt Romney's meme-worthy claim to have "binders full of women," politics has been a central staging ground in the United States for debates about gender. The 2016 presidential campaign was no exception. For the first time in the nation's history, a woman received a major party nomination to head the ticket as candidate for president. As it happens, the Republican Party nominee also served as a lightning rod for discussions of gender issues, particularly in the days following revelations of his vulgar boasting about the sexual assault of women. The eventual outcome of the 2016 presidential election took many experts by surprise, revealing that many observers had badly misjudged how women would cast their votes. In the end, the 2016 campaign season confirmed not just the ongoing centrality of gender in the U.S. politics but also that we still have a long way to go in understanding *how* gender matters—to each of us as individuals and as members of a shared polity.

The *Gender Matters in U.S. Politics* series pushes the boundaries of existing research on gender and politics. Traditionally, political scientists have engaged the subject of gender primarily by looking at differences in the way men and women behave—as voters, candidates, leaders, policymakers, activists, and citizens. Today, there is growing recognition—within the field of political science and beyond—of the critical need to think more broadly, and more deeply, about gender. Across the social sciences, researchers now recognize that gender is not only an individual attribute but also a "socially constructed stratification system" that plays a central role in determining an individual's place in the social order.[1] At the same time, scholars are bringing a more intersectional perspective to the study of gender in recognition of the influence of race, sexuality, and other axes of social difference on gender identity and gender politics.[2] These new ways of conceptualizing gender have far-reaching implications for political scientists with interests in topics ranging from electoral behavior to social movement mobilization to media and politics.

The books in this series address a wide array of topics—from conservative women pundits to political cartoons—to demonstrate the far-reaching, and sometimes quite unexpected, ways that gender is mobilized in contemporary political discourse. Some authors bring new insight to the study of gender in familiar settings, such as grassroots political campaigning. Others take a closer look at gender politics in less-well-studied contexts, like media coverage of political sex scandals, thereby reminding us that politics doesn't stay neatly within the boundaries of official institutions. And while some books in this series highlight the persistence of gender inequalities, others draw attention to the distinctive ways women's political roles have changed in the wake of second-wave political activism and legal reforms, as well as technological advances that have given new forms of voice and visibility to historically marginalized groups.

Finally, while the terms "women and politics" and "gender and politics" have, in the past, sometimes been used synonymously, the authors in this series emphasize that gender impacts the lives of women *and* men. The books presented in this series are intended to inform, engage, and inspire our readers to think in new ways about issues of deep importance to all of us. In making clearly written, empirically grounded, and thoughtfully argued research available to interested audiences, this series aims to spark conversation and produce new understanding.

—Juliet A. Williams
Department of Gender Studies, UCLA

CHAPTER 1

The Gender Gap throughout History

On October 21, 2012, about two weeks before the 2012 presidential election, political predictions expert Nate Silver wrote in his blog, *FiveThirtyEight*, "If only men voted, Mr. Obama would be biding his time until a crushing defeat at the hands of Mitt Romney, who might win by a similar margin to the one Ronald Reagan realized over Jimmy Carter in 1980."[1] Silver went on to correctly predict the largest gender gap in history, with women deciding the election for Obama. If more men than women had voted in 2012, Mr. Romney would have become President Romney. However, as with every election since 1980, that was not the case. Nearly 10 million more women than men voted in 2012, and they overwhelmingly supported Obama. The 2012 election serves as a prime example of the power of women voters, and that power has only grown over the last three decades.

The so-called women's vote and gender gap have been frequent topics of discussion for media, political pundits, and candidates since the 1980 presidential election. The gender gap refers to the differences in the number of women and men who support a candidate or political party. The 1980 election between Ronald Reagan and Jimmy Carter was notable because it marked the beginning of the modern gender gap in vote choice and party affiliation. The gender gap in 1980 was eight points, with 54 percent of men and only 46 percent of women voting for Reagan. While some gender differences in vote choice and policy preferences existed prior to 1980, this election marked the emergence of a clear and consistent gender gap with women tending to prefer the Democratic candidate.

The gender gap is more than an interesting topic of discussion for media and pundits; it has a significant effect on election outcomes. Women vote in higher numbers and proportions than men, and in many recent elections, women have been more likely to be swing voters. Campaigns and news media often focus on a specific subset of women voters as the most persuadable or most likely to have the greatest impact on the outcome of the election. The subgroup has varied over time; there have been soccer moms, security moms, *Sex and the City* voters, Beyoncé voters, and Walmart moms, just to name a few. This chapter explores the gender gap and women voters' influence on election outcomes, media coverage, and political campaign strategies.

WOMEN VOTERS: THE BEGINNING

Women gained the right to vote in 1920, after a nearly century-long battle to win that right. Led by Elizabeth Cady Stanton and Susan B. Anthony, suffragettes first argued that women deserved the right to vote because they were equal to men, and a few states began granting voting rights to women prior to 1900, with Wyoming being the first (1890) followed by Colorado (1893), Utah (1896), and Idaho (1896).

However, the argument that women and men were equal did not gain much traction nationally, so by the early 20th century, suffragettes tried a different strategy and argued that women deserved the right to vote because they were different from men. They claimed that women's unique roles in the domestic sphere gave them important insights into politics that men could not offer, and this argument gained more traction. As president of the National American Woman Suffrage Association, Carrie Chapman Catt implemented what she titled a "Winning Plan" for women's suffrage.[2] The plan included a unified push from state and local suffrage organizations across the country to gain acceptance and support at the local and national levels.

Finally, on August 26, 1920, the Nineteenth Amendment to the Constitution was ratified, and women across the country were able to vote in the 1920 election. Despite the long struggle to gain voting rights, relatively few women turned out to vote in the 1920 election.[3] Estimates put women's turnout at about 50 percent and men's at about 75 percent. Estimates of the number of women voters from 1920 to 1964 indicate a slow but steady increase. The 1964 election was the first time the Census Bureau tracked national voter turnout by sex; at this time, 67 percent of women and 71.9 percent of men voted. From 1964 to 1974, men made up a larger portion of voters, but that gap closed with each election.

Prior to the 1980 election, women tended to align with Republicans. From 1952 to 1964, women were more likely to identify with the Republican Party. Women were more likely to vote for the Republican presidential candidate from 1952 to 1960, and from 1956 to 1966, women were more likely to vote for Republican congressional candidates. The likely cause of women's preference for Republicans is that women tended to be more religious and more conservative on traditional moral issues such as sexuality, abortion, and civil liberties for atheists, racists, and communists.[4]

The 1960s brought important changes in the party identification and policy positions of men and women, which continued into the 1980s. Analysis of social survey data from the early 1960s to the early 1980s reveals some important differences in the policy positions of men and women. First, women became much less likely than men to support the use of force or violence. These issues included the use of foreign force, such as military involvement, and domestic force or violence, such as capital punishment and gun rights. For example, between 1960 and 1983, women were on average nine percentage points more likely to oppose the use of force and violence.[5]

Second, women became more supportive of compassion issues, which are defined as issues related to the government's care of citizens, such as income inequality, health care, and student loans. Third, in the two decades leading up to 1980, women became more supportive of government regulation and protection; these issues included their opposition to nuclear power as well as support for seat-belt laws and cigarette-advertising bans.

While men and women's issue positions were diverging, so were their political party affiliations. Women were growing more liberal on many issues, but men, particularly Southern white men, began moving from the Democratic to the Republican Party.[6]

THE 1980s GENDER GAP

While the tides had been changing for some time, the 1980 election truly marked the emergence—or stabilization—of the gender gap. The 1980 election was the first time that the percentage of female voters was greater than that of male voters, with 61.9 percent of eligible women voting and 61.5 percent of men voting. This change was particularly notable because women make up a slightly greater proportion of the U.S. population and, therefore, a greater number of eligible voters. In 1980, 1.7 million more women than men voted.[7]

Prior to 1980, there had been minor differences in how men and women voted, but it was generally assumed that married women voted the same way as their husbands. However, the 1980 election made clear that a significant gender gap was emerging, and the increased number of women voting amplified the importance of this gap. Women were significantly

Table 1.1   The Gender Gap in Presidential Elections, 1980–2012

Year	Presidential Candidates	Women	Men	Gender Gap
1980	Ronald Reagan (R)	46%	54%	8%
	Jimmy Carter (D)	45%	37%	
	John Anderson (I)	7%	7%	
1984	Ronald Reagan (R)	56%	62%	6%
	Walter Mondale (D)	44%	37%	
1988	George H. W. Bush (R)	50%	57%	7%
	Michael Dukakis (D)	49%	41%	
1992	Bill Clinton (D)	45%	41%	4%
	George H. W. Bush (R)	37%	38%	
	Ross Perot (Reform)	17%	21%	
1996	Bill Clinton (D)	54%	43%	11%
	Bob Dole (R)	38%	44%	
	Ross Perot (Reform)	7%	10%	
2000	George W. Bush (R)	43%	53%	10%
	Al Gore (D)	54%	42%	
	Ralph Nader (Green)	2%	3%	
2004	George W. Bush (R)	48%	55%	7%
	John Kerry (D)	51%	41%	
2008	Barack Obama (D)	56%	49%	7%
	John McCain (R)	43%	48%	
2012	Barack Obama (D)	55%	45%	10%
	Mitt Romney (R)	44%	52%	
2016	Donald Trump (R)	41%	52%	11%
	Hillary Clinton (D)	54%	41%	

Note: The gender gap is the difference between the number of men and women who voted for the winning candidate.

Source: Center for American Women in Politics (CAWP), Eagleton Institute of Politics, Rutgers University, 2012.

less likely to vote for the Republican candidate and winner, Ronald Reagan; 54 percent of men and only 46 percent of women voted for Reagan. This eight-point difference marked the first significant gender gap in vote choice where women were more likely to support the Democratic candidate and men the Republican candidate.

There are several possible explanations for the development of this gap. The women's movement of the 1970s had highlighted issues and positions distinct from the concerns and positions of men. For example, legal abortion, equal pay, and the Equal Rights Amendment were important issues for feminists. Women were also working outside the home in increasing numbers, which gave them a new perspective on politics and the issues that mattered to them. Furthermore, Ronald Reagan's conservative positions on issues like the Equal Rights Amendment and abortion pushed women toward Jimmy Carter.[8]

Traditional women's issues were not the only driving force in women's support for Carter. Women disapproved of Reagan's foreign policy and feared that his presidency would increase the risk of war.[9] Reagan did win the election, but his win was due to male voters. Females were relatively equally split in their support with 46 percent voting for Reagan and 45 percent for Carter. Independent candidate John Anderson drew the remaining votes.[10]

After the 1980 election, women's organizations took the opportunity to draw attention to women's issues. With a clear gap emerging and an increase in the number and proportion of women voting, organizations like the National Organization for Women promoted the gender gap as something politicians must pay attention to if they hoped to win elections. While some argued at the time that the 1980 gender gap was a fluke, it was clear by the end of the 1980s that the gap was real and persistent. The 1984 and 1988 elections produced a gender gap of six and seven points respectively (see Table 1.1).

In both cases, a slight majority of women still voted for the winning Republican candidate, but the difference in vote choice was much smaller among women than men. In 1984, Ronald Reagan knew he had a problem with women voters and attempted to attract them by announcing that he would name a woman to the Supreme Court, launching his Fifty State Project examining discriminatory laws at the state level, and emphasizing policies that would help women in business.[11] Ultimately Reagan won the 1984 election with a slightly smaller gender gap than in 1980.

THE GAP IN PARTY IDENTIFICATION

The gender gap in presidential vote choice since 1980 is clearly illustrated in Table 1.1. From 1980 to 2016, the average gender gap was 8.1 points. The lowest gap was in 1992, in the three-way race between Democrat Bill Clinton, Republican George H. W. Bush, and Independent Ross Perot. The largest gap of 11 points was seen four years later in 1996,

Table 1.2   Gender Gaps in Party Identification, 1984–2014

Year	Democrat Women	Republican Women	Female Gap	Democrat Men	Republican Men	Male Gap
1984	40%	28%	12%	37%	31%	6%
1986	40%	29%	11%	35%	28%	7%
1988	41%	29%	12%	32%	31%	1%
1990	38%	30%	8%	28%	32%	4%
1992	36%	32%	4%	29%	34%	5%
1994	38%	25%	13%	34%	29%	5%
1996	44%	26%	18%	33%	29%	4%
1998	35%	27%	8%	28%	30%	2%
2000	37%	29%	8%	30%	35%	5%
2002	39%	30%	9%	29%	29%	0%
2004	39%	28%	11%	31%	30%	1%
2006	41%	25%	16%	30%	30%	0%
2008	42%	25%	17%	32%	29%	3%
2010	38%	25%	13%	30%	23%	7%
2012	38%	30%	8%	25%	31%	6%
2014	36%	20%	16%	27%	23%	4%

in the election between Bill Clinton and Republican Bob Dole. This record was tied in 2016, in the race between Hillary Clinton and Donald Trump.

This gap in presidential voting was a symptom of the changing tide in party affiliation. While women in the 1950s were more likely to identify as Republicans, women in the early 1960s were more likely to identify as Democrats, and by the early 1980s, a significant gender gap had emerged. For example, in 1983, 43 percent of women identified as Democrats compared to only 32 percent of men, and only 21 percent of women identified as Republicans compared to 25 percent of men. In fact, according to the Center of American Women and Politics, in every year since 1983, more women than men have identified as Democrats, and in each year, significantly more women identify as Democrats than Republicans.[12]

During this time, men as well as women were changing their party affiliation. While women's identification with the Democratic Party increased slightly from 1964 to 1988, men were moving in large numbers to the Republican Party. Table 1.2 shows the party gap for men and women since 1984. Since 1952, men had been more conservative on many social welfare issues, but their party identification shifted to align with these beliefs between 1966 and 1978.[13]

This trend continued into the 1990s, with women moving to the Democratic Party and men moving away. The gap was greatest in 1999, with a 24-point difference; the gap was lowest in 2003, with a 1-point

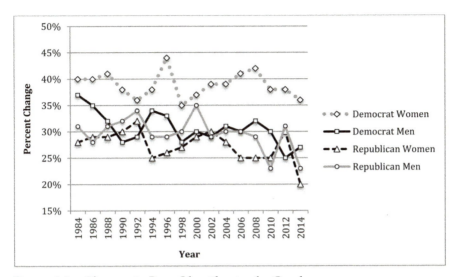

Figure 1.1   Changes in Party Identification by Gender

difference. On average, from 1983 to 2014, women identified as Democrats by 11.4 percent. While the gap has ebbed and flowed since 1980 (see Figure 1.1), the average gap in party identification from 1983 to 2014 was 11.38 points.[14] By 1996, gender predicted party identification better than all other social cleavages except for race.[15]

CAUSES OF THE GENDER GAP

There are many possible explanations as to why the gender gap emerged and has persisted. Feminism and the women's movement led to greater group consciousness and political activism among women, and these led to distinct issue positions.[16] Group position was also a likely cause of party realignment; as a subordinate group, women began challenging the dominance of men, and men began moving to the Republican party in an effort to preserve their dominance.

Karen Kaufmann, associate professor at the University of Maryland's Department of Government and Politics, has conducted several studies on the nuances of the gender gap. She states,

> I argue that white men have become increasingly resistant to the liberal cultural agenda of the Democratic Party. Social policies that advocate for greater female equality and expanding legal protections for gays and lesbians—particularly in the workplace, and in the family—pose substantial challenges to a traditional social order in which white men have been largely privileged.[17]

Kaufmann makes an important point here, because women's changing societal roles have led them to hold distinct issue positions and priorities and, at the same time, to challenge the dominance of men. For example, women's increasing levels of education have corresponded to women's shift to the Democratic Party. Since the 1980s, more and more women have obtained high school, college, and advanced degrees. Research shows that education makes women as a group more liberal and that the liberalizing effect of education is significantly greater for women than men.[18] Education may have this unique effect on women because it exposes them to ideas about feminism, income inequality, and autonomy from men.[19]

Women's increasing representation in the workforce prior to and since 1980 is likely another contributing factor to the gender gap. As women entered the workforce, the importance of and their interest in the political world increased. Furthermore, issues related to their working conditions and pay became more salient, and since women tend to earn less money than men, they may be more supportive of government assistance programs. Additionally, women are more likely than men to be in jobs related to servicing the community and/or government-based social welfare, which may increase their support of such programs and issues.[20]

Finally, the socialization of men and women may contribute to different positions and priorities, resulting in differing party affiliations and vote choices. Since women and men are socialized into different sex-typed societal roles, this may lead to learned psychological differences that help them perform those roles. For example, women are socialized to be more caring and nurturing, partially because childcare is still their primary responsibility. Research also shows that women show greater people orientation, meaning that they prioritize the welfare of others. Women also value egalitarianism more, which is related to more liberal attitudes.[21] These elements of socialization then led women to have distinct issue positions and priorities. Generally, women prioritize compassion issues (those issues that relate to caring for others) and tend to be more opposed to issues related to force and violence.

THE ISSUE GAP

The gender gap in presidential vote choice and party identification was symptomatic of women developing issue positions and priorities distinct from their male counterparts. The most important issues contributing to the gender gap have to do with cultural attitudes and social welfare policies. Cultural attitudes have been an increasingly important determinant of party identification among women, with women expressing more liberal positions. So-called culture war issues—such as affirmative action, gay rights, abortion, childcare, and education—have had a larger impact on women's party affiliation than men's.[22] In other words, these cultural attitudes have been a driving force behind women's move to the Democratic Party since 1980.

Social welfare policies are often tied to cultural attitudes, as they relate to equality and opportunity. Social welfare policies include the compassion issues mentioned previously. In fact, these two terms, "social welfare" and "compassion issues," demonstrate the differing views on these issues. The phrase "social welfare" can bring with it negative connotations of giving handouts to people who don't deserve them, but "compassion issues" implies showing empathy and care for others.

These issues relate to the government providing services to its citizens. Oftentimes, the largest debates about these issues center around whether tax dollars should be spent on these programs and whether the government should provide such services. These compassion issues include programs such as education, childcare, elder care, health care, unemployment assistance, and affirmative action.

In general, women show a greater support for government social services and greater support for policies that help the disadvantaged, even if it means increasing spending.[23] Women are more liberal on a range of issues, including greater support for health care, education, children's programs, maternity leave, and assistance to racial minorities. The gender gap on compassion issues has remained over time, even after accounting for political ideology. Regardless of how conservative or liberal women are, they show greater support than men for social welfare programs. Furthermore, women are more likely to break with their ideological constraints or party affiliation when the welfare of a group is at stake.[24]

The gap in opinions regarding social welfare policies grew in the 1980s and 1990s, and it has remained rather stable into the 21st century. However, there are important differences in the weight men and women give these issues when choosing a party or candidate. For men, opposition to social welfare programs, particularly government spending, is a significant predictor of party affiliation. In other words, men are more conservative on these issues and give them more weight in deciding whom to vote for and which party to support.[25]

The most significant differences in men and women's issue positions can be seen in cultural attitudes and social welfare programs, but some other differences do exist. Since the 1950s, women are more likely to oppose military spending and the use of military force. For example, Gallup reports that women were less likely to support the war in Vietnam and both Iraq wars.[26] Women are more supportive than men of the use of military force if the stakes are humanitarian and there is approval from the United Nations, but they are far less supportive if the conflict is economic or strategic and unilateral. On the other hand, men's approval of the use of force does not vary based on these conditions.[27]

Men and women also have different foreign policy goals. Men are more concerned with protecting weaker nations from foreign aggression, maintaining superior military power, and defending the security of our allies, and women are more concerned with combating world hunger, strengthening the United Nations, and improving the global environment.[28]

THE 1990s AND SOCCER MOMS

By the early 1990s, it was clear that the gender gap was no fluke. Women were more likely than men to identify as Democrats and to vote for Democratic candidates for president and Congress. In the 1990, 1992, and 1994 elections, the gender gap was consistent across a variety of demographic factors, including race, age, income, religion, and region.[29]

The gender gap was intensified in the wake of the Clarence Thomas hearings. In 1991, President George H. W. Bush nominated Clarence Thomas to the Supreme Court to replace retiring Justice Thurgood Marshall. Women's organizations opposed Thomas's nomination from the start, based on his conservative positions on issues like abortion, but opposition peaked when allegations surfaced that Thomas had sexually harassed Anita Hill when they had both worked at the Equal Employment Opportunity Commission (EEOC).

Hill was called to testify in front of an all-male Senate committee and was asked detailed, embarrassing questions about the alleged harassment. Thomas vehemently denied the allegations and called the hearings a "high-tech lynching."[30] Despite Hill's allegations and those of three other women who were not allowed to testify, Thomas was confirmed in a 52 to 48 vote.

However, the hearings themselves highlighted two important issues for women: sexual harassment and the lack of women in Congress. Hill's testimony politicized sexual harassment by giving a name to what many women had experienced and encouraged women to speak up, evidenced by a doubling in sexual harassment claims to the EEOC from 1991 to 1998.[31]

Furthermore, millions of Americans watched Hill, a 35-year-old African American woman, testify in embarrassing detail about sexual advances made by her supervisor and defend against attacks from the committee composed of all white men. The optics of the hearings made it abundantly clear that women were gravely underrepresented in Congress. The Hill-Thomas hearings are often credited as a major force behind the 1992 Year of the Woman, when the number of women in the Senate doubled (from 2 to 4) and women in the House grew from 28 to 47.

The 1992 election also brought a new president, Bill Clinton, to the White House. The gender gap in vote choice was smaller in 1992 than many other years, with 45 percent of women and 41 percent of men voting for Clinton. However, the presence of a third-party candidate, Ross Perot, may have pulled votes for the other two candidates and contributed to a smaller gender gap in 1991.

Despite all the attention given to women voters and women candidates in 1992, there was little to no discussion of women by the media in the 1994 midterm elections. In fact, as Susan J. Carroll argues, the 1994 election could be called the "Year of the Angry White Male."[32] In 1994, men were significantly more likely to vote Republican than in the previous two elections, while women's allegiances remained about the same.

This movement to the right by male voters was likely the result of more conservative positions on social welfare policies; for the first time since the New Deal era, positions on these issues were the biggest difference between the two parties. Women also turned out to vote in much smaller numbers in 1994. In fact, women's turnout in 1994 was the lowest since 1974, and this likely won Congress for the Republicans.[33]

The media may not have focused on women in 1994, but they certainly did in 1996. The media and candidates focused their attention on a specific subgroup of women: the soccer mom. The term can be traced back to a 1995 local election in Denver, when candidate Susan B. Casey used the slogan "A Soccer Mom for City Council."[34] The first use of the term by the news media appeared in a July 21, 1996, *Washington Post* article by E. J. Dionne, when he quoted Republican political consultant Alex Castellanos. Dionne argued that Clinton had resurrected FDR's Democratic themes of emphasizing working people and families. About Clinton's attempt to sway female voters, Dionne wrote,

> Castellanos has a shrewd view of what Clinton is up to in pushing such initiatives as school uniforms, teen curfews, crackdowns on truancy, gun restrictions and the V-chip to block obscene programming on television. The president, following the advice of consultant Dick Morris among others, is sending a message to a voter Castellanos calls "soccer mom": the overburdened, middle income working mother who ferries her kids from soccer practice to scouts to school. Clinton's message is, the government

will do what it can to help her raise her kids and establish some order in her family life.

Castellanos adds that Clinton's specific (and putatively liberal) spending commitments—to Medicare and Medicaid for the parents of "soccer mom" and student loans for her children—reinforce the message that Clinton and by extension the federal government is a "protector" of her family.[35]

The soccer mom theme soon dominated media discussions of women voters in the 1996 election. The media reported that these women were the key swing voters and defined them generally as married, busy, stressed middle-class white women, who lived in the suburbs, worked outside the home, and drove a minivan (or a similar family vehicle). The belief was that soccer moms viewed the world through the lens of motherhood and childcare. The soccer mom voter was partially based in reality. Given a mother's need to care and provide for her children and the fact that many women are also tasked with caring for aging parents, social welfare policies can be particularly important to women.

Women in general were also more liberal on social spending issues, and these issues were more salient to women in 1996, making them important deciding factors for female voters. However, the actual soccer mom demographic was a rather small percentage of the voting population—only about 10 percent.[36] Based on the quantity of news coverage soccer moms got in 1996, one would assume they were a much larger proportion of voters.

The 1996 presidential candidates, incumbent Bill Clinton (D) and challenger Bob Dole (R-KS), both made pointed efforts to campaign to women in general and soccer moms in particular. While Clinton never used the term "soccer mom," he did focus on the shared demographic characteristics associated with them. Clinton also had a strong record of supporting issues important to women in his first term, and he used this record to court their votes in 1996. Clinton touted his accomplishments related to violence against women, family medical leave, early childhood learning, and pay equity.[37] He also campaigned on issues Dionne mentioned in his *Washington Post* article, including school uniforms, teen curfews, V-chips, and education.

Contrary to Clinton, Bob Dole did use the term "soccer mom" when campaigning; he referred to them in a debate and asked audiences at rallies if there were soccer moms in the crowds. Dole also tried to appeal to soccer moms by discussing such issues as the home-office tax deduction so that women could work from home and tax cuts that, he argued, would allow one parent to stay home.[38]

Whether or not soccer moms or women in general decided the 1996 election, Clinton won with the largest gender gap of the 20th century. Clinton won 54 percent of women voters, while Dole won only 38 percent and Ross Perot picked up 7 percent. Male voters, on the other hand, were relatively equally split between Clinton (43 percent) and Dole (44 percent). Ultimately, Clinton won the popular vote by 8.51 points, meaning Clinton's 11-point advantage among women was essential to his victory.

THE BUSH YEARS: SOCCER MOMS TO SECURITY MOMS

The presidential election of 2000 was no doubt one of the most interesting in history, with the Supreme Court ultimately deciding the outcome. One *St. Louis Post-Dispatch* article titled "Undecided Women May Hold Key to the Election"[39] highlighted the importance of winning women voters, who were proportionately more likely to be undecided. Both candidates attempted to win their votes.

Al Gore campaigned on many issues important to women, such as health care and education. He had the support of Planned Parenthood, and the organization helped to mobilize women voters against Bush.[40] Gore also focused on the theme of "working families" in an effort to attract women voters.[41] Women were central to Gore's campaign strategy. As one *Washington Post* headline stated, "Strength among Women Is the Atlas of Gore's Campaign."[42] Polling six weeks out from the election showed that Gore's strategy was working, and he had a 10-point lead among women.

Bush also made efforts to sway women voters by discussing family values and appearing on TV shows like *Oprah*. Bush also campaigned as a "compassionate conservative" in an effort to appeal to women his Republican predecessors could not.[43] The media regularly reported on Bush's trouble with women and attempts to win them with headlines like "Even Softening GOP's Tough Image Isn't Helping Bush Bridge Gender Gap" and "Bush Working to Win Back Women's Support."[44] In the end, Bush won the election but lost women voters by a 10-point margin. Gore did particularly well among women in states with poor scores for women's health, employment, and earnings. Had the election been decided on national plurality, Gore would have been elected because of women; 8.4 million more women than men voted in 2000, and 54 percent of them voted for Gore.[45]

The context of the 2004 election was very different than that of 2000. Terrorists had attacked the United States on September 11, 2001; the United States was engaged in two wars, Iraq and Afghanistan; and George W. Bush was running for reelection. Given the heighted discussion and concerns surrounding terrorism and the Bush administration's War on Terror, issues of national security and military action were foregrounded in both the media's discussion of the 2004 election and the candidates' campaign messaging.

Interestingly it was Democrat Joe Biden who first labeled the new group of swing voters as "security moms." The 2002 midterms proved to be difficult for Democrats, and Biden noted that the issue priorities in the wake of 9/11 had changed and that "soccer moms are security moms now."[46] The media was quick to run with the security mom label during the 2004 presidential election, and articles with titles like "Presidential Race May Hinge on Undecided 'Security Moms'" and "Security Moms: Bush's Secret Election Weapon"[47]made it seem that they favored Bush.

Security moms were married women with children under the age of 18, and since 9/11, they were more concerned with protecting their families against terror attacks and had hence moved to support Republican George W. Bush.[48] It was believed that the security mom possessed the same demographic characteristics of the 1990s soccer mom (married, white, and lived in the suburbs), but her issue priorities were different. These demographic characteristics represented about 26 percent of women voters, and they were actively courted by both George W. Bush and John Kerry during the 2004 election.

Representing a very different group of women was the so-called *Sex and the City* voter. The label came from the popular HBO television show featuring four 30-something white, financially comfortable, single women. These women were distinct from the married security mom, whose primary concern was security for her family. The media loved this catchy title for this group of women voters, and get-out-the-vote ad campaigns were designed to mobilize this part of the electorate. A large portion of this group of women hadn't turned out to vote in 2000, and they represented 24 percent of the voting age population. The belief was that these single, younger women were more liberal and that if they voted, they could swing the election in favor of Kerry.[49] Public service announcements targeting the *Sex and the City* voter featured celebrities like Jennifer Aniston and Christina Aguilera pleading for single women to go vote.

With two alleged groups of female swing voters both candidates made specific efforts to campaign to women voters and numerous activist women's organizations became involved in persuading women voters. The activist organizations came from both the right and left and included groups such as Moms4Bush, Mainstream Moms Oppose Bush, Granny Voters, Axis of Eve, and the Democratic Women's Leadership Foundation. Bush ran his "W Stands for Women" campaign, which focused on six key issues: making America more secure, reducing the tax burden on families, providing affordable health care, reforming education, empowering faith-based groups, and building a culture of responsibility.[50] First Lady Laura Bush also actively campaigned for her husband in ads targeted to women, and Vice President Cheney's daughter campaigned as a security mom on behalf of the Bush-Cheney ticket. A key part of Bush's 2004 campaign was focused on security and his ability to keep Americans safe.[51]

John Kerry also attempted to win over female swing voters. He held events like a women and security rally in Iowa, and he recruited mothers and wives of service personnel to campaign against Bush. His Web site contained a Women's Action Kit to help grassroots efforts, and on Women's Equality Day, he launched a national Women for Kerry-Edwards Initiative including a report on the status of women. Kerry also campaigned on several issues he hoped would win women voters, including increasing the minimum wage, expanding after-school programs, closing the pay gap, strengthening women's reproductive rights, increasing the childcare tax credit, and strengthening the Violence Against Women's Act.[52]

In the end, Bush won the popular vote 50.73 percent to 48.26 percent, but he did not win over women voters. Kerry won 51 percent of women voters compared to Bush's 48 percent of women. The 2004 election again revealed a gender gap in how women and men vote, with 53 percent of men supporting Bush, resulting in a seven-point gender gap. This gap was slightly smaller than the 10-point gap of 2000, but it was still significant.

The push of the so-called security moms did not pan out; in fact, analysis of women's 2004 voting patterns reveal the security mom was a myth. Women with children were no more likely to vote for Bush in 2004 than they were in 2000, and nonmothers were actually more likely to vote for Bush in 2004 than were mothers.[53] The slight shrinkage of the gender gap in 2004 was likely due to the changing votes of southern white women, who favored Bush more in 2004 than they did in 2000, but this trend was contained to the South. These women were significantly more likely than nonsouthern women to approve of Bush's national security policy, and they were more likely to believe that he "cares about people like you."[54] Removing southern women from the equation shows that the gender gap actually grew slightly in the rest of the country.

The reality of 2004 was that women's issue positions had not drastically changed post-9/11 and the *Sex and the City* voter did not turn out to vote in greater numbers than 2000. When it came to defense and security issues, women were less likely than men to support increased defense spending and the War on Terror, and they rated these issues as lower priorities. Women were also less likely to believe that the Iraq and Afghanistan wars were worth it and less likely to think the Bush administration had made the country more secure.[55] Not only were mothers not supportive of Bush on military issues; they were also more liberal than nonmothers on many social welfare issues, such as health care, government support for jobs, assisting the poor, and gay rights.[56]

The media and candidates should have learned an important lesson in 2004; assuming a small segment of women are single-issue voters who can sway an election is dangerous. Neither the security mom nor the *Sex and the City* voter behaved as the media and pundits expected. As it turned out, women, even a small segment of women, were not single-issue voters, and it was incorrect to assume that mothers would become drastically more conservative after 9/11.

This election highlighted the importance of examining the issue positions of a variety of subgroups of women with a variety of demographic characteristics. Furthermore, focusing solely on one or two groups of women allows both the news media and candidates to ignore a much larger segment of voting women. Despite the fact that these assumptions about women were incorrect in 2004, similar generalities were made in following elections.

THE OBAMA YEARS: GENDER IN THE 2008 ELECTION

The real news of the 2008 election of Barack Obama was not as much about women voters as about minority and young voters, whose turnout reached record numbers. Of particular note was the turnout of black women, who voted in significantly higher numbers than previous elections, with 63.7 percent of eligible black women voting in 2004 and 68.8 percent in 2008. A larger proportion of eligible black women voted than any other demographic subgroup.[57] Women voters in general were also still an important portion of the electorate and were given special attention because of Hillary Clinton's primary race and Sarah Palin's Republican nomination for vice president. Some pundits argued that women would simply vote for a female candidate regardless of party, but this proved to be far from the truth.

Hillary Clinton's historic run for the Democratic presidential nomination brought gender to the foreground of the primary and general elections, and Clinton held unique appeal to female voters. Early polling indicated that gender was an important factor in opinions of Clinton. In April 2007, there was a clear gender gap in Clinton's favorability ratings; men were equally split (47 percent favorable, 49 percent unfavorable), but she was significantly more popular among women, with 58 percent giving her a favorable rating and 36 percent an unfavorable rating.[58] While

Clinton's favorability was highest with Democratic women, the gender gap was present among Democrats, Republicans, and Independents.

In 2007, it seemed that Clinton was the inevitable Democratic candidate for president, and polls were looking at how she would fare against potential Republican nominees. One Pew study found that Clinton's support was strongest among women under the age of 50, and in a hypothetical race between her and Rudy Giuliani, Clinton ran 13 points better among female voters than male voters. Echoing earlier polling, the gender gap was evident among Independents, with Independent women favoring her by 12 points.

The same poll indicated the importance of Clinton's gender in her candidacy. Not only did young women disproportionately support Clinton in early polls, but 47 percent of women under the age of 50 believed it would be good to elect a female president, compared to 34 percent of women over 50 and 24 percent of men. This gap was most apparent among younger voters (age 18 to 29); 50 percent of these women said it would be good to have a woman president compared to only 24 percent of men in this age group. Of those Independents who said that electing a woman would be a good thing, 70 percent supported Clinton.[59] This indicates that Clinton's gender was a factor for female voters, especially younger women.

As the primary season pressed on, it seemed that Clinton was not a sure thing after all. After the Iowa caucuses, it became clear that Barack Obama would be tough competition for Clinton, and gender played an important role in the outcome. Obama was favored among the highly educated (those with postgraduate degrees) regardless of gender, and Clinton was favored by the least educated. However, for voters in the middle of the education scale (those with some college but no degree to those with a college undergraduate degree), gender was found to be a strong predictor of candidate preference; women in these groups tilted toward Clinton, while men favored Obama.[60]

This gender gap was very apparent in early 2008 polling, when Clinton had 48 percent support among Democratic women and 38 percent of Democratic men. Women's support proved to be a key element necessary for Clinton's success. Obama's later gains came primarily from women, and by the end of January 2008, the gender gap was disappearing. In the course of two weeks, Clinton went from having a 13-point gap between male and female support to a 6-point gap. During the same period, Obama's support among women, which had been 10 points less than male support, became only a 3-point gap.[61] These polls suggest that the gender gap was essential for Clinton's success; as she began to lose female supporters, Obama began to gain them and ultimately win the nomination.

The 2008 presidential election is a prime example of candidates' attempts to court women's votes, with both Obama and McCain specifically targeting women. They employed a variety of strategies in 2008, many of which have been used in previous elections.[62] First, the candidates emphasized the importance of women in their lives; for example, Obama frequently recalled his mother's influence. Second, they highlighted issue differences that were of particular importance to women (e.g., women's economic issues, discrimination in the work place, childcare). Third, they appeared on television shows with large female audiences, such as *The View* and *Ellen*. Fourth, and most notably, they made well-known women a key part of their campaign. Obama campaigned with Hillary Rodham Clinton, Claire McCaskill, Kathleen Sebelius, and even Oprah Winfrey. Carly Fiorina, former CEO of Hewlett-Packard, campaigned for McCain, and McCain even selected a female vice presidential candidate, Sarah Palin, arguably in an attempt to increase support from female voters.

Many pundits believed that McCain's selection of Sarah Palin was a Hail Mary play to win over women voters, particularly disgruntled Clinton supporters and female Independents. Palin was relatively unknown at the time of her nomination, but in some ways, she was a good complement to John McCain. Like McCain, she was a "maverick." She was also a Washington outsider, and she was young. Initially announcement of Palin resulted in increased favorability of McCain and the Republican presidential ticket. In fact, 50 percent of viewers rated Palin's convention speech as the highlight of the event, compared to only 17 percent rating McCain's speech as the highlight.[63]

While women tend to be more liberal and more likely to vote Democratic, the selection of Palin on the ticket was meant to appeal to women. This was evidenced in some of the language Palin herself used in campaign speeches; for example, she referred to herself as a "hockey mom" and "mama grizzly" and appealed to mothers to support the McCain-Palin ticket. While there is evidence that female voters sometimes prefer a female candidate,[64] this usually happens within the same political party. In other words, Republican women may have preferred Palin over a male candidate, but it was unlikely that Democratic women would prefer Palin over a Democratic male candidate.

However, there was some hope in the McCain camp of drawing votes from disgruntled Hillary Clinton supporters. The Democratic primary was long and contentious, and many Clinton supporters, particularly women, were upset that Clinton lost the nomination. Yet, it was a mistake to believe that these women would cross party lines because of their disappointment.

Polling in 2008 shows a gender gap in regard to the likeability of Palin and the McCain-Palin ticket in general. A CNN/Opinion Research Corporation poll conducted in September 2008 found that 62 percent of men had a favorable view of Palin compared to 53 percent of women, and the gap was even greater when it came to views of her qualifications. Among men, 57 percent believed that she was qualified compared to only 43 percent of women.[65]

As the election grew closer, Palin's favorability decreased with both sexes, likely caused in part by her major gaffes in media interviews. Additionally, her favorability among those the McCain camp had hoped to attract, mainly white women, fell dramatically as the campaign went on, falling 21 points among white women from September to the end of October and falling 24 points among Independent women voters.[66]

The cause of the gender gap is still somewhat unclear. It could have been the women were simply more liberal than men and therefore had a less favorable view of a conservative candidate. It could also have been Palin's conservative positions on certain women's issues, such as reproductive rights. The cause also could have been a fear among women that Palin's lack of qualifications would hurt women's chances of making it to the White House in the future.

In the end, the 2008 presidential election resulted in a gender gap of seven points. Obama won 56 percent of women voters and 49 percent of male voters, and McCain won 43 percent of women and 48 percent of men.[67] These numbers demonstrate that women were an important factor in the outcome; men were relatively equally split between McCain and Obama, but women overwhelmingly preferred Obama. Unlike 2004, where Kerry won women voters by only 3 points, Obama won women's votes by 13 points, and the 2008 election was not the last time women would catapult Obama to victory.

THE OBAMA YEARS: WOMEN REELECT OBAMA IN 2012

The 2012 election did not feature a woman on either party's presidential ticket, but women and women's issues were still at the foreground of the election. The so-called Republican War on Women was a central theme in both the presidential and Congressional elections, and both parties actively campaigned to women voters. Leading up to the 2012 election, Republicans in the U.S. Congress and many state legislatures had pushed through conservative legislation limiting women's reproductive rights and weakening protections from domestic violence. For example, the *New York Times* reported in May 2012[68] that House Republican's had recently pushed through a bill that weakened the Violence Against Women Act (VAWA) and denied the District of Columbia's delegate (a Democratic woman) the opportunity to testify on legislation that would ban nearly all abortion in D.C. after 20 weeks. While the U.S. Senate ultimately approved reauthorization of VAWA, they omitted protections for gay, Native American, student, and immigrant abuse victims.

Equal pay was also a hot issue, with Obama campaigning on his record of supporting the Lily Ledbetter Equal Pay Act, while Republicans, like Governor Scott Walker of Wisconsin, repealed laws that allowed women to bring lawsuits about pay discrimination to the state court. Additionally, abortion rights were under fire from Republicans at the state level. Arizona banned abortions after 18 weeks, and several other states enacted similar legislation that restricted women's access to abortion and did not allow for exemptions in the case of rape or incest. Several states also attempted to defund Planned Parenthood and began requiring intrusive sonograms for women seeking abortions.

Democrats jumped on the opportunity to label these actions as a "war on women," and they targeted campaign messaging on these issues toward women. Republicans refuted the label, arguing that being pro-life is not antiwoman and that Republicans do not believe that men should control women's bodies or take away birth control.[69] However, the label stuck and became a frequent topic in the news media. This was exacerbated by a few Republicans ranging from insensitive to outright sexist.

Most memorable was Todd Akin, the Republican candidate for the U.S. Senate running against incumbent Claire McCaskill in Missouri. In an interview, Akin stated that he believed abortion should be illegal in the case of rape because "if it's a legitimate rape, the female body has ways to try to shut that whole thing down."[70] This was quickly picked up by the media and discredited by scientists. The Akin-McCaskill race went from close to a landslide in favor of McCaskill.

GOP members of the U.S. House, including Akin and vice presidential nominee Paul Ryan, also attempted to pass federal legislation that would only allow abortion funding for "forcible rape" in an attempt to limit subsidized abortions. Idaho Senator Chuck Winder argued that women should have to go through two forced ultrasounds before obtaining an abortion and stated his concern that women would claim they were raped just to get an abortion. He went on to say, "Rape and incest was used as a reason to oppose this. I would hope that when a woman goes into a physician with a rape issue, that physician will indeed ask her about perhaps her marriage, was this pregnancy caused by normal relations in a marriage or was it truly caused by a rape."[71] Additionally Rick Santorum and Mike

Huckabee argued that women should "make the best" of their rape and have the child.

The attention given to these comments as well as the legislative actions regarding abortion and equal pay made women voters central to the 2012 presidential campaign. Both President Obama and Republican challenger, Mitt Romney, attempted to persuade women voters. Obama ran several ads directly targeting women, including one titled "First Law" touting Obama's signing of the Lilly Ledbetter Fair Pay Act. Other ads focused on the benefits of the Affordable Care Act to women and attacked Romney's positions on funding Planned Parenthood, abortion rights, and contraception.

In all, Obama ran nine different ads focused on reproductive rights and health, compared to only one ad from his opponent, which featured a female speaker assuring viewers that Romney did not oppose contraception and supported abortion in certain circumstances.[72] Obama also ran these ads on channels and during programs that had large female audiences, including cable networks like Hallmark and the Food Network and daytime talk shows and reality shows.[73]

Romney took a different approach to targeting women voters; he primarily focused on the economy as a women's issue. Romney ran a series of ads, each featuring a different female speaker stating that the economy was her biggest concern. While this approach was consistent with Romney's overall campaign strategy, research suggested it was not as successful at persuading female voters as Obama's advertising.[74] Romney also emphasized the economy as a women's issue in his speeches and debates, and his wife, Ann, discussed this issue in many of her campaign speeches, including her speech at the Republican convention.

These efforts to appeal to women voters (particularly Independent women) were relatively unsuccessful, and a gaffe during the second presidential debate made Romney appear out of touch. During the town-hall-style debate, Romney was asked what he would do to address gender inequalities in the workplace, and he responded by referring to the creation of his cabinet when he became Massachusetts governor.

He stated, "I had the chance to pull together a cabinet, and all the applicants seemed to be men." He went on, "I went to a number of women's groups and said, 'Can you help us find folks?' and they brought us whole binders full of women."[75] While Romney chose his words poorly, he intended to say that he actively recruited women to leadership positions. However, the statement "binders full of women" went viral immediately and became a persistent joke throughout the campaign.

The news media also made clear that women were key to winning the 2012 presidential election. A few headlines emphasizing the importance of women voters included "Women Seen as the Key to November Victory"; "Election 2012 Examining the Gender Gap; Women Hold Balance of Power"; "It's the Women, Stupid: Romney Repels Female Voters"; "Did Debate Woo or Irk Women"; and "Why American Women's Votes Matter More Than Ever in This Election."[76]

Not all women were key to the 2012 election. In all elections, some women are firmly Republican or firmly Democratic, but in 2012, women were more likely than men to be swing voters[77] and made up the majority of undecided voters. With less than three weeks left before the election, approximately 60 percent of undecided voters were women.[78]

Young women and unmarried women made up the bulk of swing voters, and media coverage was quick to give these women catchy labels. For example, US News and World Report ran an article titled "Walmart Moms Could Swing 2012 Election." Based on a study published by Public Opinion Strategies, the article defined these women as "women with children 18 or younger who shop at Walmart at least once per month."[79] What was most important about this group was that they made up 27 percent of all female registered voters, were evenly split between the parties, were likely swing voters, and were concerned with the economy and wages.[80]

There were also the "single ladies" or "Beyoncé voters," who were important to the election's outcome. An ABC News headline in April 2012 read, "Put a Ring on It: Obama Wins Women, but Not the Married Kind,"[81] emphasizing the focus on unmarried women voters, who historically vote in lower numbers than married women but also overwhelmingly supported Obama in 2008.

Despite Romney's efforts to focus on the economy, women's issues, like birth control and abortion, were extremely important in women's vote choice in key battleground states. A Gallup poll of women in 12 battleground states found that 60 percent considered government policies on birth control to be a very important issue, and 39 percent said abortion was the most important issue in the 2012 election.[82] Ultimately, according to NBC News, Obama won reelection largely due to the votes of women, particularly unmarried women, with 67 percent of their vote.[83]

Obama won 55 percent of female voters compared to only 45 percent of male voters, resulting in one of the largest gender gaps in history. What is even more noteworthy was that the majority of men voted for the losing candidate (Romney won 52 percent of men's votes), and the majority of women voted for the winning candidate. This has happened only one other time in history: Bill Clinton's 1996 election. In 1996, the men's vote was much more evenly split between the two major party candidates and also included a third-party candidate. In 2012, women decided the election by overwhelmingly voting for Barack Obama, and the gender gap widened across racial groups.[84] However, it is important to note that Romney did win some groups of women; he won white women by 14 points (56 percent to 42 percent), and he won married women by 7 points (53 percent to 46 percent).

Two important lessons can be learned from the 2012 election: women voters can swing an election and women are not a monolithic voting bloc. The next few chapters explore both of these lessons to uncover the similarities and differences among female voters. Specifically, I examine the influence women's gender identity has on their political leanings as well as differences between feminist and nonfeminist women. Later, I explain how these variables can be used to identify what issues women voters find important, what traits they want in a candidate, and how to persuade specific subgroups of women.

2016: THE WOMAN CARD AND LOCKER ROOM TALK

It is hard to imagine an election where gender could be more central than the 2016 presidential race. Hillary Clinton won the Democratic nomination, becoming the first woman in history to win a major party's nomination for president. Unlike her 2008 primary campaign, Clinton made her gender a part of her 2016 campaign. She did not hide from her "first-woman" status and instead embraced it. On the other hand, Donald Trump, a political novice and reality TV star with a reputation for poor treatment of women, became the Republican Party's candidate for president. Trump could not seem to stop himself from saying things that many voters, particularly women, found offensive, and he did little to target women voters, who many believed would overwhelmingly back Clinton.

From the time Clinton announced her candidacy, she embraced her identity as a woman and used to it to appeal to women voters. In her official campaign launch on June 13, 2016, she spoke at Four Freedoms Park in New York City and addressed women's issues and women directly, saying of Republicans, "They shame and blame women, rather than respect our right to make our own reproductive health decisions."[85] Later in the speech, she identified another issue affecting women that she planned to address as president: "And it is way past time to end the outrage of so many women still earning less than men on the job—and women of color often making even less. This isn't a women's issue. It's a family issue."[86] Toward the end of the speech, she even explicitly discussed her "first-woman" status, saying,

All our Presidents come into office looking so vigorous. And then we watch their hair grow grayer and grayer. Well, I may not be the youngest candidate in this race. But I will be the youngest woman President in the history of the United States! And the first grandmother as well. And one additional advantage: You won't see my hair turn white in the White House. I've been coloring it for years![87]

Clinton continued these themes throughout her campaign and specifically targeted women voters, like many presidential candidates before her, in her speeches, advertisements, and online communication. This is not to say she only addressed women's issues or targeted women, but women were a central part of her campaign. For example, when her opponent, Donald Trump, claimed she was "playing the woman card" to win the election, she responded, "If fighting for equal pay, and paid family leave, and raising the minimum wage and affordable childcare, is playing the woman card, then deal me in."[88]

She also ran numerous advertisements targeting women voters and attacking Trump, often using Trump's own hateful words about women. For example, in the ad "Mirrors," young women are shown looking at themselves in the mirror while pieces of Trump's interviews or speeches are played and he says things like, "I'd look her right in that fat, ugly face of hers" and "A person who's flat-chested is very hard to be a 10."[89]

Donald Trump had a problem with women voters very early on. Prior to his political career, which began when he announced his candidacy on June 16, 2015, Trump was known as a businessman and reality star who sometimes criticized Barack Obama on Fox News and Twitter. He had also made many disparaging comments about women throughout his time in the public eye, which Clinton used in her advertising. Trump had other woman problems as well, and they weren't all from the past. After a Republican primary debate, Trump said of Megyn Kelly, one of the debate moderators, "You could see there was blood coming out of her eyes. Blood coming out of her wherever."[90] Only a month later, Trump said of Republican primary opponent Carly Fiorina in a *Rolling Stone* interview, "Look at that face! Would anyone vote for that? Can you imagine that, the face of our next president."[91]

Trump did little to target women voters during his campaign, setting him apart from nearly every other presidential candidate in modern history. He did run some ads featuring his daughter, Ivanka Trump, that attempted to speak to women and addressed issues like childcare and family leave.

However, the negative press Trump had related to women and gender issues far outshone the good. As the general election neared, *The*

Washington Post published an October surprise, which included a video of Trump discussing with *Access Hollywood* reporter Billy Bush how he, as a celebrity, could do whatever he wanted to women, including grabbing them by their genitals.[92] Trump dismissed the recording as "locker room banter," but for many, that defense was inadequate.[93] Adding fuel to the fire, more than a dozen women came out of the woodwork and accused Trump of sexual misconduct, ranging from harassing comments to unwanted touching and kissing, all allegations Trump denied.[94]

It was not just the candidates themselves who made gender matter in 2016; it was voters as well. There was clear sexism in attacks against Clinton, and research found that holding sexist beliefs was a strong predictor in whether or not someone supported Trump.[95] On the other hand, women who had experienced sexual harassment in their own lives were significantly more likely to support Clinton. This summary only scratches the surface of gender in 2016; scholars will be sorting out the role gender played in the 2016 presidential election for years to come.

When it was all said and done, the United States did not elect its first woman president. Despite a lead of nearly 3 million votes, Clinton lost the electoral college vote to Trump 306 to 232. However, Clinton won women voters by an 11-point margin. Post-election analysis was quick to jump on the story that Clinton lost white women voters, but they story was not so simple. Clinton lost married white women without a college education, but this was a group who had been increasingly voting Republican over the past 15 years. The majority of women, 54 percent, voted for Clinton.

What the 2016 election taught us was that gender still matters, and it matters a lot. Female candidates still face sexism, particularly when running for the presidency. It also showed us that a large segment of the population was willing to overlook or simply did not care about the sexist comments and behaviors of a presidential candidate. On the other hand, Trump's victory spurred a renewed activism among women.

The day after Trump's inauguration was the first Women's March. Touted as the largest demonstration in U.S. history, it included approximately 4 million people in the United States and more abroad. This was followed by movements like #MeToo and #TimesUp, which focused on calling out and ending sexual harassment. A record number of women attended campaign training following the 2016 election and reported plans to run for office in the near future.[96] While Clinton did not win the presidency, her candidacy, as well as Trump's, had a historic impact on women in American politics.

CHAPTER 2

Women's Group Connectedness and Political Behavior

The consistent gender gap in vote choices, political party identification, and issue positions demonstrates that men and women are distinct voting blocs and that when it comes to politics and government, the majority of women see things differently than the majority of men. This indicates that these differences are the result of women and men's membership in their gender group. This chapter outlines how women's feelings of connection to their gender group explain their distinct views on politics. Membership in a group, particularly if that group is disenfranchised in some way, is an important part of a person's personal and political identity. Nearly all major social movements in American history have been centered around a specific group of people, and the group identity of those people was politically important. Examples include the abolition of slavery, suffrage for African Americans and women, fair and safe workplaces for laborers, and equal rights for African Americans, women, and LGBTQ people. In each of these cases (and many more), the group, rather than the individual, was (or is) at the heart of the political and social issues.

Women's identification with their gender group results in specific group-based political beliefs and preferences. This theory of group identification is based on the work of social psychologist Henri Tajfel and his theory of social identity.[1] Tajfel's research found that when people are put into groups, even extremely arbitrary groups, they show a preference for their own group and attempt to maximize benefits for the in-group. Tajfel argued that humans have a natural tendency to put themselves into one or more groups and then base part of their identity on that group membership. Furthermore, identifying with social groups allows people to better understand who they are and to gain self-esteem. Tajfel's social identity

theory has been important in shaping social psychological theories related
to group behavior, intergroup relations, stereotyping, and prejudice.

According to social identity theory, women are members of a distinct
social group. In addition to their gender group, women may be members
of many social groups, including racial, socioeconomic, educational, and
geographical. For the purposes of understanding the gender gap and politics, we must focus on membership in the group "women." Tajfel's work
suggests that an important part of women's identity is membership in that
group and exclusion from the group "men." Researchers Patricia Gurin,
Arthur Miller, and Gerald Gurin have built on Tajfel's work by examining members' identification with their social group(s). They define group
identification as "the awareness of having ideas, feelings, and interests
similar to others who share the same stratum characteristics."[2] Put simply,
identification occurs when one recognizes similarities between one's self
and other members of a group.

For a woman, this means feeling that she has meaningful similarities
and shared interests with other women and that being a woman makes her
different from men. Identification with a group has also been described
as a willingness to say "we" as opposed to "I" or "they."[3] A wonderful
example of this is the famous Rosie the Riveter poster depicting a woman
showing her muscle and reading, "We Can Do It!" This is a call to all
women, not an individual woman. The term "we" implies a similarity and
link between the individual and the group. Women who speak of what
is good for "us" or what "we" might do are demonstrating identification
with their gender group. With this feeling of group identification comes a
sense that the group shares a common future, particularly when it comes
to government or social issues.

Pamela Johnston Conover has explored the role of group identification
in vote choice among a variety of groups. Her 1984 work looked at several
groups including African Americans, women, business people, and the
middle class. She examined the relationship between group identification
and issue positions and found that group-identified people have distinct
group-based issue positions and that the positions of the identified tend
to be more extreme.[4] To explain the role of group identification in political thinking, Conover proposed a cognitive-affective model. This model
contended,

> In summary, three key assumptions underlie our cognitive-affective model
> of the role of social groups in political thinking: the assumption that people
> organize their information about social groups in terms of group sche-
> mata; the assumption that people's *political* thinking about social groups

is purposive, being guided by their desire to know what various groups are getting and whether it is deserved; and the assumption that people react affectively to social groups based on stored affective tags and causal attributions, and that these affective reactions influence how and what people think about social groups.[5]

In other words, people think of themselves and others in terms of what groups they do and do not belong to. They have feelings about those groups based on experience and perceived fairness. In the case of women, an individual woman will think of others as either part of the in-group (women) or the out-group (men). She will also consider her experiences as a member of that group and evaluate the social positions of the in-group and out-group. Additionally, the model suggests that individuals will favor their own group(s) and that if an issue is framed in group terms, they will react in group terms. Conover's model suggests that women have distinct positions on some issues because of their membership to the group "women" and the framing of those issues. In many cases, the issues where women differ from men are issues that have been culturally framed (and often framed in campaigns) as women's issues or issues with which women should be concerned.[6] These include issues such as women's reproductive rights and pay equality as well as issues related to women's traditional role as caregivers, such as care for the elderly and children. Additionally, research that has shown women's preference for female candidates (given all else is equal) can partially be explained by the salience of a candidate's gender in a mixed gender race.

While group identification can occur in any type of social group, it is particularly strong among members of disadvantaged groups, such as women and racial minorities. Group members' sense of group connectedness can result in distinct political beliefs and behaviors important to the group. Gender group identification is less likely among males, because they have little reason to think of themselves in political terms as members of the group "men." This is particularly true of white men, because their social position is the norm against which other groups are measured. Men also have little reason to voice a unique political position because their position is that of the system. This is supported by empirical research that has found no support for male gender-group identification, and no link has been found between male gender-group identification and political behavior.[7]

On the other hand, women have been addressed by the political system, for better and worse, as a distinct group, so women have more social and political reason to see themselves in terms of being part of the group "women." History is ripe with examples of women being treated as a group and often excluded because of that group membership. Women have been explicitly barred from owning land, voting, attending universities, applying for certain jobs, and getting a credit card. Much of the early women's movement centered around gaining these and other rights for women as a group. Women's ability to give birth has further distinguished them from men. With that distinction has come discrimination and governmental policies that apply specifically and uniquely to women. For example, until 1978, a woman could be fired when she became pregnant. Today policies regarding reproductive rights, access to contraceptives, and paid maternity leave affect women directly and differently than men. Historically, gender group membership has been a socially and politically important part of women's identity.

While membership in a gender group does not change day to day, identification with a subordinate group has a stronger influence on political beliefs and behaviors if that group membership is politicized in some way.[8] For example, a woman may feel identified to her gender group, but that identification may not affect her decision making on a daily basis. However, if there is a female candidate running for office or issues pertaining to the voter's gender group membership are salient, then identification may lead her to vote for a particular candidate or support certain issues.

In elections with large gender gaps, issues relevant to women as a group were salient for women voters. For example, in 1980, Reagan was opposed to the Equal Right Amendment and abortion rights, and these two issues were uniquely relevant to women and politicized women's gender group membership. The Clarence Thomas–Anita Hill hearings in 1991 politicized sexual harassment and highlighted the drastic underrepresentation of women in Congress. In 1992, a record number of women were elected to the U.S. Congress, and Democrat Bill Clinton won the presidency. In 1996, Clinton politicized issues important to women in general and mothers in particular. He campaigned on issues such as equal pay, violence against women, early childhood education, V-chips, and school uniforms; Clinton also won with the largest gender gap in recorded history.

The 2012 presidential election saw the second largest gender gap in history, and it was the second time women decided the outcome of the election. Women's issues were highly politicized as Democrats spoke of the Republican War on Women and issues such as pay equity and reproductive rights were central issues in the election. Each of these elections demonstrates that in years where issues uniquely important to women are politicized, the majority of women tend to unite as a group and vote in the best interest of that group.

THE INFLUENCE OF CANDIDATE GENDER

The political implications of gender group identification go beyond the politicization of certain issues. The presence of viable female candidates for office can also tap into women's gender group identification. Women are more involved in politics when there are female candidates running for office.[9] Women also demonstrate greater political knowledge during elections that include a viable female candidate, indicating that they pay more attention and are more interested in these elections.[10] The presence of a female candidate is also related to internal political efficacy in women such that the presence of a female candidate is associated with women feeling more capable of participating in politics.[11] Finally, when a woman is on the ballot, women are more likely to discuss politics and attempt to persuade others to vote for the female candidate.[12]

Women voters are more involved in elections with a female candidate because the presence of the female candidate taps into their gender group identification. Since women still run for office less frequently than men, their presence makes their gender differences noticeable, and this therefore makes women voters' gender group membership more relevant. This is not to say that women will simply vote for any female candidate; rather, it indicates that when their group membership becomes relevant and noticeable, women are politically mobilized. While this research suggests that in general women are more involved in politics when there is a female candidate, the true effect a female candidate will have on women voters depends on the particulars of the race, candidate, political party, office, and election cycle.[13]

Identification with their gender group can also lead to a gender affinity in vote choice among women. Research indicates that in certain circumstances, women show a preference for female candidates over male candidates. One study found that women show a slight preference for female candidates, whereas men were equally likely to vote for a female as a male; gender affinity was even more noticeable in open-seat races, where women show a significantly stronger preference for female candidates.[14] Since political party affiliation is an extremely important factor in vote choice, gender affinity is most frequently seen when party is not a factor, such as in a primary race. For example, looking at Democratic candidates and voters, women display higher affect toward female candidates than male candidates, translating into an increased likelihood to vote for the female.[15]

Women do not support female candidates simply because they are women but because their group identification means that they feel a similarity to other women and a connection through shared concerns. This sort of group identification is related to a well-established concept of homophily. Homophily is the perceived similarity between two people. Previous research has established two important types of homophily concerning public figures: attitudinal homophily, the perceived similarities in attitudes, beliefs and values; and background homophily, the perception of shared educational or social background.[16] Numerous studies have demonstrated that homophily, particularly attitudinal homophily, is one of the strongest factors in vote choice.[17]

The connection between homophily and group identification is clear. Women who identify strongly with their gender group perceive similarities, shared experiences, and common values among all women. In a political sense, homophily is the perceived similarity between a voter and a candidate, specifically with regard to shared attitudes and shared background. The reason women are more likely to prefer a female candidate is because they believe the female candidate is more likely to share their concerns.[18] This is true even when the female and male candidates have similar issue positions. For example, in the 2008 Democratic primary, while Hillary Clinton and Barack Obama had very similar positions on the issues, Clinton, at least early on, enjoyed a lead among women voters.

GENDER GROUP IDENTIFICATION IN THE 21ST CENTURY

Most scholarly research on women's identification with their gender group came in the 1980s and early 1990s, when the gender gap emerged and more women began running for and winning elected office. One of the most thorough examinations of gender group identification was the work of Susan Tolleson Rinehart in her 1992 book, *Gender Consciousness and Politics*. Rinehart examined women's identification with their gender group from 1972 to 1988, using data from the American National Election Study, which asked participants to indicate which social groups they felt close to. A variety of potential social groups were listed including women, men, working people, labor unions, Catholics, African Americans, and young people. They were then asked to identify which group they felt closest to. This research revealed that as many as 60 percent of women felt close to other women and that they felt closer to other women than to men. Women also generally identified with groups thought to be of particular concern to women, such as the poor, elderly, and young people.

Another cleavage between women and men was that women indicated they did not feel close to groups associated with the white male status quo.

The American National Elections Study (ANES) stopped including the group closeness items used in Rinehart's research, so understanding women's gender group identification in the 21st century required an original survey. Conducting a survey specifically focused on women and their group connectedness allowed for a more in-depth exploration of the topic than was possible with the items included in the ANES, but it also meant that the sample would not be as large or as diverse as that of an ANES study. Throughout this chapter, I share the findings of the Women's Political Involvement (WPI) survey[19] conducted in the fall and winter of 2011, and I compare those findings to previous research on women's group identification. In the coming chapters, I use the WPI data and ANES data to further explain women's group identification and its relationship to a variety of political beliefs and behaviors.

The first step in understanding women's gender group identification was to find a suitable means of defining and measuring it. Identification includes recognition of similarities between one's self and the group and feeling that group membership is an important part of one's identity. The ANES was limited in its ability to tap into the complexities of identification, but the WPI allowed the opportunity to better measure and understand the components of group identification and its presence in the 21st century. The WPI included two measures of group identification that had been successfully used in previous research. The first measure was Mael and Tetrick's Identification with a Psychological Group (IDPG) scale.[20] This scale was developed to measure identification as defined by Tajfel's social identity theory.[21] The scale was used by Mael and Tetrick to measure individuals' identification with an organization, but it applies to any group with which people might feel a connection.

Mael and Tetrick define identification with a psychological group as "a feeling of oneness with a defined aggregate of persons," and they state it "involves the perception of shared prototypical characteristics, virtues, and flaws."[22] The IDPG scale consists of two elements of group identification: shared characteristics and shared experiences. The scale consists of four items that measure the shared characteristics component, which is defined as "the perception that one shares the attributes and characteristics of prototypical group members."[23] The scale also includes six shared experience items designed to measure "the perception that one shares the experiences, successes, and failures"[24] of one's gender group and the belief that "these successes and failures apply to and reflect"[25] the gender group. The IDPG scale has proven reliable in testing individuals' identification with a variety of groups including political party,[26] nationality,[27] and organizations.[28] In this study of gender group identification, the IDPG scale achieved acceptable reliability (α = .82).

Respondents were asked to think about their gender group and indicate their level of agreement with each statement ranging from "strongly disagree" (1) to "strongly agree" (7) for each of the ten IDPG items. The mean score on the IDPG was 4.69 on a 7-point scale, indicating that women have a moderate-to-high level of identification with their psychological group. To better examine the percentage of women who could be considered gender group identified, categories of women were created and analyzed based on IDPG score. Women with a mean IDPG score greater than or equal to 4 on the 7-point scale were classified as Identified, meaning they reported a high level of gender group identification. Those women with a mean score less than 4 on the IDPG were classified as Individualist, meaning they reported a low level of gender group identification. This revealed that the large majority of women had strong feelings of gender group identification; in fact, 82.22 percent of women could be considered Identified.

The IDPG results were further analyzed to better understand what attitudes and beliefs make up Identified women. Each item of the IDPG scale was recoded so that responses to each item fell into one of three categories: disagree, neutral, and agree. Table 2.1 displays the percent of women who agreed or disagreed with each item.

The IDPG scale demonstrates that the majority of women have some level of identification with their gender group. While the mean score showed an overall moderate level of identification, Table 2.1 demonstrates that when specific indicators of group identification are examined, a large majority of women have feelings of group identification. Most notable is that 87.2 percent of women said they had a number of qualities typical of their gender group, indicating a strong sense of shared characteristics. Furthermore, over 70 percent of women demonstrated a group orientation by indicating they use the term "we" to describe their gender group and that they feel like criticism of the group is a personal insult. Finally, two-thirds of women demonstrated feeling that women have a shared fate by indicating that they believe the group's successes are their successes. These results demonstrate that the majority of women possess feelings of shared characteristics and shared experiences, which are the key components of identification with a psychological group.

In addition to feelings of shared characteristics and experiences, gender group identification requires an emotional attachment to the group. In other words, people have to care about the group and their membership

Table 2.1   Women's Identification with a Psychological Group

	Agree	Neutral	Disagree
When someone criticizes this group, it feels like a personal insult.	74.9%	10.6%	14.5%
I *don't* act like the typical person of this group.	25.1%	26.5%	48.5%
I'm very interested in what others think about this group.	53.2%	28.1%	18.7%
The limitations associated with this group apply to me also.	51.8%	21.2%	27.0%
When I talk about this group, I usually say "we" rather than "they."	71.3%	16.4%	12.3%
I have a number of qualities typical of members of this group.	87.2%	8.6%	4.2%
This group's successes are my successes.	66.3%	23.1%	10.6%
If a story in the media criticized this group, I would feel embarrassed.	45.4%	24.2%	30.4%
When someone praises this group, it feels like a personal compliment.	52.9%	25.9%	21.2%
I act like a person of this group to a great extent.	61.8%	22.6%	15.6%

Table 2.2   Gender Group Attachment

Survey Item	Agree	Neutral	Disagree
I like being a member of my gender group.	93.3%	2.8%	3.9%
I am proud to be a member of my gender group.	93.0%	4.2%	2.8%
My gender group membership is central to who I am.	80.8%	13.9%	5.3%
I believe that being a member of my gender group is a positive experience.	90.5%	5.3%	4.2%

in that group. To measure this component of group identification, survey respondents were asked four questions used in previous research.[29] Respondents indicated their level of agreement with four statements on a 7-point scale ranging from "strongly disagree" (1) to "strongly agree" (7). The scale had high reliability ($\alpha = .90$). The results demonstrate that women have a strong attachment to their gender group. The mean score was 6.03 on a 7-point scale. Responses were collapsed into three categories to demonstrate the percentage of women who agreed, disagreed, and were neutral for each item. As Table 2.2 demonstrates, the overwhelming majority of women have a strong attachment to their gender group. On three of four items, over 90 percent of women agreed with the statements. This level of group attachment indicates that the majority of women consider gender to be an important part of their identity. Furthermore, attachment to the group is a necessary component of gender group identification and the politicization of that identification.

IDENTIFICATION AND DEMOGRAPHICS

To better understand which women were group identified, I analyzed women's gender group identification across a variety of demographic factors, including political party affiliation, liberal-conservative ideology, race, age, income, and education. Results indicate that gender group identification is not confined to a particularly political party. The mean scores on the IDPG and Gender Attachment scales were tested for a statistically significant difference based on political party affiliation (see Table 2.3). The only statistically significant difference was that Democratic women scored slightly higher on the Identification with a Psychological Group scale than Republican women, but the three groups were statistically similar on the Gender Group Attachment scale.[30] In other words, women of each political party demonstrate similar levels of gender group identification.

Gender group identification and liberal or feminist political beliefs have sometimes been conflated. Feminism is certainly one manifestation of gender group identification, and many feminists fall on the more liberal side of the political spectrum. However, there are also plenty of more conservative women who do not identify as feminists. One might assume that most of these women would identify with the Republican Party, but their placement on a conservative-liberal political-ideology scale provides more nuanced information on their political beliefs. Survey participants were asked to place themselves on a 10-point scale ranging from

Table 2.3 Gender Group Identification by Political Party

	IDPG Mean	Gender Attachment Mean
Democrat	4.84_a	5.97_a
Republican	4.56_b	6.08_a
Independent/other	4.65_{ab}	6.06_a

Note: Means in the same column that do not share subscripts differ at $p < .05$ in the LSD method.

"extremely liberal" (1) to "extremely conservative" (10). Placement on this scale was not correlated with any element of gender group identification; women across the liberal-to-conservative spectrum possess similar levels of identification.

Women belong to more groups than their gender group, and a woman's racial group is certainly an important part of her political identity. Since women of color are members of both a disadvantaged gender group and racial group, many identify strongly with both their race and gender. Since white women are not racially disadvantaged, it is possible that white and nonwhite women have different levels of gender identification. White women did score slightly higher on the Gender Group Attachment scale than did nonwhite women, likely because nonwhite women have dual attachments to both their gender group and their racial group. However, across all racial categories, women scored high on both group identification measures. These findings indicate that women, regardless of race, have an attachment to their gender group and feel that women share common characteristics and experiences.

Several additional demographic variables were examined to determine if they influenced women's group identification. Regression analysis revealed that women's levels of gender group identification could not be explained by age, income, or education. In other words, there was no correlation between gender group identification and these demographic factors, which indicates that women's gender group identification crosses generational, educational, socioeconomic, and political lines. Some previous research has found slight differences based on education and age.[31] As women age, they gain more life experience, which may make them feel closer to other women, and education, particularly college education, can provide women with knowledge and relationships that can enhance their feelings of group connectedness. However, much of that research was from the 1980s and early 1990s. Since that time, it has become much more common for women to seek higher education and to work outside the home, which may contribute to greater gender group identification across demographic lines.

IDENTIFICATION TO CONSCIOUSNESS

Group consciousness is a more complex theory of group-based thinking than gender group identification. Identification is one ingredient in consciousness, but group consciousness includes additional variables and occurs when social beliefs and actions arise out of identification with a group.[32] Rinehart defined women's gender consciousness as:

One's recognition that one's relationship to the political world is at least partly but nonetheless particularly shaped by being female or male. This recognition is followed by identification with others in the "group" of one's sex, positive affect toward the group, and a feeling of interdependence with the group's fortunes. It is suffused with politics when women's fortunes are assessed relative to those of other "groups" in society, women's particular contributions to politics and policy are weighed, and political orientations are constructed according to what the individual believes will be in the group's interest or expressive of the group's point of view.[33]

Group consciousness is an even stronger influence than identification on the social beliefs and behaviors of women because of how it structures political thinking. For example, Pamela Johnston Conover found that group consciousness creates more political sympathy for one's own group and more progroup positions.[34] In the case of women, this would mean that gender conscious women care about other women and take political positions they believe most benefit their gender group. Group consciousness also promotes political participation, especially when the individuals strongly identify with the group, prefer members of their own group, are dissatisfied with the group's status, and believe there are systematic inequalities that disadvantage their group.[35]

Based on previous research, there are three clear components of gender consciousness: identification with the group, polar affect, and collective orientation.[36] As demonstrated in the previous section, identification with the group is the feeling of connectedness, similarity, and a shared fate with one's gender group. Polar affect is a preference for members of one's own group. This could be seen in a preference for policies that benefit women, a prioritization of political issues that uniquely affect women, or a gender affinity in vote choice. The third component, collective orientation, is the belief that women must work as a group for the betterment of that group.

Pamela Johnston Conover's cognitive-affective model of group consciousness highlights the distinction between identification and consciousness. She argues that identification is the seed that grows into consciousness, because identification creates an in-group bias resulting in an increased evaluation of the in-group; it also leads one to attribute positive outcomes to the in-group and negative outcomes to external factors, and it enhances the personal relevance of group outcomes for the individual.[37] In other words, group identification is the first step toward group consciousness. This influences political participation by creating a progroup position on issues, especially if candidates or the media have used group cues to frame the issues.

Table 2.4 Polar Affect

Survey Item	Agree	Neutral	Disagree
Women should have more power in government and business than men.	15.6%	44.0%	40.4%
Men should have more power in government and business than women.	4.5%	35.4%	60.1%
In most families, women should have more power and influence than men.	20.9%	49%	29.8%
In most families, women are better suited for making important decisions than men.	13.3%	46.8%	39.8%
In government and business, women are better suited for making important decisions than men.	13.6%	52.6%	33.7%

For women whose group identification has grown into group consciousness, they may also express polar affect and collective orientation. Polar affect is the preference for the in-group over the out-group. This can be displayed in a woman's preference for a female candidate over a male candidate and prioritization of issues important to women or issue positions that most benefit women. This is not to say that women with polar affect dislike men; rather, it is a positive feeling toward women and their unique perspectives and positions. For this study, polar affect was measured using five items based on the 1992 American National Election Study (ANES)[38] where respondents indicated their level of agreement on a five-point scale ranging from "strongly disagree" (1) to "strongly agree" (5). The polar affect scale achieved acceptable reliability ($\alpha = .83$).

Results show an overall mean score of 2.67, with a maximum score of 5, indicating that women have a relatively low-to-moderate level of polar affect. The responses were collapsed to show the percentage of women who agreed, disagreed, or felt neutral for each item; the percentages are displayed in Table 2.4. The majority of women land in the neutral category for all but one of the items. A majority (60.1 percent) of women disagree with the idea that men should have more power in business and government than women. The high percentage of neutral and disagree responses is likely due to the polar affect statements requiring participants to indicate a preference for one gender over the other. It is likely that these results reflect a desire for equality rather than dominance.

Table 2.5   Collective Orientation

Survey Item	Agree	Neutral	Disagree
It is not enough for a woman to be successful herself.	60.2%	21.4%	17.8%
While individual effort is important, the best way for women to really improve their position is if they work together.	56.0%	30.4%	13.1%

Table 2.6   IDPG as a Predictor of Consciousness

Consciousness Variable	B	SE β	β
Polar affect	.24	.04	.30*
Collective orientation	.37	.05	.36*

Note: $p < .01$.

The final element of gender consciousness is collective orientation. This is the belief that women must work together to overcome discrimination and inequality. Collective orientation was assessed with the two items used in previous research.[39] The scale achieved acceptable reliability ($\alpha = .76$). Survey results demonstrate that women have a moderate to high level of collective orientation, with a mean score of 3.54 out of 5. As is reflected in Table 2.5, the majority of women agree that women must work together for the betterment of the group.

Since previous research indicates that group identification is the seed that grows into group consciousness, regression analyses were conducted to test whether a woman's identification with her psychological group (IDPG) and her attachment to her gender group predicted levels of polar affect and collective orientation. Regression analysis (see Table 2.6) revealed that IDPG was a significant predictor of both polar affect and collective orientation. In other words, as a woman's identification with her psychological (gender) group increases, so do her polar affect and collective orientation. IDPG explained 9.2 percent of the variance in polar affect and 13.7 percent in collective orientation. However, attachment to her gender group was not a significant predictor of either polar affect or collective orientation. These findings suggest that gender group attachment is, in and of itself, not a strong enough seed to sprout into gender consciousness. On the other hand, identification with a psychological group is more likely, but not certain, to result in consciousness.

DEMOGRAPHICS AND CONSCIOUSNESS

While results indicate that women generally have a high level of group identification, their level of polar affect and collective orientation is lower. In order to understand what factors besides group identification contribute to gender consciousness, analysis was conducted on several demographic factors, including education, age, race, and placement on a liberal-conservative political-ideology scale (see Table 2.7). Results indicate that none of these variables explain polar affect, but regression analysis revealed a relationship between collective orientation, age, and political ideology. As women's age increases, so does their level of collective orientation, and more liberal women demonstrate greater levels of collective orientation. Together, age and political ideology explained 14 percent of the variance in collective orientation. These findings should not be surprising. As women grow older, they encounter more experiences of sexual discrimination and are more likely to recognize systematic inequalities, which require a group-based response to be solved. Liberals are also more likely to support group- and government-based solutions to inequality.

Analysis of gender consciousness based on political party revealed that Republican women have significantly lower levels of collective orientation than both Democratic and Independent women[40] (see Table 2.8). There are two possible explanations for this. First, Republican women are more likely to accept traditional gender roles and therefore not to believe that sexual discrimination is a widespread problem requiring group action. Second, Republicans tend to believe in a smaller government, so Republican women are less likely to support group-based responses that call for government action.

This is not to say that Republican women do not identify with their gender group. In fact, as the results on party and group identification indicate, Republican women have moderate levels of identification with their psychological gender group and high levels of group attachment. Furthermore, Republican women's level of group attachment is slightly higher than that of Democratic and Independent women. What this indicates is that group identification and attachment can, and does, exist without the components of group consciousness. Since collective orientation is associated with liberal women, the difference might be related more to feminism than gender group identification. In other words, women in all parties might feel connected to their gender group, but the way that becomes politicized might be different based on their political ideology and beliefs about the feminist movement.

Table 2.7 Collective Orientation and Demographics

Demographic Variable	B	SE β	β
Age	.01	.01	.26*
Liberal-conservative placement	−.11	.02	−.27*

Note: *p < .00.

Table 2.8 Gender Consciousness by Political Party

Party	Collective Orientation Mean		Polar Affect Mean	
	Mean	Standard Deviation	Mean	Standard Deviation
Democrat	3.69$_a$	.85	2.75$_a$	.63
Republican	3.24$_b$	.81	2.61$_a$	.69
Independent/other	3.73$_a$	.85	2.66$_a$	.69

Note: Means in the same column that do not share subscripts differ at p < .05 in the LSD method.

GENDER CONSCIOUSNESS OR FEMINIST CONSCIOUSNESS?

As the results of this study indicate, gender consciousness is not found in all group-identified women, and it may manifest in different ways depending on a woman's beliefs. Of all types of group consciousness studied, gender group consciousness has been one of the more difficult to measure and understand. The primary reason is that gender differs as a group from many other groups (e.g., African Americans, Latino Americans, the working class) because sexes are interdependent. Many theories related to group consciousness assume that members have much more contact with the in-group than the out-group, bolstering consciousness. In other words, people tend to interact more with members of their own social groups.

This is not the case for women. Women often interact with men as much as or more than they interact with other women, and this complicates the development of group identification into consciousness. Furthermore, women and men's lives are often intertwined and interdependent. In the case of heterosexual married women, their economic and family lives are deeply tied to the lives of men. This relationship between men and women makes it difficult for strong gender consciousness to develop. Despite the complicated nature of gender consciousness, research has shown it does exist and has very real consequences for politics.

As my results demonstrate, gender group identification can be found across all demographic factors, but gender consciousness, particularly as a collective orientation, varies. This is likely because existing gender-consciousness research has focused more on what could be defined as a "feminist consciousness," not a general women's consciousness.[41] In fact, much of the existing research has focused on women who self-identify as feminists, and this research has demonstrated the strength of feminist consciousness in political decision making. Feminist consciousness is characterized by identification with the group "feminists" (rather than women), egalitarian sex-role attitudes, and a positive feeling towards the feminist movement.[42] Anne Reid and Nuala Purcell argue that exposure to feminism increases identification with feminists and that feminist identification involves the belief in a common fate for women and a positive evaluation of feminists.[43] Research has shown the largest predictors of feminist consciousness are education (high) and church attendance (low).[44] A variety of intrapersonal variables including personality traits, life experiences, and education also contribute to feminist consciousness.[45]

Feminist consciousness has been shown to predict warmer feelings towards Democrats,[46] positive feelings toward women, feelings of interdependence with other women, the dislike and fear of war, and support for social programs.[47] There is also a strong positive relationship between feminist consciousness and particular positions on women's issues.[48] Additionally, women with high feminist consciousness have distinct political and basic values; they are more liberal, less racist, more egalitarian, and more sympathetic to the disadvantaged.[49] Previous research has found that the influence of feminist consciousness on issue positions remains even after controlling for partisanship and ideology and is second only to party identification in its influence on issue stances.

While this research reveals important information on feminist women, it fails to address the gender group identification and consciousness of nonfeminist women. As my research demonstrates, gender identification is not confined to a particular subgroup of women; it is present in women from all political parties and across demographic characteristics. Sue Tolleson Rinehart argues that gender consciousness is not a variable that can be measured; rather, it is the political manifestation of group identification.[50] Furthermore, she argues that all women can be gender conscious. While all feminists are gender consciousness, not all gender-conscious women are feminists. Women on the right of the political spectrum may be concerned with individual liberty and economic freedom, but they may not consider themselves feminists. However, they can still be gender conscious if they identify with their gender group and have political preferences linked to their group membership and identity. The following chapter discusses how a woman's beliefs about gender roles intersect with gender group identification to shape two types of gender-conscious women. These women have important group-based similarities, but they also have important differences that often put them on different sides of the political aisle.

CHAPTER 3

Gender Identity, Gender-Role Beliefs, and Politics

The gender gap in vote choice and political beliefs makes clear that women and men, in general, see at least some political issues differently. Women occupy a distinct social position shaped by their gender identity, and cultural norms reinforce that identity. Whether it is expectations about women's roles, such as being a mother and primary caretaker, or the real-life experiences of women in a still-male-dominated world, gender is an important part of many women's self-identity. That identification with their gender group has a clear influence on how women view political issues and engage in politics. Women with greater levels of group identification are more likely to think and act on behalf of their gender group. As explained in chapter 2, group consciousness is an even stronger, more politicized, form of group connectedness. While there are trends and similarities among women's political beliefs and behaviors, not all women hold the same political beliefs or support the same candidates.

While group identification and consciousness provide one explanation for differences and similarities among women voters, another important part of women's identity must be considered if we are to truly understand the differing ways women see issues and behave politically. A woman's beliefs about gender roles are an extremely important part of her identity. A woman who believes in traditional gender roles will see the world and politics very differently than a woman with egalitarian beliefs. Women with traditional gender-role beliefs see women and men as having different roles in family and society, and they often believe that women's primary role is as a caretaker in the private sphere of home and family. For example, women with traditional beliefs are likely to believe that women and men have complementary roles, where men are the breadwinners and women are the caretakers.

This is not to say that traditional women consider women to be the lesser sex or believe that women should abstain from the public sphere; rather, they see the sexes as fundamentally different and believe that they have different strengths. On the other hand, women with egalitarian gender-role beliefs see men and women as equally able to fulfill both private and public sphere duties and believe that women should be given the same opportunities as men. For egalitarian women, the genders are equal; it is like comparing apples to apples. However, for traditional women the genders are fundamentally different, like comparing apples to oranges. These two competing worldviews lead to differing positions on issues, candidate preferences, and political engagement.

Much existing research on group identification and consciousness has focused primarily on feminist women but has neglected the role of gender-based consciousness on the political beliefs and behaviors of nonfeminist women. In her book *Gender Consciousness and Politics*, political scientist Sue Tolleson Rinehart argues that all women can be gender conscious; even women who do not consider themselves feminist may be aware of sex discrimination and sympathetic to feminist goals, and women who hold and embrace traditional gender roles may still believe that women have a unique perspective and valuable role to play in the political world.[1] Women who identify with their gender group, particularly those with gender consciousness, act on behalf of the group, and both feminist and nonfeminist women can act for the group.

The political issue of abortion provides a clear example of both the division between traditional and egalitarian women and their similarity in terms of group-based political beliefs. On one hand, there are egalitarian woman fighting for abortion rights because they believe that women, not the government, should have the right to make decisions about their bodies and reproduction. On the other hand, women with traditional gender-role beliefs may fight against abortion because they believe it is the role of women to protect and care for children and see abortion as contradictory to those beliefs. Rinehart explains, "It is difficult to question the existence of real gender consciousness in either kind of activist, one a consciousness grounded in protection of traditional roles and the other grounded in a challenge to the validity of those same roles."[2] While these two groups of women belong to the same gender group and may identify with that group, their views about what that identity is or should be differ and lead them to differing political positions and priorities.

This approach to gender consciousness is particularly relevant today, when there are more women entering the political arena who do not identify themselves as feminists and who hold more traditional gender-role beliefs. From the 1970s through the 1990s, many of the women active in the political world represented the feminist movement and were fighting for change that reflected their egalitarian gender-role beliefs. These women were often associated with the Democratic Party and included such notable women as Barbara Boxer, Dianne Feinstein, Carol Moseley Braun, Barbara Mikulski, Shirley Chisholm, and Nancy Pelosi. In addition to women serving in elected office, there have been many politically active feminist women since women's suffrage, including Elizabeth Cady Stanton, Betty Friedan, Gloria Steinem, and bell hooks, just to name a few.

There have always been politically active conservative women holding traditional notions of gender roles, such as Phyllis Schlafly, but by the 1990s and continuing into the 21st century, women of the new political right also became more engaged in politics and started running for office in higher numbers than they had previously. Such women who have served in office include Sarah Palin, Michele Bachmann, Jackie Walorski, and Joni Ernst. The rise of the conservative woman can also be seen in political media, with women like Ann Coulter, Laura Ingraham, and Maggie Gallagher voicing conservative, traditional beliefs. There has also been a growth of vocal conservative women leading women's political organizations, such as Marjorie Dannenfelser, president of the Susan B. Anthony List, and Penny Nance, CEO of Concerned Women for America. While liberal women still outnumber the conservative in terms of voters, there has been a notable rise in politically active conservative women who articulate very different positions on a variety of issues and reflect a different type of gender group identity than liberal women.

Women on both sides of the spectrum can feel connected to their gender group, and as was demonstrated in the previous chapter, a significant number of women from both political parties indicate feelings of shared experiences, shared characteristics, and group attachment. Furthermore, a sense of collective orientation and polar affect can be found in women across party lines at varying levels. Despite this, little research has accounted for women with more conservative beliefs or compared the political beliefs and actions of conservative group-identified women with those of liberal group-identified women.

It is important to note, and will be discussed later in the chapter, that political party is not a sufficient means for understanding women's gender-role beliefs. There are women who identify as Republican who also consider themselves feminists, and there are Democratic women who also believe in traditional gender roles. The purpose of this chapter is to identify and compare two types of group-identified women: those with egalitarian beliefs and those with traditional beliefs. These two groups will also be compared to those women who do not display the key elements of gender group identification.

GENDER AND MODERN CAMPAIGNING

The 2008 election demonstrated the importance of identity politics in contemporary elections. The differences among female candidates were blatant in 2008, with two prominent women fighting to break the glass ceiling to the White House: Hillary Rodham Clinton and Sarah Palin, very different women with very different beliefs. In 2008, Clinton represented the second wave feminists of the baby boom generation and gained much support from older working-class women.[3] Palin represented something different; she did not share many issue positions held by traditional feminists, resulting in attacks from many women on the left.[4] Palin's focus on her role as a mother and her traditional beliefs led some to call her the antithesis of feminism,[5] but others considered Palin a new archetype in the third wave of feminism.[6] The split among women who supported Palin and those who despised her represent an opportunity to explore different types of gender identification and consciousness. As Rinehart's work demonstrated, women may identify with and act on behalf of all women, but they may do so in considerably different ways with strikingly different goals.

Clinton and Palin exhibited their gender-role ideologies and gender identity in their campaign speeches and advertisements. Clinton gave a speech on May 31, 2007, a few months after she had announced her 2008 candidacy, to the Silicon Valley Leadership Group where she specifically addressed the underrepresentation of women and minorities in STEM fields and to compliment a specific woman:

> Sixth, we have to open the doors of science and engineering to more people, especially women and minorities. We've done a great job bringing the best and brightest from around the world but we have to do more to get women and minorities to be involved, and as president I will try to promote that, to tap new sources of talent and to set examples by having a greater public awareness of what awaits. You know, one of my favorite people is the president of RPI in New York who previously was the head of the Nuclear Regulatory Commission. She's the first or the second African American woman to receive a PhD in nuclear physics. Well, I don't know if enough people know about her and know about what she has done with her life and how she can, perhaps, serve as an example for others.[7]

Clinton emphasized women and women's issues in a variety of speeches and advertisements. In one advertisement titled "Thank You," an unnamed woman speaks in support of Clinton: "She is a symbol for the females. I'm sixty years old, and I want her to win and I will continue to support her the best I can." The ad then cuts to a video clip of Clinton stating, "I love that sign—'Pennsylvania women for Hillary.' Thank you very much. There's also a great sign back there—'Our mamas for the mama.' I like that." After Clinton lost the Democratic nomination in 2008, she tried to rally her supporters and women behind Barack Obama. In her speech at the Democratic National Convention, she not only attacked McCain's position on a variety of issues affecting women but also reminded the audience of women's history in politics and the importance of fighting for equality:

> I'm a United States Senator because in 1848 a group of courageous women and a few brave men gathered in Seneca Falls, New York, many traveling for days and nights, to participate in the first convention on women's rights in our history.
>
> And so dawned a struggle for the right to vote that would last 72 years, handed down by mother to daughter to granddaughter—and a few sons and grandsons along the way.
>
> These women and men looked into their daughters' eyes, imagined a fairer and freer world, and found the strength to fight. To rally and picket. To endure ridicule and harassment. To brave violence and jail.
>
> And after so many decades—88 years ago on this very day—the Nineteenth Amendment guaranteeing women the right to vote would be forever enshrined in our Constitution.
>
> My mother was born before women could vote. But in this election my daughter got to vote for her mother for President.
>
> This is the story of America. Of women and men who defy the odds and never give up.[8]

Sarah Palin also spoke specifically to women and focused on her gender and traditional gender-role beliefs. This began when she was announced as John McCain's running mate on August 29, 2008. She began by introducing her family and noting that it was her 20th wedding anniversary. She went on to further emphasize her role as a mother and wife, saying, "I was just your average 'hockey mom' in Alaska. We were busy raising our kids. I was serving as the team mom and coaching some basketball on the side. I got involved in the PTA and then was elected to the City Council and then elected mayor of my hometown, where my agenda was to stop wasteful spending and cut property taxes and put the people first."[9]

Palin's speech at the Republican National Convention provides another example of her emphasis on traditional gender roles. When speaking of McCain's expertise in military affairs, she tied the topic to her own experience as the mother of a solider:

> He's a man who wore the uniform of this country for 22 years, and refused to break faith with those troops in Iraq who have now brought victory within sight.
>
> And as the mother of one of those troops, that is exactly the kind of man I want as commander in chief. I'm just one of many moms who'll say an extra prayer each night for our sons and daughters going into harm's way.
>
> Our son Track is 19.
>
> And one week from tomorrow—September 11th—he'll deploy to Iraq with the Army infantry in the service of his country.[10]

These examples of Clinton and Palin in the 2008 election demonstrate how both women with egalitarian and traditional gender-role beliefs can politically identify with their gender group. Clinton's 2016 campaign provided even more explicit examples of egalitarian gender-group identification because she made gender an even larger part of her campaign. For example, in several ads, she discussed the pay gap and paid family leave. In her ad "Paygap" Clinton clearly embraced the idea of fighting for and with women, stating, "In 2015, many women are paid less than men for doing the same work. Your fights are my fights, and I won't quit until Americans have a chance to get ahead and stay ahead."[11] Numerous examples exist of female candidates evoking group identification and their gender-role beliefs, and they come from women on the left, such as Claire McCaskill and Kirsten Gillibrand, and from women on the right, such as Kelly Ayotte and Joni Ernst. This sort of political rhetoric exists for a reason; it reflects two distinct types of women voters.

MEASURING GENDER-ROLE IDEOLOGY

As should be clear at this point women are not a monolithic voting bloc. Rather there are important divisions among women, and gender-role beliefs are one division that shapes political attitudes. Furthermore, as established in chapter 2, women's identification with their gender group also influences political attitudes. To better understand women voters, this study examines the relationships between gender-role beliefs, group identification, and political orientations. To begin the analysis, women's gender-role beliefs had to be measured. The Ambivalent Sexism Inventory (ASI)[12] was used because it best captures the multifaceted nature of gender role beliefs. Developed by psychologists Peter Glick and Susan T. Fiske to measure the complicated and sometimes contradictory beliefs about women and men, this scale has proven to be a reliable measure of modern gender-role beliefs.

Consistent with past research using the ASI, this study examined gender-role ideology as a composite sexism score and then more specifically along the ASI's two distinct factors. As a composite sexism score, a high ASI score indicates more sexist—or traditional—beliefs about women's roles, and a low score indicates more egalitarian attitudes about women's roles. The ASI consists of two distinct factors: hostile sexism (HS) and benevolent sexism (BS). Hostile sexism reflects beliefs that are commonly considered sexist and is characterized by a feeling of hostility toward women. Hostile sexism includes beliefs that women exaggerate unfair treatment at work and are looking for special treatment and that feminist are seeking to gain control over men. The ASI measures three components of hostile sexism: dominate paternalism, competitive gender differences, and heterosexual hostility. Dominant paternalism refers to the belief that women are not capable on their own and are in need of a dominant male in their life. Competitive gender differences reflect the belief that only men have the necessary traits for leadership, and heterosexual hostility is the idea that women use sex to control men.

Distinct from hostile sexism but related to it is benevolent sexism. Benevolent sexism is a subtler form of sexism and is defined by Glick and Fiske as "a set of interrelated attitudes toward women that are sexist in terms of viewing women stereotypically and in restricted roles but that are subjectively positive in feeling tone (for the perceiver) and also tend to elicit behaviors typically categorized as prosocial (e.g., helping) or intimacy-seeking (e.g., self-disclosure)."[13] Examples of benevolent sexist beliefs include the belief that women have a superior moral sensibility and that women should be protected and cherished by men. The ASI also measures three components of benevolent sexism, reflecting the more positive side of the hostile sexism components. Benevolent sexism consists of protective paternalism, the belief that men need to protect and care for women; complementary gender differences, the belief that men and women complement each other through the traditional divisions of labor and traits; and heterosexual intimacy, the belief that men need intimate relationships with women to be complete.

Research has demonstrated that HS and BS are correlated but distinct factors,[14] and both viewpoints demonstrate a preference for a traditional gender-role ideology.[15] Since this study attempted to understand the relationship between gender-role ideology and other variables, the ASI provides the best available means to capture the full picture of modern sexism and gender role beliefs. The ASI is composed of 22 items, 11 BS and 11 HS items, with responses ranging from "disagree strongly" (0) to "agree strongly" (5) with no neutral midpoint. Examples of hostile sexist statements include the following:

- Women are too easily offended.
- Most women fail to appreciate fully all that men do for them.
- When women lose to men in a fair competition, they typically complain about being discriminated against.
- Women seek to gain power by getting control over men.

Examples of benevolent sexism statements include the following:

- No matter how accomplished he is, a man is not truly complete as a person unless he has the love of a woman.
- Men should be willing to sacrifice their own well-being in order to provide financially for the women in their lives.
- Women, compared to men, tend to have a superior moral sensibility.
- A good woman should be set on a pedestal by her man.

The ASI and its individual components (HS and BS) have all had high reliability in previous research.[16] The composite scale proved reliable in this study ($\alpha = .90$), as did the individual components (HS $\alpha = .86$, BS $\alpha = .86$).

WOMEN'S GENDER-ROLE BELIEFS AND DEMOGRAPHIC CHARACTERISTICS

To understand the factors that might influence women's gender-role ideology, the relationships between the ASI scores with age and level of education were examined using regression analysis. The findings regarding age were particularly interesting; age was a significant predictor of gender-role ideology, such that younger women were associated with more traditional, or sexist, gender-role beliefs on the ASI and its two components, BS and HS. However, this finding was explained by the influence of education on gender-role beliefs. After accounting for education, age was no longer a significant predictor, indicating that it is not so much a woman's age that predicts her gender role beliefs but rather her level of education. In fact,

Table 3.1   ASI, Education, and Political Ideology Correlations

	ASI Composite	Hostile Sexism	Benevolent Sexism	Age	Education	Ideology
ASI composite	–	.87*	.88*	–.28*	–.45*	.39*
Hostile sexism	–	–	.53*	–.23*	–.43*	.35*
Benevolent sexism	–	–	–	–.26*	–.34*	.33*
Age	–	–	–	–	–.10	–.01
Education	–	–	–	–	–	.30*
Ideology	–	–	–	–	–	–

Note: *p < .01.

education explained 20 percent of the variance in ASI scores, which is a rather large proportion.[17] In other words, as a woman's education level increases, she is more likely to have egalitarian beliefs.

These findings are consistent with previous research on feminist beliefs. For example, one study found that as women are exposed to feminism, usually through college course work, they become more likely to identify as feminist and to articulate feminist beliefs.[18] Rinehart found a similar relationship between egalitarianism and education; however, she also found that older women tended to hold more traditional beliefs.[19] These contradictory findings suggest that the relationship between age and education has changed since Rinehart's study over 20 years ago. This change is likely the result of a more highly educated female population. In other words, the older women in Rinehart's study were less likely to have a college education than the older women in this study. This, in turn, resulted in a more educated and egalitarian group of women in older age groups. Table 3.1 displays the correlations between the variables of interest and clearly demonstrates the strong correlation between education and gender role beliefs.

In addition to age and education, political ideology has been tied to gender-role beliefs. Study participants indicated their political ideology by placing themselves on a scale ranging from "extremely liberal" (1) to "extremely conservative" (10). Analysis revealed that placement on the conservative-liberal ideology scale predicts over 15 percent of the variance in composite ASI scores.[20] The relationship demonstrates that women who identify as politically conservative are more likely to hold traditional gender-role beliefs. Furthermore, examinations of correlations, as shown in Table 3.1, indicate a positive relationship between conservative ideology and both benevolent sexism, which reflects positive yet

Table 3.2   Sexism Scores by Political Party

	Democrats	Republicans	Independents
ASI composite	2.97$_a$	3.45$_b$	3.25$_b$
Hostile sexism	2.91$_a$	3.38$_b$	3.14$_{ab}$
Benevolent sexism	3.03$_a$	3.52$_b$	3.36$_b$

Note: Scores are based on seven-point scales with lower scores associated with egalitarian sex-role beliefs. Means in the same row that do not share subscripts significantly differ at $p > .01$ in the Bonferroni method.

limiting stereotypes about women, and hostile sexism, which reflects a negative view of women, particularly in the public sphere.

Related to political ideology is identification with a political party. Given that the Republican's party platform is based on a conservative ideology and the Democrat's on a liberal ideology, it would be expected that women with more traditional gender-role beliefs would be more likely to identify as Republicans. As is demonstrated in Table 3.2, women who identify as Democrats report significantly lower levels of sexism on the ASI and its two factors, BS and HS. Most interesting are those women who do not identify with either party and are categorized as Independents. Women in this group fall between Republicans and Democrats on the ASI, and the only significant differences found were that Democrats expressed more egalitarian beliefs than Independents on the composite ASI and on the benevolent-sexism factor. These findings suggest that there is a relationship between gender-role ideology and political party affiliation but that the differences between groups is not as large as one might expect. Put simply, egalitarian women are not all Democrats, and traditional women are not all Republicans; the spectrum of gender-role beliefs can be found in both parties and among Independents.

These analyses help to paint a picture of egalitarian and traditional women. Egalitarian women tend to be more educated and consider themselves to be more liberal. On the other hand, traditional women tend to have less education and identify more strongly as politically conservative. Democratic women express slightly more egalitarian gender-role beliefs than Republican and Independent women, but there is little difference between the gender-role beliefs of Republicans and Independents. Now that a profile of egalitarian and traditional women has been created, a more nuanced examination of women based on a combination of the gender role beliefs and level of group identification is possible. The combination of these two variables provides a more complete picture of the nuances among women voters.

GENDER-ROLE IDEOLOGY, GROUP IDENTIFICATION, AND CONSCIOUSNESS

As the central variables of this study are a woman's identification with her gender group and her gender-role ideology, these variables were tested for correlations with each other as well as with the gender-consciousness variables. Previous research found similarities among women based on these categories, specifically that egalitarian women were more likely to identify with their gender group.[21] However, few scholars have revisited this connection since. Therefore, my analysis reveals, first, what the relationships are between gender-role ideology, gender identification, gender consciousness and, second, if women with high gender-group identification are more likely to have a particular gender-role ideology.

In order to determine the relationships between variables, bivariate correlations were computed among the sexism (ASI, HS, and BS), gender group identification (IDPG), gender attachment, and gender-consciousness variables (polar affect and collective orientation) for the entire sample of women. As demonstrated in Table 3.3, a significant correlation emerged between BS and IDPG such that higher levels of benevolent sexism were correlated to higher levels of identification. In other words, stronger benevolent sexist beliefs were associated with greater gender group identification. While a statistically significant relationship exists, it is rather weak and is likely caused by a specific subset of women. This relationship is explored further when Egalitarian-Identified and Traditional-Identified women are compared later in this chapter.

Additionally, the group consciousness variables of polar affect and collective orientation were correlated with ASI scores (see Table 3.3). Polar affect was significantly correlated with all three components of the ASI, indicating that traditional gender-role beliefs are associated with a greater preference for members of one's own gender group. The strongest relationship was between benevolent sexism and polar affect. Since benevolent sexism includes beliefs that women are more moral, should be protected, and needed by men, it is not surprising that this variable would be associated with polar affect, as it reflects a preference for one's own gender group and often a sense of superiority over the out-group.

Previous research has revealed a relationship between feminist attitudes and polar affect, but these findings suggest that women who hold more traditional gender-role beliefs might also feel greater affect for the in-group (women). However, the reasons behind polar affect may differ based on whether women hold more egalitarian or traditional gender-role beliefs; this will be examined later in this chapter. On the other hand, consistent with previous research on gender and feminist consciousness,

Table 3.3   Group Identification, Consciousness, and Sex-Role Ideology Bivariate Correlations

	IDPG	Gender Attachment	Polar Affect	Collective Orientation	ASI	Hostile ASI	Benevolent ASI
IDPG	–	.44*	.30*	.36*	.10	−.03	.19*
Gender attachment	–	–	.09	.24*	.01	−.05	.07
Polar affect	–	–	–	.25*	.26*	.15*	.30*
Collective orientation	–	–	–	–	−.17*	−.27*	−.04
ASI	–	–	–	–	–	.87*	.88*
Hostile sexism	–	–	–	–	–	–	.53*

Note: *$p < .01$.

the analysis in this study revealed a negative correlation between collective orientation and both the ASI and HS. Thus, egalitarian gender beliefs are associated with a greater sense that women must work as a group to overcome discrimination. These findings are consistent with a major tenet of the feminist movement—that collective action through protest and politics is necessary to better women's place in society.

These findings indicate interesting relationships between gender-role beliefs, group identification, and consciousness when looking at women as a whole. However, as previous research and analysis in this study have found, these variables may not operate the same way for all women. Gender-role beliefs and gender consciousness may have differing relationships depending on how strongly a woman identifies with her gender group. In order to more specifically understand the interaction of these variables, women were analyzed based on their level of gender group identification to explore whether these groups varied in their gender-role ideology and gender consciousness.

GROUPING WOMEN BASED ON GROUP IDENTIFICATION

The only previous research that examined women based on both group identification and gender-role ideology was Rinehart's 1992 work. Her analysis began by splitting women into two groups: those with high levels of gender group identification (the Identified) and those with low levels of gender group identification (the Individualists). My analysis begins by grouping women in this way. To categorize women based on their level of group identification, scores on the Identification with a Psychological Group were used. This measure was chosen over the Group Attachment scale because it contained two factors of identification (shared experience and shared characteristics) rather than one and the IDPG responses had more variance. Women with a mean IDPG score greater than or equal to four on the seven-point scale were classified as Identified, meaning they reported a high level of gender group identification. Those women with a mean score less than four on the IDPG were classified as Individualist, meaning they reported a low level of gender group identification.[22]

Identified versus Individualist Women

To test whether or not Identified women differed significantly from Individualist women in their gender-role beliefs, the ASI, HS, and BS scores of the two groups were compared.[23] Analysis revealed no significant differences in the gender-role ideologies of women who feel that their gender is an important part of their identity as compared to those who do not. This means that group identification does not explain gender-role beliefs and that these two variables are distinct. In other words, women who identify with their gender group are equally likely to hold traditional as egalitarian gender-role beliefs.

However, analysis did find that Identified women ($M = 3.56$, $SD = .84$) reported significantly higher levels of collective orientation than Individualist women ($M = 3.12$, $SD = 1.23$). Identified women ($M = 2.72$, $SD = .68$) also reported higher levels of polar affect than Individualist women ($M = 2.44$, $SD = .56$).[24] Previous research argued that group identification was linked to both polar affect and collective orientation to form group consciousness, and this study confirms that Identified women of the 21st century still show higher levels of these gender consciousness variables.[25] Put simply, Identified women are more likely to have positive feelings about their gender group, favor that group, and believe that women must work together to overcome inequality.

There are clear differences between Identified and Individualist women in terms of gender consciousness, and this warrants further comparative analysis between these two groups in order to answer two questions. First, what are the relationships between sexism (ASI, HS, and BS), group identification (IDPG), gender group attachment, and gender consciousness (polar affect and collective orientation) for Identified and Individualist women? Second, how do those relationships differ between Identified and Individualist women? To address these questions, bivariate correlations were conducted for both groups on the variables of interest and are reported in Table 3.4.

For Identified women, many of the variables correlated with each other. The relationships were such that higher levels of group identification (IDPG) were associated with higher polar affect, collective orientation, and benevolent sexism. Interestingly, higher polar affect was associated with more traditional, or sexist, gender-role beliefs on all three sexism variables (ASI, BS, and HS). On the other hand, collective orientation negatively correlated with all three sexism variables. As was noted previously, these findings are contrary to previous research that found both polar affect and collective orientation to be associated with more egalitarian attitudes. However, much of that previous research was focused on feminist women, not women with traditional gender-role beliefs. Perhaps the components of gender consciousness are present among women with traditional beliefs but operate differently.

These findings paint a complicated picture of the Identified woman; she is someone who has an emotional attachment to her gender group, cares about the group as a whole, and believes that women must work together for equality, but she may also hold restricting beliefs about women's gender roles. While many of these characteristics can be defined as feminist and are specifically related to second-wave liberal feminism, benevolent sexist beliefs do not. It is quite likely that Identified women as a group may hold some contradictory beliefs, and this warrants a more nuanced analysis of Identified women.

Bivariate correlations (reported in Table 3.4) were also conducted for Individualist women. A positive correlation emerged between gender group identification and gender attachment as well as between identification and collective orientation, indicating that even Individualist women who feel more connected to their gender group have an emotional attachment to the group and are more likely to believe that women must work together to overcome discrimination. However, by definition, Individualist women have lower levels of group identification, so it is important to note that the correlations that existed for Identified women were very different. Identified women showed a more complex relationship between these variables, as can be seen by the numerous correlations.

In fact, there are more differences than similarities in how the variables of interest operate for Identified and Individualist women. While the relationship between identification (IDPG), attachment, and collective orientation existed for both groups, Identified women were distinct in that they also displayed relationships between IDPG, polar affect, and ASI scores. In other words, while Individualist women may care somewhat about women as a group, it is not a defining part of their identity. Identified women, however, do feel that their gender is an essential part of their identity, and that feeling is related to their gender-role beliefs, feelings towards other women, and feelings towards men.

The profiles of Identified and Individualist women show some similarities between the two groups, but they show many more differences.

Table 3.4   Identification, Consciousness, and Sex-Role Ideology
Bivariate Correlations by Group Identification

	IDPG	Gender Attachment	Polar Affect	Collective Orientation	ASI	Hostile ASI	Benevolent ASI
Identified							
IDPG		.30**	.29**	.26**	.05	−.06	.14*
Gender attachment			.08	.15**	.05	−.05	.06
Polar affect				.25**	.26**	.15**	.29**
Collective orientation					−.23**	−.32**	−.09
ASI						.86**	.87**
Hostile ASI							.50**
Benevolent ASI							
Individualist							
IDPG		.28*	.13	.28*	.11	.07	.13
Gender attachment			−.11	.21	−.08	−.08	−.07
Polar affect				.05	.12	.14	.23
Collective orientation					−.09	−.12	−.03
ASI						.92**	.93**
Hostile ASI							.70**
Benevolent ASI							

Note: * $p < .05$, ** $p < .01$.

Furthermore, the complex and sometimes contradictory beliefs expressed by Identified women necessitates further exploration of the characteristics and beliefs of this group. In order to better understand women voters, particularly group-identified women, analysis was conducted based on whether women held more egalitarian or more traditional gender-role beliefs.

GROUPING WOMEN BASED ON IDEOLOGY AND IDENTIFICATION

Rinehart's 1992 work further divided women based on both their gender-role ideology and level of group identification. My analysis uses a similar

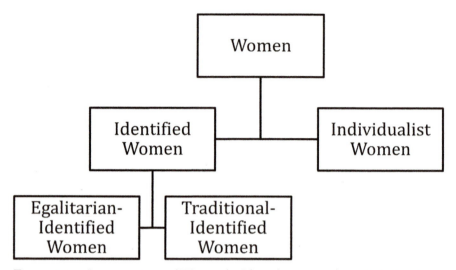

Figure 3.1   Categorization of Women by Identification and Sex-Role Ideology

method to compare and describe three types of women: those who identify with their gender group and have egalitarian beliefs (Egalitarian-Identified), those who identify with and have traditional beliefs (Traditional-Identified), and those who do not identify with their gender group (Individualist).

After women were categorized based on whether they were Identified or Individualist, they were further divided based on their gender-role ideology (see Figure 3.1). Women with a mean score on the ASI greater than 3.5 were categorized as Egalitarian, meaning they reported more egalitarian beliefs about women's roles. Those women with a score less than or equal to 3.5 were categorized as Traditional, meaning they reported more traditional or sexist beliefs about women's roles. This produced 176 (40.39 percent) Egalitarian-Identified, 119 (33.15 percent) Traditional-Identified, 44 (12.27 percent) Egalitarian-Individualist, and 20 (5.57 percent) Traditional-Individualist women. Since this study was most concerned with the political participation and beliefs of Identified women and the total number of Egalitarian-Individualist and Traditional-Individualist was low, for the purpose of analysis, these two groups were collapsed into one group labeled "Individualist women" ($n = 64$, 17.83 percent). The categorization of women based on their level of gender group identification (Identified and Individualist) and gender-role ideology (Egalitarian-Identified and Traditional-Identified) allowed each group to be examined independently as well as compared to the other groups. This method provided a more robust analysis of women's political participation, as is reflected in the results of this study.

DEMOGRAPHICS OF IDEOLOGY-IDENTIFICATION GROUPS

The three ideology-identification groups can be described based on demographic characteristics. Since preliminary analysis found education to play an important role in women's sex-role ideology, the educational makeup of each group was analyzed, and Table 3.5 displays the highest level of education completed by each group. The majority of women in each category had a college degree of some sort, but it is noteworthy that Traditional-Identified women were the least likely to have a graduate degree. This might be because graduate education requires a great deal of time working away from the home, may delay marriage and children, and often encourages women to shed traditional gender roles. What is unclear is if women with traditional gender-role beliefs are less likely to pursue a graduate degree or if through the process of graduate education, women's gender beliefs become more egalitarian.

This relationship is further emphasized by the fact that Egalitarian-Identified women were the most likely to have a graduate degree, followed closely by Individualist. Additionally, Traditional-Identified women were significantly more likely than the other two groups to indicate that they had less education than a college degree. The relationship between education and egalitarian, or feminist, beliefs has been documented in previous research. For example, Rinehart found that higher levels of education were associated with both egalitarian attitudes and greater group identification.[26] The four-year college experience has also been shown to create more egalitarian beliefs, and these beliefs were related to students' academic engagement, women's studies courses, and diversity experiences.[27]

As previous analysis demonstrated, education and age are related in terms of their relationship to gender-role beliefs. In this study, Traditional-Identified women ($M = 28.87$, $SD = 14.51$) were significantly younger than Egalitarian-Identified ($M = 35.52$, $SD = 16.42$) or Individualist women ($M = 35.91$, $SD = 16.81$). As was found in the earlier analysis, this age difference is likely related to corresponding educational differences, with younger women having completed less of their education and having less exposure to feminist ideals. The marital status of women from each ideology-identification group reflected earlier findings on women as a whole, in that women from each group were equally likely to be married or in a domestic partnership. In other words, marriage does not seem to be related to a woman's gender-role ideology or level of group identification.

Previous research, as well as the analysis in chapter 2, makes it clear that gender group identification transcends party lines, but analysis of gender-role beliefs revealed differences based on political party.

Table 3.5 Highest Level of Education of Ideology-Identification Groups

Education	Egalitarian-Identified	Traditional-Identified	Individualist
Some high school	0%	2.4%	0%
High school graduate	6.9%	14.3%	2.7%
Some college or specialized training	14.9%	26.2%	10.8%
College graduate	36.6%	40.5%	45.9%
Graduate degree	41.6%	16.7%	40.5%

Table. 3.6 Political Party Affiliations among Identification-Ideology Groups

Party	Egalitarian-Identified	Traditional-Identified	Individualist
Democratic	50%	31.9%	28.1%
Republican	26.1%	42.0%	48.4%
Independent/other	23.9%	26.1%	23.4%

Table 3.6 demonstrates differences and similarities among women from each ideology-identification group. Not surprisingly, Egalitarian-Identified women associate most frequently with the Democratic Party, but nearly one-quarter identify as Republican. This indicates that, contrary to what some may assume, egalitarian or feminist beliefs among women cross party lines and are not exclusively a characteristic of Democratic women. The affiliations of Traditional-Identified women support the idea that gender-role beliefs and group identification are not tied to any particular political party. While a slight majority of Traditional-Identified women are Republicans, women with these beliefs are well represented in the Democratic Party and as Independents.

Last, Individualist women most frequently identify as Republicans, possibly because the Republican Party less frequently emphasizes gender as a political issue. Much existing research and media coverage of political behavior focuses on political party as a primary motivation, but gender-role beliefs and group identification are also significant contributors; these findings demonstrate that political party affiliation alone does not adequately describe the beliefs of women, particularly as they relate to their gender identity. Furthermore, the ability to describe these groups of women and identify similarities that transcend party lines can provide insights into their political priorities and beliefs and can aid in understanding what political messaging is likely to appeal to particular female voters, regardless of political party.

Egalitarian-Identified, Traditional-Identified, and Individualist Women

It is important to understand the specifics of the differences between women. In order to better understand the relationships between gender-role ideologies and levels of group identification, group attachment, and consciousness, the two subgroups of Identified women (Egalitarian-Identified and Traditional-Identified) were compared to each other and compared to Individualist women (see Table 3.7). First the gender-role ideologies of the three groups were compared.[28] By definition, the Traditional-Identified women have more traditional beliefs than the Egalitarian-Identified women, but the analysis also revealed that these two groups differed in both their hostile and benevolent sexism scores. These findings demonstrate that women's levels of hostile and benevolent sexism vary and that the two components work together to make up women's gender-role beliefs. Furthermore, this indicates that hostile and benevolent sexist beliefs are more prevalent among Traditional-Identified women than Egalitarian-Identified women.

Like the previous analysis of Identified and Individualist women, bivariate correlations were computed for Egalitarian-Identified and Traditional-Identified women to determine how the variables of interest related to each other for each group (see Table 3.8). Many correlations emerged among Egalitarian-Identified women. Identification with their gender group and emotional attachment to that group were correlated with a greater sense of collective orientation. Group identification was also positively associated with polar affect. For Egalitarian-Identified women, the previous research on gender-consciousness theory was confirmed by the results in this study,[29] including the finding that for Egalitarian-Identified women, consciousness includes a progressive view of gender roles and a belief that women face societal inequalities that must be overcome through collective action. In other words, among women with egalitarian gender-role beliefs and high gender-group identification, the theories developed 20 to 30 years ago still apply today.

The bivariate correlations revealed some notable relationships for Traditional-Identified women. First, gender group identification (IDPG) was positively correlated with the ASI and BS such that traditional gender-role beliefs were associated with greater identification with the group. This is a key difference between Egalitarian-Identified and Traditional-Identified women. Traditional-Identified women's perception of their

Table 3.7 Ambivalent Sexism Inventory Scores by Group

	Egalitarian-Identified	Traditional-Identified	Individualist
ASI	2.82$_a$	3.84$_b$	3.10$_c$
Hostile ASI	2.73$_a$	3.72$_b$	3.14$_c$
Benevolent ASI	2.91$_a$	3.96$_b$	3.05$_a$

Note: Scores are based on seven-point scales with lower scores associated with egalitarian sex-role beliefs. Means in the same row that do not share subscripts significantly differ at $p < .01$ in the Bonferroni method.

Table 3.8 Identification, Consciousness, and Sex-Role Ideology Bivariate Correlations by Ideology-Identification Group

	IDPG	Gender Attachment	Polar Affect	Collective Orientation	ASI	Hostile ASI	Benevolent ASI
Egalitarian-Identified							
IDPG	—	.31**	.28**	.24**	−.11	−.12	−.07
Gender Attachment			.11	.17*	.07	−.00	−.11
Polar affect			—	.23**	.20**	.07	.25**
Collective orientation				—	−.34**	−.37**	−.20**
ASI					—	.83**	.83**
Hostile ASI						—	.37**
Benevolent ASI							—
Traditional-Identified							
IDPG	—	.30**	.28**	.40**	.20*	−.21*	.45**
Gender attachment			.07	.12	.08	−.04	.14
Polar affect			—	.35**	.24**	.05	.23*
Collective orientation				—	.06	−.25**	.32**
ASI					—	.59**	.55**
Hostile ASI						—	−.35**
Benevolent ASI							—

Note: * $p < .05$, ** $p < .01$.

group identity is tied to traditional but seemingly positive gender beliefs. The second important finding was a negative correlation between polar affect and HS, which indicates that a preference for one's own group is associated with lower levels of hostile sexism, a relationship that did not exist for Egalitarian-Identified women. Third, and most interesting, a negative correlation between BS and HS emerged, indicating that among Traditional-Identified women, higher levels of benevolent sexism were associated with lower levels of hostile sexism.

The components of gender consciousness exist among Traditional-Identified women, but they seem to operate differently for this group. First, Traditional-Identified women do not have egalitarian or feminist gender-role beliefs; in fact, their beliefs are even more traditional, or sexist, than women who feel little connection to their gender group. Furthermore, benevolent sexist beliefs correlated with group identification for these women, indicating that their group identity is strongly linked to restrictive yet seemingly positive traditional gender-role beliefs. However, their identity is not linked to the more hostile forms of sexism. In fact, further analysis of the individual BS and HS items revealed that all but 2 of the 11 BS items were associated with greater group identification, and none of the HS items positively correlated with identification.

Finally, the gender-role beliefs of Traditional-Identified women seem to be particularly complex, as is indicated by the finding that this group displayed a negative relationship between benevolent sexism and hostile sexism. Previous research using the Ambivalent Sexism Inventory has found that benevolent and hostile sexism were two positively related factors.[30] In other words, high benevolent sexism was associated with high hostile sexism, and the same was found in this study among Individualist and Egalitarian-Identified women. However, this was not the case for Traditional-Identified women, and the influence of benevolent sexism appears to be particularly important in the gender identification and consciousness of this group. Benevolent sexism, as measured in Glick and Fiske's Ambivalent Sexism Inventory, reflects a belief in positive but restricting beliefs about women. For example, benevolent sexism reflects the beliefs that marriage between a man and a woman is important, that men need women and should cherish and support them, and that women have a superior moral and cultural sensibility. Among Traditional-Identified women, benevolent and hostile sexism were negatively correlated, indicating that the less these women accept hostile sexist beliefs, the more they accept benevolent sexist beliefs. This is an important difference between Traditional-Identified women and Egalitarian-Identified women.

Since the ASI was found to be reliable and to relate to other variables, it seems that the benevolent-sexism component was the driving force of Traditional-Identified women's traditional gender-role beliefs. This conclusion is supported by the fact that the composite ASI and BS were positively correlated. One explanation for this may be that benevolent sexism serves as a coping strategy for women that embrace traditional gender roles. Protecting their gender-role beliefs may be easier for women if they accept seemingly positive stereotypes more than the hostile and less socially acceptable stereotypes.

Previous research does provide some possible explanations. First, the subgroup of women the survey participants are thinking about may influence their responses. For example, one study found that if respondents were thinking of a woman fulfilling traditional gender roles, such as a homemaker, they were more likely to agree with benevolent sexism beliefs. Furthermore, if women thought that the BS statements described them, they were more likely to agree with them. Since Traditional-Identified women by definition hold more traditional gender-role beliefs, then it is likely that many of these women felt that BS statements represented them. Furthermore, the same study found that self-described traditional women were more likely to apply hostile sexist statements to women who were nontraditional, such as feminists and career women.[31]

In other words, traditional women are more likely to identify and agree with benevolent sexism statements, and they are more likely to associate hostile sexist statements with women who do not conform to traditional gender roles. As Glick and Fiske stated, "Women who are hostile sexists are likely to be traditionalists who also hold negative views of nontraditional women because such women (e.g., feminists, career women) threaten to do away with the gender-role distinctions that are integral to traditional women's identities."[32] This statement clearly reflects the fundamental difference between Traditional-Identified women and Egalitarian-Identified women articulated at the beginning of this chapter; this difference is not in the degree of connection a woman has to her gender group but in the relationship between that connection and her beliefs about appropriate gender roles. Traditional-Identified women feel a connection to other women—but to other women who hold similar gender-role beliefs, not women who reject those beliefs. The finding that for Traditional-Identified women, higher levels of benevolent sexism was associated with a belief in greater collective orientation highlights this difference between the two groups. For Traditional-Identified women, collective orientation is the belief that women must work together to protect their traditional views and the political policies that reflect those views.

CONCLUSION

It should be clear at this point that women are not a monolithic group of voters and political party affiliation does not provide sufficient explanation for women's political beliefs. By examining how women feel about their gender identity and their role in society, a more nuanced picture of women voters emerges. Women who consider their gender to be an important part of their identity are distinct from those who do not. Women who have egalitarian beliefs about gender roles are distinct from those with traditional beliefs. When we look at women in terms of these beliefs, we can better understand specific groups of women voters.

While political party affiliation is an important characteristic in understanding voters, their beliefs, and their candidate preferences, my analysis demonstrates that group identification and gender-role beliefs cross party lines, which may explain why women are often swing voters. As one might expect, Republican women tended to have more traditional gender-role beliefs than Democrats, but this differences was not nearly as large as one might expect. In fact, nearly one-third of Traditional-Identified women were Democrats. Furthermore, when looking at women who identify with their gender group, over one-quarter of those with egalitarian beliefs classify themselves as Republicans and only slightly less as Independents. Finally, when looking at political Independents, those most likely to be swing voters, we find a similar amount of women from each category, a finding that could help candidates target their messaging to female swing voters.

As with Rinehart's 1992 analysis, this study of 21st-century women confirmed that there are two distinct categories of gender-identified women: the Egalitarian-Identified and the Traditional-Identified. Both types of Identified women consider what is best for the group of all women and believe that women have a unique perspective on the world. Furthermore, it is clear that the relationship between group identification and gender-role beliefs operate differently for these two groups of women. The profile of Egalitarian-Identified women is most similar to previous research on women voters, likely because much previous gender-consciousness research has assumed that gender group identification and consciousness were associated with egalitarian or feminist beliefs. Egalitarian-Identified women express feelings of polar affect, preference for their in-group, and collective orientation, a belief that women must work together to better their social position. These feelings of identification, feminist beliefs, polar affect, and collective orientation have been qualities established by much earlier research on feminist women voters.

The most noteworthy findings of this study deal with the profile of Traditional-Identified women. First and foremost, even women with more traditional gender-role beliefs can identify with their gender group and possess gender consciousness. However, the motivating factors behind group identification and gender consciousness for Traditional-Identified women is very different from Egalitarian-Identified women. For Traditional-Identified women, gender identity is strongly linked to benevolent sexist beliefs, which is also related to polar affect. These women do feel connected to their gender group, and that group is an important part of how they understand their identity. This connection to their gender group is based on embracing traditional gender roles that may seem positive, such as believing that women and men complement each other through their differing traits and traditional divisions of labor.

Traditional-Identified and Egalitarian-Identified women are distinct groups of voters with differing motivations and beliefs. Candidates courting the votes of Egalitarian-Identified women may want to emphasize issues of greater concern to women with more egalitarian or feminist beliefs. Previous research has found that women with feminist beliefs who also identify with their gender group are more likely to support social programs and women's issues (e.g., equal rights, abortion) and to dislike war, so candidates courting the votes of Egalitarian-Identified women may find success if they emphasize those issues in their campaign messaging.[33]

The earlier examples from Hillary Clinton's 2008 and 2016 campaigns reflect this type of strategy, but female candidates are not the only ones who can utilize such a strategy. Barack Obama successfully targeted these women voters in 2012 in his campaign advertising. Obama's ads included one titled "First Law" that touted his signing of the Lilly Ledbetter Fair Pay Act, as well as several ads that highlighted the benefits of the Affordable Care Act to women's health and ads that attacked Romney's positions on abortion rights and insurance covered birth control.

Candidates courting Traditional-Identified women voters will want to emphasize issues of concern to women who value elements of traditional gender roles. For example, Traditional-Identified women are more likely to be concerned with issues that emphasize their unique and traditional roles as women, such as mothers, caretakers, and wives. Female candidates looking to gain votes from Traditional-Identified women should consider emphasizing their common gendered social roles (e.g., mother, wife) as well as issues that connect to those roles. These issues might include juvenile violence, teen pregnancy, drugs, and elder care.

Additionally, as has been demonstrated by Tea Party women in recent years, candidates can tie women's traditional roles to a variety of issues that might not at first seem to be associated with traditional gender roles. Melissa Deckman, professor of public affairs at Washington College, notes that the Tea Party has successfully made the federal budget a women's issue by arguing that women take care of their family budget and hence are best suited to address the federal budget. They have also tied the role of motherhood to protecting children from future government debt and a growing federal government that harms the traditional family.[34] Strategies such as these are likely to be effective in persuading and mobilizing Traditional-Identified women voters. Some of these strategies can be seen in Romney's unsuccessful 2012 campaign. Romney's primary message to women was that the economy was the most important women's issue, and he ran ads like the one titled "Sarah," which featured a woman speaking of her concern about the debt left to her children.

There is no such thing as the "women's vote," but women voters are important in deciding the outcome of elections, particularly presidential elections. Candidates hoping to win over women voters must first know which women they can and should be targeting. Campaigning specifically to women voters is nothing new, but campaigns attempting to persuade women voters should take into account the importance of gender to those women's identity as well as the gender role beliefs of those women. Understanding those qualities will help candidates best target their message to the women whose votes they hope to win. Furthermore, news media and political pundits should look beyond women as a monolithic voting bloc and instead examine the nuances among women voters. Those nuances are more complicated than soccer moms and Walmart moms, and they include deeply held beliefs about gender and society.

CHAPTER 4

Mobilizing Women Voters

In a 1776 letter to her husband urging him to think about the rights of women when establishing the nation's independence from Great Britain, Abigail Adams, the future first lady, wrote, "Do not put such unlimited power into the hands of the husbands. Remember all men would be tyrants if they could. If particular care and attention is not paid to the ladies we are determined to foment a rebellion, and will not hold ourselves bound by any laws in which we have no voice, or representation."[1] It was nearly 150 years later when women finally won the right to vote and the Nineteenth Amendment to the U.S. Constitution was ratified. Women in the United States and abroad have been politically active for as long as history remembers. They were not always able to engage in the same ways as men, but they were active. One of the biggest barriers women faced was the belief by men, and some women, that women should not be involved in public affairs and should not be public speakers. The public sphere was considered unfit for proper women, but that did not stop the founding mothers of women's suffrage.

As Susan B. Anthony stated, "No advanced step taken by women has been so bitterly contested as that of speaking in public. For nothing which they have attempted, not even to secure the suffrage, have they been so abused, condemned and antagonized."[2] Despite opposition, many strong-willed women spoke anyway. They could not vote, but they could speak, even if it was protested. Women like Lucy Stone spoke frequently in favor of both women's rights and abolition. In 1848, Elizabeth Cady Stanton and Lucretia Mott participated in the Seneca Falls Convention, which resulted in the Declaration of Sentiments, a document based on the U.S. Declaration of Independence. In this document, women argued for equal civil and political rights. It would be another 72 years before women gained the right to vote and even longer before they were legally guaranteed equality in education and employment.

Women of the 1960s and 1970s fought hard for women's equality in and outside of the voting booth. Led by women such as Betty Friedan and Gloria Steinem, women of the second-wave feminist movement fought for women's equality in the workplace, pay equality, and antidiscrimination laws. They voted, but they were engaged in many other ways, including protest marches and petitions. Through political activism, these women helped to secure women's protection under the Civil Rights Act of 1964, which prohibited discrimination on the basis of sex in schools and workplaces, and they won reproductive rights under the *Roe v. Wade* decision.

Furthermore, there are numerous political organizations specifically focused on women's role in politics and their rights. Established in 1920, the League of Women Voters is still active today and is a nonpartisan organization that encourages women's participation and discussion of political issues. The National Organization for Women, established in 1966, continues to fight for gender equality. These two organizations are some of the most well known, but there are numerous other organizations focused on women and their role in politics. Despite the activities of these organizations and those that came before, research has consistently found that women are less politically engaged than men; this has been true of their level of activism, their involvement with parties and candidates, and their level of political discussion. This chapter explores the gender gap in political engagement and its historical roots, and it argues that, like the activism of suffragettes and second wave feminists, women's political engagement is strongly tied to their gender identity.

GENDER DIFFERENCES IN POLITICAL ENGAGEMENT

"Political engagement" is a broad term that includes a variety of activities, including voting, interest, discussion, volunteering, and donating. Women have voted in higher numbers than men for decades, but women have consistently reported lower levels of other types of engagement.[3] For example, one foundational study on gender and political engagement conducted by a team of political scientists in the late 1990s found that women were significantly less likely than men to say they were interested in politics, discuss politics frequently, and sought out political media.[4] This phenomenon is difficult to explain, but Nancy Burns, political science professor at the University of Michigan, attempts to interpret some of the differences. She argues that resource disparities between men and women—such as income, education, free time, and control of money—might be partially to blame for differences in political involvement, and she claims that "marriage, motherhood, and homemaking socialize women out of politics."[5]

According to Burns, while marital status may not have a direct effect on political involvement, it does have an indirect effect due to the division of labor in the home that either keeps women at home with children or forces them into a double shift as worker and homemaker. While there is greater equality in home and childcare responsibilities than there was in the 1970s, women still spend more time than their male partners taking care of the home and children. In fact, one study found that women who have children under the age of six have about two hours' less leisure time than their husbands.[6] Such disparities in time available for participating in politics are one likely cause for gender differences in engagement, particularly in activities that require a time commitment, like volunteering or attending political meetings.

Childhood socialization is another likely cause of women's lower levels of political engagement. Parents, peers, and education all contribute the political socialization of men and women. Socialization starts at a young age, and it influences many political beliefs and behaviors, including interest, knowledge, discussion, and ambition. Political socialization is linked to gender socialization, which encourages boys to be competitive, aggressive breadwinners and girls to be nurturing, polite caregivers. These gender norms then make politics seem like an appropriate realm for boys but too dirty, competitive, and unpleasant for girls. These norms have existed since before Abigail Adams wrote her husband in 1776, and they have since served as a way to steer women away from politics.

The link between gender socialization and political socialization has been supported by much research. For example, boys are exposed to and participate more in political talk in the home. So while little Jimmy is eating dinner with his parents, he is more likely to hear them talk about politics, and in turn, he is more likely to participate in that political discussion. However, little Sarah is not as likely as Jimmy to hear her parents talk about politics at the dinner table, so she in turn has less knowledge about politics, is less interested, and sees it as less important.

Political scientists Jennifer Lawless and Richard Fox highlight the importance of encouraging girls to be involved in politics in their report "Girls Just Wanna Not Run."[7] They found that not only are girls less likely to be exposed to political talk than boys but they are also significantly less likely to participate in political activity with their parents, such as following an election, discussing political issues, and sharing political stories online. Furthermore, Lawless and Fox found that boys were significantly more likely than girls to be encouraged by their father and mother to run for office, while girls were more likely to be encouraged to pursue a non-political career. These gender differences persist into young adulthood. In college, women are exposed less to politics in their classes and peer groups. For example, college women are significantly less likely than their male counterparts to take a class in politics or government, to participate in student government, and to discuss politics with their friends.

Gender differences in political engagement have persisted over time, and to better understand these differences, I analyzed data collected in the American National Election Study (ANES) from 2000 to 2012. The ANES is a large national survey conducted during election years, and many of the same questions are asked over the course of several years, which enables researchers to analyze longer-term trends. To begin, I look at gender differences in political interest. Interest in politics will likely determine whether that person discusses, learns about, and participates in political activities. The ANES asked participants to indicate their level of interest as either "very much interested," "somewhat interested," or "not much interested." As is reported in Table 4.1, analysis revealed that men were significantly more likely to report high interest in the election.[8]

In addition to expressing less interest in the election, women also reported a lower level of interest in public affairs. When asked how closely they follow government and political affairs, 74.9 percent of men said that they followed most or some of the time compared to only 60.5 percent of women. On the other hand, 39.6 percent of women said they followed public affairs "only now and then" or "hardly at all" compared to 25.1 percent of men. In 2012, the ANES also asked how often men and women pay attention to politics and the election, with responses on a five-point scale ranging from "never" (1) to "always" (5). Given that gender played an important role in presidential and down-ballot campaigns and given the so-called Republican War on Women, one might expect for women to have paid attention at least as frequently as men. However, ANES data from this election indicates that women still paid less attention than men. The difference was not large, but it was statistically significant.[9] From this data, it's clear that women are simply less interested in elections and public affairs than are men.

Related to political interest is political discussion. Previous research has found that women participate less frequently in political discussions with their friends and family. Political discussion is an extremely important component of political engagement because it increases knowledge and gives people a chance to hear others' viewpoints and to learn more about issues. Participating in political discussion also makes people more confident in their own political views and relates to other types of engagement,

Table 4.1 Level of Interest in the Election by Gender

	Men	Women
Very much interested	50.1%	42.9%
Somewhat interested	42.2%	46.6%
Not much interested	7.7%	10.7%

such as volunteering and persuading others. Analysis of ANES data from 2000 to 2012 shows a small but significant gender difference when participants were asked if they ever discuss politics with their family or friends; 64.1 percent of men and 60.6 percent of women indicated they had. Participants were also asked how often in the past week they had discussed politics, and again men discussed politics significantly more than women.[10]

Exposure to political media is also related to political interest and discussion. Those who are interested are more likely to seek out information, and those who have more information can feel more competent in discussing politics. During the 2012 election, women were less likely than men to be exposed to political news on certain media; specifically, men were more likely to get information from the radio, newspapers, and the Internet. Participants also indicated if they got information from each source "a good many" times, "several" times, or "just one or two" times. Since frequency was measured on a three-point scale, the mean values are rather small, but there were still statistically significant gender differences. Women used all media types except candidate Web sites less frequently than did men. Table 4.2 shows the percentage of women and men who got political information from each source and the average frequency of use for each source.

While a relatively small number of people engage in politics by trying to influence others' votes or working for a candidate, these types of activities are an important type of political engagement. They indicate a deeper level of interest and commitment than voting and reading a newspaper. These activities are also a good way for men and women to gain recognition in their community and local political party, which can lead to encouragement to run for office and increased interest in running for office. In other words, when a person works for a candidate or attends political meetings, it increases the chances that others will encourage him or her to run for office, and it increases the chances that he or she will be interested in running for office. Given that women are still drastically underrepresented at all levels of government, women's participation in these activities can help create a stronger pipeline of women that are

Table 4.2   Use of Political Media by Gender

Media	Media Used		Frequency of Use	
	Men	Women	Men	Women
Watch campaign programs on TV	78.4%	78.1%	1.98**	1.86**
Hear radio speeches/ discussion	41.1%**	32.1%**	1.97**	1.86**
Read the newspaper	53.0%**	47.5%**	2.04**	1.92**
View/hear Internet information	60.8%**	51.7%**	2.14**	1.97**
Visit a candidate's Web site	15.2%	14.6%	1.61	1.55

Note: Items marked with ** indicate a significant difference between columns in the same category at $p < .01$. Frequency of use responses were measured on a three-point scale, with higher scores indicating more frequent use.

Table 4.3   Political Participation by Men and Women, 2000–2012

Activity	Men	Women
Try to influence votes of others	39.6%**	34.5%**
Attend political meeting or rally	7.4%*	6.3%*
Work for party or candidate	4.3%	3.8%
Display candidate button/sticker	16.2%	15.4%
Donate money to party or candidate	14.6%**	10.8%**
Contribute to a political party	9.2%**	6.6%**
Contribute to a PAC	5.7%**	3.0%**
Give money to an individual candidate	11.0%**	8.1%**

Note: Items marked with ** indicate a significant difference between columns at $p < .01$. Items marked with * indicate significant differences between columns at $p < .05$.

willing to run for office. However, analysis of ANES data from 2000 to 2012 reveals that women are significantly less likely than men to partici-pate in these types of activities. Table 4.3 displays the percentage of men and women who participated in a variety of activities, including attend-ing meetings, working for a candidate, and contributing money. In all but two categories, women are less likely to participate.

Given the time commitment required for some of the previously men-tioned political activities, it is not surprising that a relatively low num-ber of people have participated. However, political participation can also take the form of signing petitions, using social media to share political information, or writing a letter to a newspaper. The 2012 ANES study explored some of these more common political activities, and the results

Table 4.4 Political Participation in 2012

Activity	Men	Women
Joined a protest march	7.6%	5.1%**
Attended city/school board meeting	20.1%	19.3%
Signed an Internet petition	26.3%	23.8%*
Signed a paper petition	24.9%	24.2%
Gave money to a religious organization	49.1%	52.4%*
Gave money to a social/political organization	24.4%	25.9%
Called a radio/TV program about a political issue	4.3%	2.4%**
Sent a message on Facebook/Twitter about a political issue	20.5%	20.8%
Wrote a letter to a newspaper or magazine about a political issue	5.8%	3.3%**

Note: Items marked with ** indicate a significant difference between columns at $p < .01$. Items marked with * indicate significant differences between columns at $p < .05$.

are displayed in Table 4.4. The good news is that women are not significantly different from men in attending city and school board meetings, signing paper petitions, donating to a social/political organization, or discussing politics on social media. However, there are a few notable differences. Men are significantly more likely to participate in activities that make their political positions known publicly, including joining a protest march, calling into a radio or TV program, and writing to a newspaper or magazine about a political issue.

There are a few likely explanations for these differences. First, as was demonstrated earlier, men show more interest and participate in more political discussion than women. These qualities likely relate to the other forms of political participation mentioned. Second, political and gender socialization encourage men to engage more in politics but can discourage women. If women do not see politics as something they should be involved in, particularly by publicly voicing their opinion, then they are less likely to participate in activities like calling into a radio show. Third, women may simply feel less confident in expressing their political opinions. Since women are exposed to less political talk and information and are socialized away from politics, many women likely feel that they are either not smart enough or not informed enough to participate in politics.

A variety of studies have found that, in addition to lower levels of political interest, discussion, and media use, women have lower levels of political efficacy than men. Political efficacy is related to political engagement and is defined as the belief that one can make a difference in politics. Researchers have identified two distinct types of political efficacy: external and internal. External efficacy has long been studied and is a measure of how responsive one feels the government is to one's needs. This is often measured by asking questions about whether or not people feel that politicians care what they think and whether or not they feel they have a say in what the government does. Internal efficacy has to do with how equipped a person feels to participate in politics. The ANES and many other studies have measured internal efficacy by asking if people feel that politics is too complicated to understand and if they feel they have a good understanding of political issues.

The ANES measures both types of efficacy, and the mean scores for each item in the 2012 survey are displayed in Table 4.5. Women were significantly less likely to feel that they had a good understanding of politics and are more likely to believe that politics was too complicated for them to understand. Internal efficacy is particularly important in terms of its effect on political engagement. If a woman believes that she simply isn't smart enough to understand politics, she will be far less likely to participate in political discussions or even bother to follow politics in the media.

On the other hand, the 2012 survey shows slightly higher levels for women in external efficacy. Women were significantly less likely to believe that public officials don't care what people think, indicating that women have greater faith in government and that politicians care about voters. This difference is important because external efficacy is related to voter turnout. If people do not believe the government or politicians care about them or that their vote matters, they are less likely to vote. However, women, at least in 2012, had a greater belief that their vote mattered, which might explain higher voter turnout numbers among women.

Table 4.5   Internal and External Political Efficacy by Gender

	Men	Women
Internal efficacy		
Politics/government is too complicated to understand.	3.10**	3.45**
I have a good understanding of political issues.	3.96**	3.71**
External efficacy		
Public officials don't care what people think.	3.67**	3.56**
I have no say about what government does.	3.20	3.18

Note: Items marked with ** indicate a significant difference between columns at $p < .01$. Each item was measured on a five-point scale ranging from "strongly disagree" to "strongly agree."

WOMEN'S POLITICAL ENGAGEMENT OVER TIME

The gender gap in voter turnout first became significant in 1980, so one might expect that women's interest in the election and public affairs would have also increased around the same time. Analysis of ANES data from presidential election years 1960 to 2012 demonstrate that even in peak years for women's voting participation, such as 1980 and 1992, men still reported higher levels of interest in the election and public affairs. Figures 4.1 and 4.2 display men and women's interest levels since 1960. In every single presidential election year, men reported significantly higher levels of interest. However, both men and women's interest in elections has increased over time, with a rapid increase between 2000 and 2012. However, the gender gap in election interest was the smallest in 2012, and women reported their highest level of interest in 2012.

In terms of interest in public affairs, again men consistently showed more interest, and that interest level remained relatively stable from 1980 to 2008. (The 2012 ANES did not ask about interest in public affairs.) On the other hand, women's interest in public affairs seems to have more variation from one election to another. Both sexes showed the greatest interest in public affairs during the 1970s, but women's interest after that time varied, with peaks in 1992, 2004, and 2008. What these trends in election and public affairs interest indicate is that the gender differences have endured over time but that women's interest in elections has slowly grown.

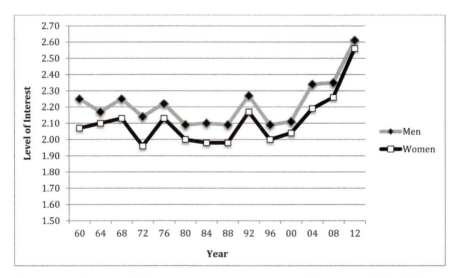

Figure 4.1   Men and Women's Interest in Presidential Elections, 1960–2012

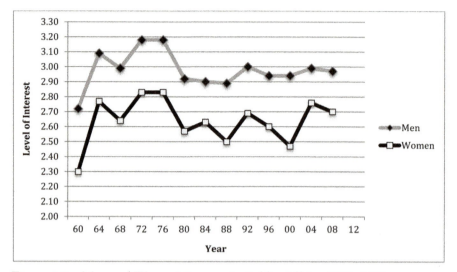

Figure 4.2   Men and Women's Interest in Public Affairs, 1960–2008

Furthermore, it seems that women's interest in public affairs varies more by the election year, so it is likely that certain issues are more likely to gain women's attention and interest. The 2012 election included a great deal of discussion of women's issues, such as equal pay, sexual assault, and reproductive rights; the prominence of these issues might explain the increased interest in the election among women. Furthermore, remember that the 2012 election was tied for the largest voting gender gap in history, which is also likely related to women's increased interest. It seems then that women's interest is very much tied to the specific electoral context and candidates, so if we are to increase women's interest, the media and candidates need to relate the issues to women. This is not to say that the focus should be solely on so-called women's issues, such as equal pay or reproductive rights, but that the media and candidates can engage voters by relating all issues to the specific experiences of women. Women's experiences are different than men's, so their experiences with the economy, health care, and a myriad of issues are slightly different. If the media and candidates addressed women's unique experiences, it is likely women would be more interested and engaged.

Political discussion is another good indicator of political engagement, and while my previous analysis indicated that from 2000 to 2012 women in general have discussed politics significantly less than men, analysis of individual campaigns reveals some interesting and positive findings. In 1984, the ANES began asking how many times per week people discussed politics with friends and family. This item was included in the majority of later ANES surveys but not all. Figure 4.3 shows the trends in the

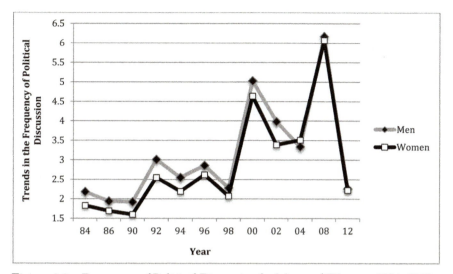

Figure 4.3 Frequency of Political Discussion by Men and Women, 1984–2012

frequency of political discussion since 1984. What is most noteworthy is that in 2004, 2008, and 2012, there was no significant difference in how frequently men and women discussed politics. In fact, in 2004, women discussed politics slightly more than men. This indicates that the gender gap in political discussion might be disappearing. Talking about politics is an important element of political engagement because it prepares citizens not only to vote but also to volunteer or even run for office themselves.

The evolution of women's political participation through activities like influencing other voters and working also indicates that women are slowly becoming more involved and that their involvement might be tied to particular election contexts. For example, ANES data from 1980 to 2012, displayed in Table 4.6, show that men were significantly more likely to try to influence the votes of others in every election except 2004 and 2008. Women were still less likely to influence voters in these years, but the difference was smaller and not statistically significant. In fact, women who said they had attempted to influence another's vote jumped by 13 percent from 2000 to 2004 and remained high through 2012.

It is impossible to isolate one specific cause for this change, but it might be explained by changes related to the September 11, 2001, terrorist attacks and the start of the 2003 Iraq War, which women were more opposed to. The jump could also be related to a backlash against conservative policies of the George W. Bush administration, or it could even be related to an increase in conservative women participating in politics. What is clear is that overall women's participation

Table 4.6 Gender Differences in Political Participation, 2008–2012

Activity by Year	1980	1984	1988	1992	1996	2000	2004	2008	2012
Try to influence votes of others									
Men	35.3*	30.4*	30.2*	39.1*	31.0*	34.1*	45.2	40.6	41.1*
Women	28.6*	25.9*	21.1*	29.7*	21.7*	27.2*	40.4	37.6	36.7*
Attend political meeting or rally									
Men	8.0	9.2	8.9*	9.2	7.3*	6.5	7.5	9.9	6.8
Women	7.2	6.8	5.9*	7.1	4.5*	4.7	7.7	8.8	5.9
Work for party/ candidate									
Men	2.9	5.3*	3.3	3.5	3.1	3.6	3.2	4.1	4.6
Women	4.0	3.1*	3.3	3.4	2.5	2.2	3.6	5.1	3.9
Display candidate button/sticker									
Men	6.8	10.3	9.1	11.9	9.9	11.9	21.7	19.5	16.3
Women	6.6	8.2	8.3	10.6	10.4	8.6	19.7	20.8	15.9
Donate money to party/candidate									
Men	8.8	9.2	10.2	8.9*	11.1*	12.5*	13.8	11.4	15.4*
Women	7.5	6.7	7.6	5.9*	7.1*	6.6*	13.2	10.9	11.8*

Note: Items marked with * indicate significant difference between rows within the category at $p < .05$.

has increased since 1980, but it does still lag behind men's. The most notable increases in women's participation have been in the form of influencing voters, displaying a button or sticker, and donating money to a party or candidate.

WOMEN CANDIDATES MOBILIZING WOMEN VOTERS

While women's political engagement has been slowly increasing, it is important to identify the conditions and contexts in which women are more likely to engage. One context is the presence of a female candidate. David Campbell and Christina Wolbrecht, professors of political science at Notre Dame, developed the role model theory, which argues the presence of female candidates is necessary to increase involvement of women and girls.[11] Their research demonstrates that the presence of viable female candidates increases the political interest of girls and changes the political socialization process of girls because politics is discussed more often in their homes, leading them to report greater interest and higher intent in participating in politics. Related to this theory is the contextual cue theory proposed by University of New Mexico political scientist Lonna Atkeson.[12] This theory posits that women's engagement is increased when there is a viable female candidate on the ballot. This happens because the female candidate's presence sends a cue to women that they are part of the political system and that the system is responsive to their concerns.

Role model theory and contextual cues theory have found support in research, but some of the results are mixed or inconclusive. Two of the most important factors are the viability and visibility of the female candidates. In races where a candidate is not highly visible, female voters are unlikely to be aware of the female candidate, so there is little chance of increased involvement.[13] For example, women voters are not likely to be affected by a female candidate running for their state House of Representatives who does not run political ads, knock on doors to meet voters, or receive media coverage. On the other hand, candidates who are seen in their community and through campaign communications or news media coverage are more likely to impact women's engagement.

Most research suggests the female candidate must also be viable; if the candidate is not viable, then female voters behave similar to those in a state with no female candidate on the ballot.[14] Viability basically refers to the likelihood that they could win their election. Viability is a frequent topic of news coverage; it is common for news outlets to focus on the horse race of who is ahead in the polls. If a female candidate is perceived as far behind and unlikely to win, women voters are less engaged. In areas where there is a visible and competitive female candidate, women's political involvement is often positively affected. Women show higher levels of interest and efficacy in elections that include a viable female candidate.

For example, Atkeson's 2003 research examined the effect of candidate gender in Senate and gubernatorial races from 1990 to 1998.[15] After accounting for differences in education, income, age, partisanship, and several other variables, Atkeson found the presence of a competitive female candidate related to a significant increase in women's discussion of politics and internal efficacy. In a similar study looking at American National Election Study data from 1984 to 2004, political scientists Beth Reingold and Jessica Harrell examined the effect of female Senate, House, and gubernatorial candidates and officeholders on women's engagement.[16] They found that in general women are more interested, more willing to discuss politics, and more willing to try to persuade others if there is a woman running. Additionally, they found that women's engagement increases most if the woman running is of the same political party. For example, these findings would suggest that Democratic women were more engaged than Republican women when Hillary Clinton was running for president. Additional research has found that competitive female candidates increase women's political knowledge, discussion, and persuasion of others.[17] However, increasing women's engagement is not always as simple as having a woman in the race. The effect a female candidate has on other women likely varies based on the candidates, election cycles, and particulars of the race.[18]

Researchers have also explored whether this effect is found when there are women holding political offices. This is often referred to as "descriptive representation," which can be defined as being represented by someone who belongs to the same social group. For women, descriptive representation at the U.S. Congressional level has been rather low, with slightly less than 20 percent of Senators and U.S. Representatives being women. The situation is not much different at the state level, where women have composed 20 to 25 percent of state legislatures for the last 25 years. However, research has shown that being represented by women in elected office can have a positive effect on women's engagement. For example, one study found that the presence of a female governor increases external efficacy of both women and men and that higher numbers of women in state legislatures increase women's efficacy relative to men's.[19] This relationship was such that the more women in office, the higher efficacy levels reported.

Another study found a similar effect with women in states with a statewide female officeholder, such as a governor or state auditor; women voters in these states have greater political knowledge and efficacy.[20]

Furthermore, female voters are more likely to approve of the job Congress is doing and more likely to approve of the incumbent when they are represented by a woman.[21] However, not all research has supported the argument that more women in office positively affect women's engagement. Other studies have shown no relationship between descriptive representation and women's engagement, suggesting that the effect is more likely to be seen during the campaign.[22] This may be due to the visibility of the candidates during the campaign season; there is a great deal of news coverage, advertising, and discussion about the candidates during the election season, which keeps gender salient, but once it is over, the spotlight is generally turned off for most officeholders.

ENGAGING WOMEN VOTERS THROUGH GROUP IDENTIFICATION

Role model and contextual cues theories demonstrate that women are more involved in politics if there are visible and viable female candidates, while group consciousness theories discussed in chapters 2 and 3 suggest that role modeling occurs because of the voter's identification with her gender group. Research conducted in the 1980s supports the connection of these two theories, finding that women who identified with their gender group were more engaged in politics.[23] Furthermore, women who had both high levels of gender group identification and egalitarian gender-role beliefs were found to be the most engaged.

A lot has changed since the 1980s. There are far more women running for and serving in elected office today, and as the analysis earlier in this chapter has demonstrated, women have slowly increased on several measures of political engagement. Women's group identification is related to their interest in politics. When there are competitive female candidates running, it taps into the group identification felt by women voters. In this section, I examine the relationship between political engagement, gender group identification, and gender-role beliefs.

Data collected from the Women Political Involvement study, cited in chapter 2, was used to better understand how group identification and gender-role beliefs relate to political engagement, confidence, and efficacy among women. Political engagement was measured using survey questions adapted from the ANES and consisted of two distinct components: interest in politics and frequency of political discussion.[24] For example, to measure political interest, women were asked to respond on a five-point scale how often and how closely they paid attention to government and politics. To measure political discussion, participants were asked how

Table 4.7   Political Engagement among Ideology-Identification Groups

	Egalitarian-Identified	Traditional-Identified	Individualist
Political interest	3.74_a	3.20_b	3.54_a
Political discussion	3.37_a	2.80_b	3.09_c

Note: Means in the same column that do not share subscripts differ at $p < .05$ in the LSD method.

often generally they discussed politics as well as how often in the past week and how often in a typical week.

We know from the earlier analysis of ANES data that women tend to have lower levels of political interest and discussion, but this analysis examines which women have lower or higher levels of engagement. First, women were compared based on their gender group identification, but no significant differences were found between Identified and Individualist women in their level of political interest or discussion. Next, women were compared based on a combination of their gender-role beliefs and level of group identification. Mean scores are displayed in Table 4.7.[25] Here we find some notable differences between groups. Egalitarian-Identified women report significantly higher levels of political interest and discussion than do Traditional-Identified women. Additionally, both Egalitarian-Identified and Individualist women discuss politics significantly more than Traditional-Identified women. In other words, Egalitarian-Identified women are the most politically interested and discuss politics the most frequently. On the other hand Traditional-Identified women are the least interested and discuss politics the least frequently. To illustrate this point, 15.3 percent of Egalitarian-Identified women said they had discussed politics with friends or family every day in the past week, compared to only 1.6 percent of Traditional Identified women.

Further analysis was conducted to see if variables were significant predictors of political engagement. In other words, of all the possible contributing factors to a woman's political engagement, (e.g., education, partisanship, age), this analysis explores the specific effect of gender-role beliefs and identification. Findings indicate that more egalitarian gender role beliefs are associated with greater political interest, and approximately 15 percent of the variance in political interest was explained by this variable.[26] In other words, as women's levels of sexism decreases, they become more politically interested.

Political discussion was also significantly related to gender-role beliefs, such that more egalitarian beliefs predicted more frequent political discussion, but group identification did not predict greater discussion. In all, gender role beliefs explained 13.5 percent of the variance in political discussion.[27] It seems that in this case it is not the level of group identification that drives political engagement but rather women's gender-role beliefs. The relationships between political interest and discussion to gender beliefs might be related to the political activist nature of feminism that encourages women to have egalitarian beliefs and to be politically active as it relates to those beliefs. On the other hand, women with traditional gender-role beliefs might generally have a lower level of engagement because traditional gender roles steer women away from politics. However, as other research has found, when issues that pertain to their traditional gender roles, such as education or abortion, are prevalent, they might be more likely to engage.

COMPETENCE TO DISCUSS POLITICS

The frequency with which one discusses politics is one measure of political engagement, but a lack of discussion might not mean the person is not engaged. Rather, a lack of discussion might by a symptom of a lack of confidence in discussing politics. Several studies have found that women possess lower levels of political knowledge than men, but there is reason to assume that this differences might be exacerbated by women's lack of confidence in their own political knowledge.[28] For example, one study found that women are more likely to answer "don't know," and men are more likely to guess on political knowledge surveys. Guessing by men and "don't know" responses by women account for almost half of the gender gap in political knowledge.[29] So while the gap in knowledge is real, it may not be as extreme as some research suggests and may be a product of women's political socialization and lack of confidence regarding political knowledge.

The Political Interpersonal Communication (PIC) index was developed to provide a better understanding of the psychological reasons women differ from men in their political knowledge and interest.[30] The PIC index measures three factors: cognitive engagement, perceived relevance, and perceived knowledge. Cognitive engagement refers to people's perception that they understand politics, are interested, and can enjoy political discussions. This is similar to political interest but goes a step deeper by getting at the reasons why someone might be uninterested in politics. It is logical to assume that if people feel that they don't understand politics or that political discussions are unpleasant, they would be less interested and less likely to discuss.

The second component of PIC is perceived relevance, which refers to how relevant a person feels politics is to his or her own life. For example, a woman who believes that politics is just about conflict and disagreement and does not have a direct impact on her would also be less likely to discuss politics or show interest. Perceived knowledge is the third component of PIC and the one most directly related to measures of knowledge and discussion. Perceived knowledge is not actual knowledge; rather, it reflects what people think they do or do not know. Women who feel that they do not have enough information might me more likely to respond "don't know" to political knowledge questions and less likely to participate in discussions with their friends and family. Furthermore, women report lower levels of political knowledge than men, even when their actual knowledge is the same. In other words, even women with high levels of political knowledge are not as confident as men in that knowledge.

Previous research has found that women are more interested and more likely to discuss politics when a female candidate is running, and this could be related to gender group identification. The presence of a female candidate makes women voters' gender more salient and might make them feel a greater sense of political relevance, perceived knowledge, and cognitive engagement. To test this hypothesis, Individualist women were compared to Identified women to determine if one group had greater levels of perceived competence. No difference was found in the overall PIC score, which combined the three factors, but examining the factors separately revealed that Individualist women reported a slightly higher level of perceived knowledge. This could be because the gender of group-identified women is a more important part of their identity and the negative stereotypes about women in politics make them doubt their own knowledge.

Another possibility is that for Identified women, gender-role beliefs also play a role in perceived knowledge. This hypothesis was tested by comparing the PIC index scores of Egalitarian-Identified and Traditional-Identified women.[31] This comparison revealed some important differences between the two groups, and these differences are represented in Figure 4.4. Egalitarian-Identified women had significantly higher PIC, cognitive engagement, and perceived relevance scores. The two groups were statistically similar in their levels of perceived knowledge.[32] Again, this result might be a result of the feminist beliefs of Egalitarian-Identified women; those who feel their gender is important and are fighting for equal rights are more likely to be cognitively engaged and to perceive what happens in politics as relevant to them. On the other hand, women with more traditional gender-role beliefs are more likely to see politics as primarily a

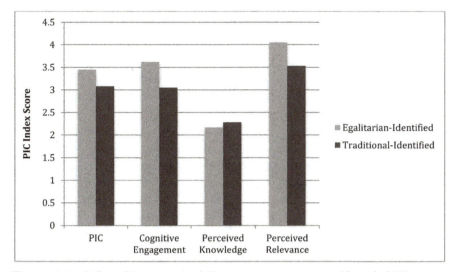

Figure 4.4 Political Interpersonal Communication among Identified Women

masculine arena and are less likely to find relevance and be engaged if the political issues are not tied to their gender identity.

It is clear that there is a relationship between gender-role beliefs and political interpersonal communication, but the impact of group identification is not as clear. Further analysis revealed that both gender-role beliefs and group identification predict PIC scores. In fact, those two variables combined explained 20 percent of the variance in PIC.[33] This is not necessarily a cause-effect relationship, but it is an important relationship. Higher PIC scores are associated with more egalitarian gender-role beliefs and increased group identification. This could be explained by the frequent politicization of gender in elections. When gender is politicized, women's group identification is stronger, and many of the issues discussed politically, particularly around the time this data was collected, relates to more egalitarian gender role beliefs.

The Women's Political Involvement Survey was conducted in the winter of 2011, as Obama and the Republican field were gearing up for the 2012 presidential election. During this time, there was a strong media narrative of the Republican War on Women. This war was fueled by Republican-controlled state legislatures tightening abortion restrictions and candidates making insensitive comments about sexual assault. The politicization of these gender-specific issues would tap into women's group identification and relate directly to their own lives, particularly among egalitarian women. This in turn can explain why these women would be discussing politics frequently and feeling more competent in doing so.

POLITICAL EFFICACY

The earlier analysis of 2012 ANES data demonstrated the existing gender gap in political efficacy, where women show lower levels of internal efficacy than men as well as slightly higher levels of external efficacy. Historically women have reported lower levels of both types of efficacy. Political efficacy is an important aspect of political engagement; without enough efficacy, people are discouraged from participating. People must feel they have enough knowledge and understanding to participate; this is internal efficacy. Voters must also have external efficacy, meaning they feel like their vote matters and have faith in the political system. Low levels of either types of efficacy have been linked to nonvoting and apathy as well as low levels of political discussion, interest, and participation.[34]

Furthermore, the presence of female candidates running for and serving in office has been shown to increase women's internal and external efficacy, which indicates there might be a relationship between efficacy and gender group identification.[35] Sue Tolleson Rinehart's work on gender group identification and politics found such a relationship; her work found that Identified women, and particularly Egalitarian-Identified women, were significantly more efficacious than the Individualist women.[36]

As it seemed that efficacy might be related to gender group identification and gender-role beliefs, women's internal and external efficacy were measured in the Women's Political Involvement Survey.[37] Internal efficacy was measured by asking participants to indicate their level of agreement on a five-point scale to the following statements:

- I consider myself well qualified to participate in politics.
- I feel that I have a pretty good understanding of the important issues facing our country.
- I feel that I could do as good a job in public office as most people.
- I am capable of participating effectively in group discussions about important political issues.
- I can't think straight about politics, regardless of how much I read or talk about the issues (reverse coded).

Participants' responses were then analyzed based on their level of group identification and gender-role beliefs. Both Identified and Individualist women expressed a moderate level of internal efficacy; the mean score was 3.41 for Identified women and 3.27 for Individualist. This difference

Table 4.8   Political Efficacy of Identified Women

	Egalitarian-Identified	Traditional-Identified
Internal efficacy	3.56	3.19
External efficacy	2.87	3.06

was not statistically significant, but Identified women did express slightly higher levels of internal efficacy. Next, Identified women were explored in more depth by comparing Egalitarian-Identified women to Traditional-Identified women, and a difference emerged; mean scores are reported in Table 4.8. Egalitarian-Identified women reported higher levels of internal efficacy, and that difference was approaching statistical significance. [38]

External efficacy refers to the belief that an individual can influence the government, and was measured by asking the level of agreement with the following statements:

- Over the years, government has paid a good deal of attention to what the people think when it decides what to do.
- Having elections makes the government pay attention to what the people think.
- I don't think public officials care much what people like me think (reverse coded).

Identified women had a slightly higher level of external efficacy than Individualist women, with Identified women's mean score at 3.0 and Individualists at 2.75.[39] Further analysis of Identified women found additional differences. As reported in Table 4.8, Traditional-Identified women actually had higher levels of external efficacy than Egalitarian-Identified women.[40] This is important to note, because on nearly all other measures of political engagement and mobilization, Traditional-Identified women have scored lower than Egalitarian-Identified women. One explanation for this difference is that Traditional-Identified women embrace traditional gender roles and a more conservative view of government, which might translate into more faith in the current political system. On the other hand, Egalitarian-Identified women are often pushing for political change that reflects their feminist beliefs, which often relates to disapproval and distrust in existing government.

Last, the magnitude of the impact identification and gender beliefs have on internal and external efficacy was explored. Analysis revealed that both gender-role beliefs and group identification explain a significant amount of variance in internal efficacy. In all, the two variables explained over 16 percent, and the relationship was such that more egalitarian beliefs and higher group identification are associated with higher levels of internal efficacy.[41] As for external efficacy, gender-role beliefs explained a small but statistically significant (1 percent) amount of the variance, and the relationship reflected the difference between Egalitarian and Traditional women found earlier; more traditional gender-role beliefs were associated with higher levels of external efficacy.[42]

CONCLUSION

Women have turned out to vote in greater numbers than men for the past 30 years, but research has indicated that other types of political involvement and interest continue to lag behind men's. Analysis of data from the American National Election Study confirms women's long-standing lack of political engagement, but there is some room for optimism. Men continue to report greater interest in elections, government, and public affairs. They seek out political news more frequently, use a greater variety of news mediums, and discuss politics more frequently. Additionally, they are more involved in political activities, such as attending a meeting, working for a candidate, and donating money.

However, analysis of gender differences over time show that women's engagement has slowly been increasing and that the electoral context may have a larger effect on women's engagement than men's. Women's interest in elections has increased and was at its highest in 2012. Additionally, women's interest in public affairs has gradually increased, but also it varies significantly more than men's, indicating that particular issues or candidates make women more interested some years than others.

Most noteworthy is that women have discussed politics equally as often or more often than men in the previous three presidential elections. This seems to indicate that women are feeling more confident in their knowledge and more engaged in the election. Related to this, women are participating in some activities in equal frequency as men, such as sharing political information on social media, attending school/city meetings, and donating to social/political organizations. However, men still surpass women in several areas of political activity that relate to making their opinion known publicly, such as calling into a radio show.

Researchers have speculated that women's political socialization, resources disparities, and responsibilities in the home are all factors that influence women's low political involvement. This study demonstrates, however, that two additional factors—gender-role ideology and gender group identification—influence women's political involvement. High levels of gender group identification and more egalitarian gender-role beliefs are associated with greater political engagement, internal political efficacy, and perceived competence to discuss politics. Egalitarian-Identified women are the most politically engaged group of women; they are the women most likely to follow politics closely and to discuss politics with friends and family. Furthermore, Egalitarian-Identified women are the most internally efficacious, indicating that they, more than other women, feel they are capable of participating in politics. Egalitarian-Identified women also perceive themselves as more competent than other women to discuss politics because they are cognitively engaged and feel that politics is relevant to them.

These findings confirm Rinehart's 1992 work, which found that Identified women were more politically engaged, efficacious, and interested than Individualist women and that egalitarianism complemented identification in increasing political involvement.[43] Gender group identification and egalitarian gender beliefs work together to increase women's political engagement. Egalitarian, or feminist, beliefs are often linked to feelings of group connectedness and the belief that women need to work together to achieve equality for all. This philosophy can be seen as far back as the work of suffragettes and second wave feminists.

Egalitarian-Identified women are the most politically engaged, but high levels of gender group identification are associated with greater political involvement for all women, suggesting that the more connected a woman feels to her gender group, the more politically involved she is likely to be. However, Traditional-Identified women, those with traditional gender-role beliefs and high levels of gender group identification, are less engaged than Egalitarian-Identified women, and gender-role beliefs may explain this difference. Traditional gender roles and socialization into those roles generally push women out of the public political sphere. However, Traditional-Identified women may be more engaged when they feel that their unique roles as women, such motherhood, make them responsible for dealing with an issue. In other words, if there was a particular issue, perhaps related to the well-being of children, that Traditional -Identified women felt their position as women made them qualified and responsible for addressing, their engagement might increase.

Additionally, Traditional-Identified women have higher levels of external political efficacy, indicating that they have faith in the government's responsiveness to issues that matter to them. This trust in government might make them less likely to feel change is needed and to feel that when needed, the government will respond to their demands. Examining the conditions or issues that influence Traditional-Identified women's political engagement would provide a more complete understanding of this group's involvement and should be the focus of additional research.

The importance of gender group identification and gender-role ideology in women's political involvement provides a deeper understanding of women voters. Campbell and Wolbrecht's role model theory posits that a viable female candidate increases women's political participation, and the findings of this study suggest this might be related to gender group identification. Since gender group identification is related to women's political involvement, it is likely that the presence of a female candidate taps into women's gender group identification and increases participation. Furthermore, these findings suggest that attempts to increase women's political involvement ought to encourage gender group identification among women. While a female candidate could most easily do this, male candidates can still tap into group identification, as Barack Obama and Mitt Romney attempted to do in their 2012 campaign advertising. This might be achieved through political messaging that aims to create a feeling of solidarity with and a sense that there are common political interests among women.

Those attempting to increase women's political participation should also consider how gender-role ideology influences political involvement. Egalitarian-Identified women are the most engaged group and thus most likely to exhibit a role model effect when a viable female candidate is running for office. Traditional-Identified women's gender-role ideology should be addressed if this group's involvement is to increase. For this group of women, traditional sex-role responsibilities should be tied to political participation. Given what is known about this group, it is likely that Traditional-Identified women may respond best to messaging that not only enhances identification but also focuses on women's unique ability to handle certain issues associated with women's traditional roles.

CHAPTER 5

The Issues Women Care About

One of the major reasons for the gender gap in vote choice stems from differing priorities and ideas as to what the role of government should be. This difference is reflected clearly in a gap in political party affiliation. The Center for American Women and Politics reports that more women have identified as Democrats than Republicans since 1983, while men have been equally split between parties or leaned Republican.[1] For example, a 2015 study by PEW Research Center found that 52 percent of women identified as Democratic and 36 percent identified as Republican. On the other hand, men were evenly divided between the two parties.[2] Over the past 20 years, more voters have described themselves as Independent, but a greater number of men (45 percent) than women (35 percent) identify as Independents.

Additionally, when Independents are asked about which party they lean towards, women report greater Democratic leanings, while men are evenly divided. Analysis of data from the American National Election Study from 2000 to 2012 reveals a significant gender gap in political party affiliation. Among women, 41.8 percent identified as Democrats, 29 percent as Independents, and 22.9 percent as Republicans. Party affiliation among men differed among all groups; 36.5 percent identified as Independents, 33.3 percent as Democrats, and 25.8 percent as Republicans. These percentages represent statistically significant gender gaps among all three affiliations, with men significantly more likely to identify as Republicans and Independents and women more likely to identify as Democrats.

The difference in political party identification is, at least partially, the result of gender differences in political philosophies. Women have historically been more supportive than men of government programs and

Table 5.1 Why the Government Has Grown

	Men	Women
All		
Involved in things people should handle themselves	56.0%	46.3%*
Government bigger because problems bigger	44.0%	53.7%*
Democrats		
Involved in things people should handle themselves	29.0%	26.7%
Government bigger because problems bigger	71.0%	73.3%
Republicans		
Involved in things people should handle themselves	87.7%	77.9%*
Government bigger because problems bigger	12.3%	22.0%*
Independents		
Involved in things people should handle themselves	59.7%	53.5%*
Government bigger because problems bigger	40.3%	56.5%*

Note: Items marked with * indicate a significant difference between columns in the same category at $p < .05$.

spending, positions that are more associated with the Democratic Party. Analysis of data from the 2012 American National Election Study confirms this gender difference in political ideology; women are more supportive of bigger government than are men. For example, when asked why the government had become bigger over the years, men were more likely to say it was because the government had become "involved in things people should handle themselves," and women were more likely to say it was because "the problems we face have become bigger."[3]

This difference in opinion clearly reflects a gender difference in how women and men view the government and indicates that women have a more favorable view of government involvement. As Table 5.1 demonstrates, this gender gap was found when looking at men and women as a whole, as well as among Republicans and Independents. It seems that Democratic men and women have similar views on government involvement, but among Republicans and Independents, gender differences exist. As expected, a greater proportion of Republicans than Democrats or Independents had a negative view of government. However, Republican and Independent women were significantly more likely than men to believe that government had grown in response to an increase in problems, and men were more likely to believe that the government had become involved in things it should not.

Another key difference between the Democratic and Republican platforms is whether the government or free market can best address economic problems. ANES 2012 data shows that 68.6 percent of women, compared to 58.2 percent of men, believe a strong government is needed to handle complex economic problems. On the other hand, 41.8 percent of men, compared to 31.4 percent of women, believe that the free market can handle economic problems without government involvement. Looking at the influence of political party affiliation, this gender gap existed among Republicans and Independents but not among Democrats. Republicans and Independent women are significantly more likely than their male counterparts to support government involvement. Among Republicans, the gap was 14.3 percent, and among Independents, the gap was 7.2 percent. Again, this difference indicates that women tend to have a more positive view of federal government action than do men.

ANES participants were also asked whether they believed "the less government, the better" or "there are more things the government should be doing." A similar gender gap emerged on this topic and is displayed in Table 5.2. In general, women were significantly more likely to say the government should be doing more, and men were more likely to want less government. Fitting with the Democratic platform, those who identified as Democrats were the most likely to support more government action, but even among Republicans and Independents, women showed more support for government than their male counterparts.

Each of these survey items indicate that women as a whole are more supportive of government involvement in solving societal and economic problems. This philosophical gender difference has two potential causes. First, women are more likely than men to need government support services and legal protection. Women are more likely to live below the poverty line and depend on government programs. Women have also benefited from government action providing legal protection from discrimination in employment and education. Second, this difference may reflect a different prioritization of issues. Women are more likely to prioritize social and cultural welfare, while men are more likely to prioritize smaller government and general economic issues.

Whatever the causes, it is clear that women from all parties show greater support for government involvement than do men, indicating that political party affiliation is not sufficient in explaining the gender gap in political-issue prioritization or positions. To best understand women voters, one must look beyond political party, because gender differences on a variety of issues exist within each party. This is particularly important for political campaigns that hope to win the votes of women; differing political beliefs could move women to cross party lines when voting. These gender gaps also help to explain why women are more often swing voters than are men.

Table 5.2   More or Less Government Action

	Men	Women
All		
The less government, the better	55.8%	44.4%*
More things government should be doing	44.2%	55.6%*
Democrats		
The less government, the better	27.8%	24.5%
More things government should be doing	72.2%	75.5%
Republicans		
The less government, the better	85.8%	75.2%*
More things government should be doing	14.2%	24.8%*
Independents		
The less government, the better	62.0%	53.2%*
More things government should be doing	38.0%	46.8%*

Note: Items marked with * indicate a significant difference between columns in the same category at $p < .05$.

ECONOMIC ISSUES

Men and women also have different views on economic and employment policies. Analysis of 2012 ANES data demonstrates that significantly more women (39.1 percent) than men (34.3 percent) believe that the Democratic Party is better at handling the nation's economy, and significantly more men (31.0 percent) than women (25.0 percent) believe that the Republican Party better handles the economy.[4] This gender difference can have real consequences on electoral outcomes, particularly in years where the economy is an important issue in voter decision making. The potential impact of this gender gap is highlighted further by examining members of the Republican Party. Even among Republicans, men are more likely to say that the Republican Party best handles the economy, and women are significantly more likely than men to say that there is not much difference in how well the two parties handle the economy.[5]

The economy in general and income inequality in particular have been central issues in the past several presidential elections, particularly in 2008, 2012, and 2016, and there are significant gender differences in views of income inequality. When asked if the government should take action to reduce income inequality, women express a significantly higher level of agreement than do men. What is most interesting is that this gender gap was greatest among Republican voters.[6] The Republican Party platform is based on less government intervention in the economy, but it seems that women in this party *do* support some level of government action to reduce income inequality.

Table 5.3   Guaranteed Jobs and Standard of Living by Gender

	Men	Women
All participants	4.81**	4.03
Democrats	3.63**	3.48
Republicans	5.34**	5.04
Independents	4.38**	3.96

Note: Items marked with ** indicate a significant difference between columns at $p < .01$.

One method for reducing income inequality that has been hotly debated by both sides of the aisle is increasing taxes for the wealthiest Americans. In fact, this was a common theme in the 2012 election, with President Obama supporting an increase in taxes for millionaires and Mitt Romney arguing that increasing taxes on this group would harm the economy. This issue was carried forward into the 2016 election, with both Democratic candidates, Hillary Clinton and Bernie Sanders, making the issue a central part of their campaigns. Given that this has been an important campaign issue, particularly for Democratic candidates, it is important to note gender differences. Analysis of 2012 ANES data demonstrates that women show significantly more support for policies that increase taxes for millionaires. Within parties, there was no gender difference among Democrats. However, a difference did emerge among Republicans and Independents; in both cases, women expressed greater support for increasing taxes on millionaires.[7]

Women and men also have different opinions on the government's role in ensuring good employment. From 2000 to 2012, the ANES has asked participants to indicate their position on the federal government's involvement in employment. The seven-point scale ranged from believing that the federal government should see to it that every person has a good job and standard of living to believing that people should be left to get ahead on their own; lower scores indicated that the federal government should be involved, and higher scores indicated that it should be left to the individual. As Table 5.3 shows, women's scores across party lines reflected more support for government intervention in employment. This gender difference might be explained by the fact that women are simply more supportive of government involvement in economic issues. It might also be related to women's economic status in the United States. Women are still more likely to occupy part-time jobs, be underemployed, and earn less than men.[8] In other words, women are more likely to need government involvement to ensure that they have a good job and standard of living.

Table 5.4   Favor and Opposition to Deficit Reduction Efforts

	Men	Women
Raising personal income taxes for those making over $250,000		
Favor	70.3%	71.0%
Oppose	17.7%	15.2%
Neither favor nor oppose	12.1%	13.8%*
Replacing Medicare with voucher system		
Favor	15.9%	10.7%*
Oppose	58.9%	63.9%*
Neither favor nor oppose	25.2%	25.4%
Increasing corporate taxes		
Favor	58.2%	61.4%*
Oppose	23.4%	16.8%*
Neither favor nor oppose	18.4%	21.8%*
Cutting military spending		
Favor	41.3%	31.7%*
Oppose	42.0%	47.5%*
Neither favor nor oppose	16.7%	20.8%*
Cutting federal employees by 10%		
Favor	60.7%	53.5%*
Oppose	18.3%	21.3%*
Neither favor nor oppose	20.9%	25.2%*
Cutting nonmilitary government activities		
Favor	65.9%	61.1%*
Oppose	18.1%	17.6%
Neither favor nor oppose	16.0%	21.9%*

Note: Items marked with * indicate a significant difference between columns in the same category at $p < .05$.

Women and men also have different views on the federal deficit and the way it should be addressed. First, men and women in all parties indicate that reducing the deficit is important, but men view it at as more important than women.[9] While the majority of women do think that deficit reduction is important, they are more likely than men to oppose spending cuts for a variety of programs in order to reduce the deficit, as shown in Table 5.4. The only deficit-reduction effort women favor significantly more than men is increasing corporate taxes. However, women are more likely than men to oppose implementing a Medicare voucher system, cutting military spending, and cutting federal employees; men, however are significantly more likely to support these efforts as well as cutting nonmilitary government activities. The only area where men and women agree is in the area of income taxes for those making over $250,000; the majority of both men and women support increasing taxes for this group. It seems then that women simply are less supportive of cutting social and military spending to reduce the federal deficit. This is consistent with previous research, which has found women to be more supportive of government spending and men to believe the government wastes tax dollars.[10]

A significant gender gap exists on a variety of economic issues, which can have a significant impact on election outcomes. The economy is one of the most frequently discussed political issues in every presidential election and in most Congressional elections. The economy is consistently an important issue in political campaigns. For example, in 2008 and 2012, economic problems were rated as the most important problem facing the country according to Gallup. In 2016, Pew Research found that 83 percent of women and 85 percent of men said that the economy was a "very important" issue to their vote.[11]

As expected, differences between political parties on economic issues exist, but what is more interesting is the presence of a gender gap on a variety of economic issues cutting across party lines. In the aggregate, women and men view economic problems and solutions differently. Men are more likely to believe that the Republican Party is best able to address economic problems, while women are more likely to believe that there is not much difference between the parties on the issue or to believe that Democrats are better at handling economic issues. Women are also more supportive of government intervention in the economy and government spending. Women express greater support for government action to address income inequality and to ensure that all Americans have a good job. Women are also more supportive of government spending in a variety of areas, and they are more likely to support increased taxes on the wealthiest Americans.

Many of women's opinions about economic issues align best with the Democratic Party, which explains why women are more likely to support this party. However, it is not only women who consider themselves Democrats who hold these views on the economy; Republican and Independent women are also more likely than their male counterparts to support government spending and intervention in the economy. Understanding differences in how women and men view economic problems and solutions is powerful knowledge for candidates crafting their campaign messaging as well as for news media and pundits reporting on campaigns and elections.

GOVERNMENT SERVICES

Women's greater support for spending on social services is well documented in political research. For example, previous research that

Table 5.5 Support for Spending on Government Services

	Men	Women
All	3.89	4.31**
Democrats	4.74	4.87**
Republicans	2.88	3.32**
Independents	3.87	4.44**

Note: Participants were asked to place themselves on a seven-point scale, with higher scores indicating greater support for government spending on services. Items marked with ** indicate a significant difference between columns in the same category at $p < .01$.

examined ANES data from 1972 to 1994 found that women were more likely to support spending on a variety of programs, including aid to the poor, health care, welfare, education, children's programs, and childcare.[12] Analysis of ANES data from 2000 to 2012 reveals similar findings. Table 5.5 shows the mean scores for men and women as a whole and by political party; women in all parties show significantly greater support for increasing spending in order to provide more government services.

It is clear that women are much more supportive of spending on government services, but men are more likely to want a decrease in spending. Table 5.6 shows men and women's support for spending on a variety of government services; the data is from the 2000 to 2012 ANES studies. The gender gap revealed here is quite remarkable. In every area of spending, women are significantly more likely than men to support an increase in spending, and in every area, men were significantly more likely to want a decrease in spending. The greatest gender gap, 9 percent, was in funding for social security. However, both men and women supported increased funding for public schools at a higher proportion than they did other services.

Further analysis of the data demonstrates that this gender gap is not restricted to certain political parties. Women from all parties are more supportive of increased spending on social programs, while men are more likely to support maintaining current levels of spending or decreasing spending. Among Democrats, a significant gender gap was present in all areas except childcare and welfare programs. Some of the biggest gender differences come from within the Republican Party, where women supported increased funding significantly more than men in all areas examined. The most notable differences were in the areas of education and social security. The majority of women, 54.9 percent, support increased funding for public schools, compared to 43.7 percent of men, and 50.9 percent of women support increased funding for social security compared

Table 5.6   Support for Spending on Government Services

	Men	Women
Aid to the poor		
Increased	41.2%	49.0%*
Same	36.6%	33.8%*
Decreased	14.7%	9.0%*
Childcare		
Increased	45.4%	51.1%*
Same	36.9%	35.6%
Decreased	15.0%	10.1%*
Public schools		
Increased	61.4%	69.1%*
Same	22.6%	18.8%*
Decreased	9.1%	4.8%*
Welfare programs		
Increased	17.3%	21.1%*
Same	40.7%	43.4%*
Decreased	39.6%	32.5%*
Social security		
Increased	52.0%	61.0%*
Same	39.3%	32.9%*
Decreased	5.8%	3.1%*
Dealing with crime		
Increased	54.9%	62.8%*
Same	35.2%	29.9%*
Decreased	7.8%	4.8%*

Note: Items marked with * indicate a significant difference between columns in the same category at $p < .05$.

to only 38.6 percent of men. Among those identified as Independents, a significant gender gap emerged in spending support for aid to the poor, childcare, public schools, and crime prevention. In all, women show much greater support for funding government services than do men, and social security, public schools, and crime prevention are the issues women show the greatest support for funding.

Health care has long been a contested issue in political campaigns, and it was one of the most talked about issues in the 2012 election; specifically, candidates from all levels of government talked about the Affordable Care Act, commonly known as Obamacare. Democrats touted the increased number of insured Americans and the guarantee of health care services to more voters, and Republicans attacked the feasibility and cost of the program while promising to eliminate the program. Given that women have historically been more supportive of increased health care services and that women were the key to Obama's reelection, one might expect a large gender gap in opinions about the Affordable Care Act, but that is not the case. Women were significantly more likely to approve of the job the president was doing on health care, but there was not a significant difference in how men and women viewed the effect of Obamacare on the quality of health care or the number of insured.[13] While women have historically been more supportive of spending on health care, it seems that Obamacare did not appeal more to women than men. In this case, political party affiliation was the strongest factor in opinions.

When it comes to social programs, women regardless of political party show a much higher level of support for the programs themselves and for government spending on those programs. This gender difference is nothing new; research going back over 30 years has found similar differences. In the 21st century, women are far more likely than men to support social programs, such as aid to the poor, education, childcare, health care, and crime prevention. For example, in 2012, 10 percent of women and only 5 percent of men listed health care as the most important problem facing the country. On the other hand, 14 percent of men, compared to 9 percent of women, indicated that the federal deficit was the most important problem.[14] Leading up to the 2016 presidential election, more women than men reported that health care, education, and social security were very important to their vote.[15]

Women's greater support for social programs can create a challenge for candidates who argue for cutting government spending. While most women do support reducing the federal deficit, they do not support cutting spending on social services to do so. Furthermore, candidates who do not support government programs like social security and education will have difficulty winning enough women voters to win the election.

GOVERNMENT REGULATIONS

The issue of government regulation has typically been a partisan issue, with Republicans more often opposing government regulations and Democrats supporting, and political party affiliation is certainly an important factor in voters' positions on a variety of regulations. For instance, a 2016 CNN/ORC poll found that 78 percent of Democrats, compared to 29 percent of Republicans, support tougher gun laws, and Pew Research found that Democratic states were significantly more likely to support environmental regulations.[16] However, important gender differences exist with

Table 5.7   Government Regulation of Access to Guns

	Men	Women
All		
More difficult	40.4%	57.4%*
Easier	8.1%	3.0%
Keep rules the same	51.5%	39.6%*
Democrats		
More difficult	58.1%	71.9%*
Easier	2.9%	1.4%*
Keep rules the same	39.0%	26.7%*
Republicans		
More difficult	19.8%	34.3%*
Easier	12.3%	4.9%*
Keep rules the same	67.9%	60. 8%*
Independents		
More difficult	37.9%	52.9%*
Easier	10.3%	3.9%*
Keep rules the same	51.8%	43.2%*

Note: Items marked with * indicate a significant difference between columns in the same category at $p < .05$.

regard to some regulations, many of them crossing party lines. In general, women are more supportive than men of government regulations.

One area of regulation where there are noteworthy gender differences is in the regulation of gun sales. During the second presidential debate of the 2012 election, Obama and Romney sparred on whether or not regulations would make Americans safer, and research by Pew Research indicates a significant gender gap in regulation of guns. In fact, in January 2013, they reported that women were more in favor, 67 percent to 48 percent, of banning semiautomatic weapons than were men, and a gender gap of 12 percent existed in support for creating a federal database to track gun sales. Pew Research explored the percentage of men and women in favor of a variety of regulations, from banning assault-style weapons and high-capacity ammunition clips to background checks for private and gun show sales; in each area, women showed greater support for regulations.[17]

The 2012 ANES had participants indicate whether they thought the government should make it more difficult to buy a gun than it is now, make it easier to buy a gun, or keep the rules the way they are. Analysis revealed a large gender gap on the issue, with significantly more women than men supporting more gun regulations. This gender difference also transcends party lines, as is demonstrated in Table 5.7. Support for making it more difficult to buy a gun has a double-digit gender gap across all parties. These findings are consistent with polling conducted leading up to the 2016 election and in the wake of several mass shootings, which found that 71 percent of women and only 46 percent of men supported a nationwide ban on assault weapons.[18]

Another area where gender gaps often emerge is crime and punishment. Previous research has found that women are more likely to support increased spending for crime prevention and drug addiction and are more likely to oppose capital punishment.[19] Women's greater support for crime prevention remains; as was discussed earlier in this chapter, women are significantly more likely to support increased spending on crime prevention than are men. Women also continue to oppose the death penalty in significantly higher frequencies than men, according to the 2012 ANES survey data. Among men, 73.5 percent approved of the death penalty, but 68.5 percent of women, a significantly lower percentage, approved. Crime prevention and the death penalty were not major themes in recent presidential elections, but these gender differences may plan an important role in persuading voters at the local and state level.

While women are more liberal than men on a variety of issues, the legalization of marijuana is an exception. In general, women are more conservative on this issue. Analysis of 2012 ANES data revealed that full legalization is favored by 42.8 percent of men, but significantly fewer women, 35 percent, support legalization. This issue is relevant in many state elections. As of June 2016, *Fortune* magazine reported that medical marijuana had been legalized in 25 states and 4 states had legalized recreational use. Furthermore, in the 2016 election, 3 states voted on medical legalization, and 5 states voted on recreational legalization.[20]

Regulation of immigration is another area where gender gaps exist. In the past several presidential elections, immigration has been a controversial topic. During the 2012 presidential election, Obama defended his immigration policies, including his support of the DREAM Act, a bill that would create a pathway to citizenship for unauthorized immigrants brought to the United States as children. Obama had also halted deportations of some immigrants who would qualify for citizenship under the DREAM Act. On the other hand, Romney opposed the DREAM Act, calling it an amnesty plan and advocated for "self-deportation" and stricter punishment for employers that hired unauthorized immigrants. Since Congress was unable to pass any type of comprehensive immigration reform during Obama's second term, immigration remained a hot issue into the 2016 election. Using strong, and sometimes offensive, language, Donald Trump argued that he would stop unauthorized immigration and build a wall between the United States and Mexico, a wall that he said Mexico

Table 5.8 Support for Immigration Policies by Gender and Political Party

	Men	Women
Democrats		
Make all unauthorized immigrants felons and send them back to their home country	12.5%	1.1%
Have a guest worker program that allows unauthorized immigrants to remain	13.5%	11.0%
Allow unauthorized immigrants to remain in the United States with certain requirements	62.1%	66.3%*
Allow unauthorized immigrants to remain in the United States without penalties	12.0%	11.6%
Republicans		
Make all unauthorized immigrants felons and send them back to their home country	25.3%	20.6%*
Have a guest worker program that allows unauthorized immigrants to remain	25.7%	22.5%
Allow unauthorized immigrants to remain in the United States with certain requirements	46.4%	53.5%*
Allow unauthorized immigrants to remain in the United States without penalties	2.6%	3.4%
Independents		
Make all unauthorized immigrants felons and send them back to their home country	21.1%	17.7%
Have a guest worker program that allows unauthorized immigrants to remain	18.1%	16.0%
Allow unauthorized immigrants to remain in the United States with certain requirements	53.3%	58.0%*
Allow unauthorized immigrants to remain in the United States without penalties	7.5%	8.3%

Note: Items marked with * indicate a significant difference between columns in the same category at $p < .05$.

would pay for. Hillary Clinton advocated for comprehensive immigration reform that included a pathway to citizenship and stated that she would work to keep families together and end family detention and deportation.

Given the importance and prevalence of the immigration issue in the past several presidential elections and the fact that it has been a fiercely contested issue, it is important to understand how voters feel about it. Generally speaking, Democrats have been more supportive of reform that includes a pathway to citizenship, and Republicans have argued against such programs and for stricter regulations and enforcement. However, not all people within each party agree, and there are some important gender differences. The 2012 ANES asked participants what the U.S. policy on immigration should be and gave them four options to choose from. Support for each program by respondents' political party is listed in Table 5.8.

Not surprisingly, the majority of Democrats support allowing unauthorized immigrants to remain with certain requirements, but women were also significantly more likely than men to support this approach. Counter to what Republican candidates often say, the majority of Republican voters also support allowing unauthorized immigrants to stay, as do the majority of Independents. Also noteworthy is the statistically significant gender gap among Republicans, with more men supporting a strict deportation policy and more women supporting letting immigrants stay. Furthermore, Republican women (49.1 percent) were significantly more likely than Republican men (39.1 percent) to favor allowing some unauthorized immigrants to gain citizenship. No gender gap existed among Democrats on this question, and among Independents, men were more likely to oppose citizenship.

A gender gap on the immigration issue might be explained by the fact that women are generally more supportive of policies that help disadvantaged groups, are more sympathetic to minorities, and support more liberal social welfare policies.[21] Immigration is sure to continue to be an important and controversial issue. For instance, 71 percent of women and 69 percent of men indicated that immigration was very important in their vote choice in the 2016 election.[22]

The environment and climate change are another controversial area of government regulations. In 2016, women were much more likely to consider the environment to be an important issue in their voting decisions. In fact, there was a 10-point gender gap in the importance of the issue, with 57 percent of women and 47 percent of men saying it was very important. The first issue of contention is whether or not climate change is happening. Despite the near consensus among scientists internationally, some in the United States still do not believe that climate change is occurring. However, the majority of men (80.3 percent) and women (82.5 percent) say that they believe global warming is happening.[23] This was true regardless of political party; the majority of voters believe climate change is happening.

The next area of contention is whether or not humans are causing climate change. ANES participants were asked to indicate if they believed the cause of climate change was "mostly humans," "mostly natural," or "about equal." As can be seen in Table 5.9, a gender gap emerged within each party on this question. Among all three groups, women were significantly more likely to believe that the cause of climate change was about

Table 5.9   Causes of Climate Change by Gender and Party

	Men	Women
Democrats		
Mostly human	48.6%	37.7%*
Mostly natural	11.5%	11.1%
About equal	39.8%	51.2%*
Republicans		
Mostly human	18.7%	21.0%
Mostly natural	35.6%	24.3%*
About equal	42.7%	54.7%*
Independents		
Mostly human	34.9%	33.5%
Mostly natural	21.8%	18.1%*
About equal	43.3%	48.4%*

Note: Items marked with * indicate a significant difference between columns in the same category at $p < .05$.

equal parts humans and nature. On the other hand, Democratic men were more likely than Democratic women to believe that the cause was mostly humans, and Republican men were more likely than Republican women to believe that it was mostly natural.

Understanding gender differences on this issue is important when considering whether or not voters will support policies to address climate change. For those who believe that the cause is mostly natural, government regulations seem unnecessary, but for those who believe that the cause is mostly or partially human, regulations make more sense. For example, ANES respondents were asked to identify their position on government regulation of the environment; the only gender gap that emerged was among Republicans, with Republican men supporting significantly lower levels of regulation than women.[24] This is not surprising, because Republican men are also the least likely to believe that climate change is anthropogenic.

In sum, women are more liberal than men on most issues related to government regulation with the exception of marijuana legalization. Women are more likely than men to favor tighter regulations on guns, drugs, and climate change. They are also more likely to oppose the death penalty and to favor immigration reform that provides a pathway to citizenship. The gender difference on these issues is likely tied to women's differing views on the role and necessity of government. Women are more likely to support bigger government and to believe that government is able to address the problems we face. Leading in to the 2016 election, both sexes rated gun policy, immigration, and the environment among the most important issues, but as the above research shows, men and women are likely to have different opinions on these issues, which may explain gender gaps in vote choices at the local, state, and federal level.

EQUALITY AND RIGHTS

Historically women have fought for their rights as well as for the rights of others. For over 70 years, women fought for their right to vote. Women were also heavily involved in the abolitionist movement of the 1800s and the civil rights movements of the 1960s and 1970s. The United States has come a long way since then, but women, minorities, and LGBTQ people still face many types of discrimination. Because of the discrimination they face, women are also more aware of what others must face and more supportive of government action to address inequality. Issues related to equality have again become topics of political discussion and campaigns. With the shootings of several unarmed black men, state laws that prohibit transgender people from using the restroom that fits their gender identity, and the sexism and sexual harassment women face, it is not surprising that equality was a much-talked-about issue in the 2016 election.

It is important to understand what men and women's perceptions about the status quo when it comes to discrimination and equality. If men and women see the current situation differently, then it is likely that they will also view government intervention into those areas differently. The 2012 ANES study asked respondents a series of questions regarding their views on equality. For example, they were asked to indicate their level of agreement to statements like "our society should do whatever is necessary to make sure that everyone has an equal opportunity to succeed"; "we have gone too far in pushing equal rights in this country"; and "one of the big problems in this country is that we don't give everyone an equal chance."

The mean scores on this six-item equality scale make it clear that there are some important gender differences.[25] Among both Democrats and Republicans, women were significantly more concerned about equality than were men, but there was not a significant difference among Independents.[26] In other words, Democratic and Republican women are more likely than their male counterparts to believe that inequality is a problem that needs to be addressed. There are two potential reasons for this difference. One is that women are a historically disadvantaged group still facing discrimination today, so women are more likely to experience inequality and view it as a problem that needs to be addressed. This is supported by the data reported in Table 5.10, which shows that women from all parties

Table 5.10 Perceptions of How Much Discrimination Exists toward
Demographic Groups

	Men	Women
Democrats		
Blacks	3.50	2.59
Hispanics	3.45	3.45
Whites	1.94	1.94
Gays and lesbians	3.86	3.90
Women	3.05**	3.21
Republicans		
Blacks	2.64**	2.87
Hispanics	2.71**	2.93
Whites	2.23	2.31
Gays and lesbians	3.11**	3.33
Women	2.35**	2.65
Independents		
Blacks	3.05	3.08
Hispanics	3.08*	3.17
Whites	2.19	2.19
Gays and lesbians	3.43**	3.63
Women	2.70**	2.84

Note: Respondents were asked, "How much discrimination is there in the United States
today against each of the following groups?" Responses ranged from "none at all" (1) to
"a great deal" (5). Items marked with * indicate a significant difference between columns
in the same category at $p < .05$; items marked with ** indicate a significant difference
between columns in the same category at $p < .01$.

are significantly more likely to believe women still face discrimination
today. Second, historically women have shown greater concern for the
inequality faced by various groups, including black Americas. When asked
how much discrimination there is in the United States against several
groups, generally women believe there is more discrimination than men.

In June 2016, the Supreme Court upheld the use of affirmative action
in universities. The case was *Fisher v. University of Texas* and dealt with
admission policies at the University of Texas that used race, among many
other factors, in their second round of admission decisions. Most students
were admitted in the first round; all in-state students who finished in
the top 10 percent of their high school class were automatically granted
admission. Ultimately the Supreme Court ruled in a four-to-three decision that the University of Texas's policy did not give an unfair advantage
to nonwhite students. Affirmative action has been a controversial topic
since its inception, but it has been upheld by the Supreme Court and
implemented in many workplaces and universities.

Opinions about affirmative action are linked to people's perception of discrimination in the world; the more discrimination people believe exists, the more likely it is that they will support laws and programs to create a more equal world. As was previously mentioned, women have historically been more supportive of policies that address inequality, and this is true in the case of affirmative action. Women in the 2012 ANES survey indicated a significantly greater level of support for affirmative action both in universities and the workplace.[27] However, affirmative action appears to be rather unpopular among both sexes, with around 50 percent of men and women opposing it. That said, many Americans do believe something needs to change in regards to how racial and ethnic minorities are treated. For example, Pew Research found in 2016 that 69 percent of women and 56 percent of men considered it to be a very important issue in their vote choice.[28]

Looking specifically at gender inequality, it is not surprising that women perceive there to be more gender discrimination than men do or that they are more supportive of equal gender roles in society. Women, as compared to men, are more likely to believe that men have greater opportunities for success than women and that the media should pay more attention to discrimination against women.[29] The ANES also asked respondents from 2000 to 2012 to place themselves on a seven-point scale indicating whether they believed more that "women should have an equal role with men in running business, industry, and government" (1) or "a women's place is in the home" (7).

Women were significantly more likely to place themselves closer to "women should have an equal role with men" than did men.[30] However, both men and women tended to place themselves closer to the "equal roles" side of the spectrum than the "women's place is in the home" side. Men were significantly more likely to believe that it is harder for a working mother than a stay-at-home mom to bond with a child and to believe that it is better if a man works and a woman takes care of the home.[31] What is also important to note is that most of these gender differences were true regardless of political party affiliation. In other words, women of all political party affiliations hold more egalitarian gender beliefs than their male counterparts and are more likely to perceive gender discrimination to be a problem that needs to be addressed.

Another gender-related issue that is always an area of political debate is abortion. Since 1972, women and men have held similar levels of support for abortion.[32] Analysis of data from 2000 to 2012 demonstrates that there is little gender gap on this issue in the 21st century; the most frequently supported position is that it is a matter of personal choice, 45 percent of men and 46.3 percent of women support this position.[33] However, polling leading up to the 2012 and 2016 elections indicate that abortion is a more important issue in women's vote choice than it is to men's. For example, in 2012, Gallup found that in a survey of 12 swing states, a plurality of women voters said that abortion was the most important issue in the election. In 2016, 52 percent of women, compared to 38 percent of men, said that abortion was a very important issue in their vote choice.[34]

When opinions on abortion regulations are explored in more detail, some small but significant gender gaps emerge. The 2012 ANES asked participants to identify what type of abortion regulation they most supported, and the results are displayed in Table 5.11. These options ranged from abortion should "never be permitted" to one should "always be able to obtain an abortion as a matter of personal choice." Among Democrats, the most frequently supported law among both men and women is that abortion should be a matter of personal choice. Among Republicans, the most frequently supported position for both men and women was that abortion should only be permitted in the case of rape, incest, or danger to the mother's life. However, Republican women were significantly more likely than Republican men to support a complete ban on abortion. Finally, among those who identify as politically Independent, the most frequently supported position was that abortion is a matter of personal choice and should not be regulated, and there were no significant gender differences among this group.

What this analysis makes clear is that there is not much of a gender gap within each party, suggesting that partisanship is more important than gender on this issue. It is worth noting that there is a gap between women; both Democratic and Independent women are far more likely to support full access to abortion than Republican women. Also worth noting is that Republican women's support covers more of the spectrum than the other two groups; a similar number of Republican women support a complete ban as do those who support unrestricted access. Since the Republican platform is pro-life, it is likely that the pro-choice women in the party simply do not see this issue as important in their decision to support a party or candidate as Democratic women. Differing levels of gender group identification and gender-role beliefs among Republican women might also explain their varying opinions on abortion; traditional gender roles embracing motherhood as a central part of women's identity are more likely to correlate with a pro-life position, but egalitarian beliefs centering on women's rights are more compatible with pro-choice beliefs.

Table 5.11 Support for Abortion Regulation by Gender and Party

Democrats	Men	Women
Never be permitted	8.2%	7.8%
Permit only in case of rape, incest, or danger to the woman	20.3%	22.0%
Permit abortion for reasons other than rape, incest, or danger to the woman	16.5%	12.4%*
Always be able to obtain an abortion as a matter of personal choice	54.9%	57.9%
Republicans		
Never be permitted	14.9%	21.9%*
Permit only in case of rape, incest, or danger to the woman	39.0%	36.1%
Permit abortion for reasons other than rape, incest, or danger to the woman	17.7%	15.2%
Always be able to obtain an abortion as a matter of personal choice	28.3%	26.7%
Independents		
Never be permitted	9.6%	10.9%
Permit only in case of rape, incest, or danger to the woman	27.2%	27.6%
Permit abortion for reasons other than rape, incest, or danger to the woman	15.6%	16.3%
Always be able to obtain an abortion as a matter of personal choice	47.4%	44.9%

Note: Items marked with * indicate a significant difference between columns in the same category at $p < .05$.

In addition to discrimination against black people and women, many Americans have faced discrimination based on their sexual orientation or gender identity. The rights of LGBTQ citizens was a topic of debate in both the 2012 and 2016 elections. In May 2012, in an interview with ABC's Robin Roberts, President Obama affirmed his support for same-sex marriage, stating, "For me personally, it is important for me to go ahead and affirm that I think same-sex couples should be able to get married."[35] This statement was followed by a massive flood of campaign donations and likely helped his image among many voters.[36] In the race for the 2016 election, Hillary Clinton also emphasized her support for equality for all people, including the LGBTQ community. For example, in her campaign-announcement video, she included two gay men who mentioned their plans to marry. While the fight for same-sex marriage had been won by the 2016 campaign, discrimination was still an important issue. In fact,

49 percent of women and 32 percent of men indicated that treatment of LGBTQ people was a very important issue.[37]

Throughout the past several decades, Americans have gradually become more accepting of LGBTQ people, and this has been especially true for younger Americans. Like many other issues related to equality, women have consistently been more supportive of policies that afford equal rights and protections from discrimination to LGBTQ Americans. Regardless of political party, women have been more supportive of laws to protect homosexuals against discrimination. ANES data from 2000 to 2012 demonstrate the gender gap on this issue; 74.8 percent of Democratic women support laws against discrimination, compared to 71.3 percent of men. Among Republicans, 62.2 percent of women and 55.9 percent of men support antidiscrimination laws. While this is not a huge gender gap, it is statistically significant, and Democratic and Republican women felt significantly stronger in their position on this issue.[38] In other words, women from all political parties are stronger supporters of antidiscrimination laws and equal rights for LGBTQ Americans.

In September 2011, Don't Ask, Don't Tell was officially repealed, and gays and lesbians were officially allowed to serve in the U.S. armed forces without hiding their sexual orientation. However, changing the policy did not change the minds of all Americans, and the issue of gays and lesbians in the military has remained a somewhat contentious issue. The majority of Americans support this policy, but women are more supportive than men. In all, 80 percent of women and 73 percent of men support allowing gays and lesbians in the military, and this small but significant gender gap can be found among Democrats, Republicans, and Independents. In each group, women are more supportive, and women indicated that they felt significantly stronger about their position than their male counterparts.[39] Women overall are stronger supporters of allowing gays and lesbians to serve in the military.

Marriage rights of gay and lesbian couples was an area of debate leading up to the 2012 election. President Obama had publicly stated his support for same-sex marriage, but many Republicans were arguing for a constitutional amendment to limit marriage to heterosexual couples. Like many other rights-related issues, a gender gap exists on this issue. Overall women are more supportive of marriage equality, with 43 percent of women and 37.6 percent of men supporting legal marriage. Men, on the other hand, were significantly more supportive of civil unions but not marriage; 35.1 percent of men and 32.3 percent of women supported such a policy. Despite the 2015 Supreme Court ruling that made same-sex marriage legal in all 50 states, the issue remains contentious. This ruling also

Table 5.12   Support for Gay and Lesbian Adoption Rights

	Men	Women
Democrats		
Yes	58.1%	62.8%*
No	37.3%	31.2%*
Don't know	2.5%	3.5%*
Republicans		
Yes	36.8%	43.0%*
No	59.2%	52.2%*
Don't know	2.2%	2.7%
Independents		
Yes	49.3%	54.6%*
No	43.8%	36.1%*
Don't know	3.5%	4.3%

Note: Items marked with * indicate a significant difference between columns in the same category at $p < .05$.

had a small effect on the issue of gay adoption, because some states require adoptive parents to be married. However, many states have stricter regulations that still bar gays and lesbians from adopting children. Like same-sex marriage, same-sex-couple adoption has been a contentious issue, and women and men have different options. As shown in Table 5.12, a greater percentage of women in each party support the right of adoption for gays and lesbians.

In nearly all issues related to equality and rights, women in the 21st century are more progressive than men. Women are more likely to see discrimination towards women, black people, and LGBTQ people as a problem that the government should address. They are also much stronger supporters of a variety of antidiscrimination laws. This is particularly important given the growing importance of equality issues in campaigns and elections. For example, the 2016 presidential campaign strongly demonstrated the importance of these issues, as candidates talked about systemic racism, pay inequality, and discrimination towards transgender people. Since Democratic candidates have shown more support for laws to address inequality, it is likely they will continue to benefit from a gender gap in political party affiliation and vote choice.

FOREIGN POLICY AND MILITARY AFFAIRS

Previous research has shown that men and women differ in their position regarding foreign policy and military issues. In general, women have been less supportive of military intervention, particularly when it is related to a conflict between two other nations or to maintaining superior military power.[40] In fact, Deborah Jordan Brooks and Benjamin Valentino, professors of government at Dartmouth University, found distinct gender differences in opinions about whether or not to go to war.[41] They found that women are less supportive of wars when the stakes are economic or strategic and wars that are not supported by the United Nations. However, wars that are based in humanitarian issues and have UN approval actually have greater support among women than men. In general though, women have been less supportive of American military action and intervention.

The gender gap in foreign policy and military affairs can also be seen in how men and women view engaging with other countries, giving foreign aid, and dealing with potential threats. Several important gender differences emerge in the 2012 ANES data related to how women and men view foreign policy. For example, men are significantly more isolationist than women, agreeing significantly more with the statement the "country would be better off if we just stayed home." This gender difference was true of both Republicans and Democrats, although the gender gap was greater among Republicans; 35.4 percent of Republican men, compared to 30.7 percent of Republican women, agreed that the country would be better off if we stayed home. Among Democrats, 37.9 percent of men and 34 percent of women agreed. This difference in opinion about how isolationist or engaged the United States should be is further highlighted by gender differences in support for foreign aid. Women regardless of political party are more likely to support keeping foreign aid at about the same level, while men of all parties are more likely to believe that foreign aid should be decreased. The size of the gap varies by political party, with Democrats having the smallest gender gap on this issue and Republicans having the greatest. However, it is important to note that this gap exists and transcends party lines.

The U.S. war in Afghanistan was the result of the September 11, 2001, terrorist attacks, and it continues today. During the 2008 campaign, Barack Obama pledged to end U.S. wars in Iraq and Afghanistan, but that proved more difficult than he'd hoped. Continued insurgencies and the growth of the terrorist organization ISIS in the region made a complete withdrawal difficult and potentially dangerous. By the 2012 election, the majority of Americans regardless of party believed that the war had not been worth the cost, and women (74.1 percent) were slightly more likely than men (71.3 percent) to believe this. The primary purpose of the war was to reduce the risk of terrorism in a post-9/11 world, but most men and women believed that the war had not achieved this goal and felt the threat had remained about the same.

Table 5.13 The War in Afghanistan's Effect on the Risk of Terrorism

	Men	Women
All		
Increased	23.7	26.8*
Decreased	28.1	21.4*
Stayed about the same	48.3	51.9*
Democrats		
Increased	22.0	23.8
Decreased	34.2	24.5*
Stayed about the same	43.8	51.7*
Republicans		
Increased	22.6	27.7*
Decreased	30.8	21.3*
Stayed about the same	46.7	51.0
Independents		
Increased	25.8	29.7
Decreased	20.9	17.4*
Stayed about the same	53.3	52.9

Note: Items marked with * indicate a significant difference between items in the same row at $p < .05$.

However, there still were some statistically significant differences in men's and women's opinions on this issue. As Table 5.13 demonstrates, the majority of women, regardless of party, believed the war in Afghanistan had not effected the terrorist threat, and Democratic women were significantly more likely than their male counterparts to believe this. Men, on the other hand, were more varied in their beliefs. While more men from each party thought the terrorist threat had remained the same, significantly more men than women from each party believed the war had actually decreased the risk of terrorism against the United States. The length of the war, along with several notable terrorist attacks around the world, explains why so many men and women felt the war effort was a failure. The fact that more women felt this way might be related to women's greater aversion to war in general, and men's greater perception that the war had decreased the risk of terrorism might be explained by their greater support for military conflict.

The United States' War on Terror has led to numerous actions by the government aimed at preventing another terrorist attack on U.S. soil and abroad. On September 11, 2012, eight weeks before the U.S. presidential election, the U.S. embassy in Benghazi, Libya, was attacked by terrorists, bringing the issue of terrorism to the foreground of the election. According to ANES data, women in 2012, particularly Republican

Table 5.14   Likelihood of a Terrorist Attack in the United States

	Men		Women	
	M	**SD**	**M**	**SD**
All	2.32	.99	2.40**	.97
Democrats	2.21	.95	2.22	.93
Republicans	2.52	.92	2.72**	.94
Independents	2.31	1.00	2.44**	.99

Note: Items marked with * indicate a significant difference between items in the same row at $p < .05$.

and Independent women, were significantly more likely to believe there would be a terrorist attack on the United States that would kill 100 or more people within a year (see Table 5.14). Given that women are more fearful of a terrorist attack, it is not surprising that women are also more likely to approve of measures taken by the government to prevent terrorism. Specifically, women regardless of party are significantly more likely to approve of the government's current wiretapping powers. However, men are more likely to say that the government has gone too far on this issue. This gender difference might also reflect differing levels of trust in government. In general, women have a more positive and trusting view of the federal government and its ability to serve its people, while men view the federal government more negatively and are less trusting.

Another controversial tactic in fighting terrorism is the use of torture when interrogating suspected terrorists. Reports of waterboarding and psychological torture, among others, made this an important issue in the 2008 and 2012 elections. Gender-based stereotypes might lead one to believe that women would be more opposed to torture than men, but this is not necessarily the case. Significant gender gaps do emerge on this issue, but they vary based on political party affiliation. As Table 5.15 demonstrates, both Democratic men and women are most likely to oppose torture. Among Republicans, more men favor the use of torture, and more women oppose it. However, Republican women vary on this issue, with about one-third each saying they favor, oppose, or have no opinion. Independents also most frequently oppose the use of torture, but significantly more Independent men favor and significantly more women oppose. The cause of these gender gaps is unclear, but it may be related to women's differing beliefs about crime and punishment; as was previously discussed, women are less supportive of capital punishment than are men, and torture is another extreme form of physical punishment.

Table 5.15   Support for the Use of Torture on
Suspected Terrorists

	Men	Women
Democrats		
Favor	18.4	16.2
Oppose	53.6	54.7
Neither	28.0	29.2
Republicans		
Favor	41.9	30.1*
Oppose	25.1	35.8*
Neither	33.0	34.1
Independents		
Favor	26.3	16.5*
Oppose	45.2	50.0*
Neither	28.5	33.5*

Note: Items marked with * indicate a significant difference
between items in the same row at $p < .05$.

Iran's development of nuclear weapons has been a foreign policy concern and point of political debate since the 2008 presidential election.
Barack Obama and John McCain sparred in the 2008 presidential debates
about how best to address the threat of a nuclear-armed Iran. In 2012,
President Obama and Mitt Romney argued about the threat Iran posed,
the effectiveness of sanctions, and the use of military force. Again in
2016, Obama's Iran nuclear deal was an issue of debate, with the Republican presidential candidate, Donald Trump, promising to tear up the agreement. According to 2012 ANES data, the majority of men (92.6 percent)
and women (91.6 percent) believe that Iran is trying to develop nuclear
weapons. However, a gender gap is present in opinions of how to handle
the situation, reflecting men's greater prioritization of the issue and/or
women's lack of confidence in taking a position on the issue.

When asked if they favored, opposed, or neither favored or opposed
a variety of government actions, women were more likely than men to
say that they neither favored nor opposed the policies. On the other
hand, men were more likely to say that they favored specific policies.
For example, men are significantly more likely than women to support
holding direct diplomatic talks, increasing economic sanctions, bombing
development sites, and invading with U.S. troops. On the other hand,
women are more likely express a neutral opinion on each of these actions.
However, the policies most frequently favored by men and women tended
to reflect partisan positions. Democratic and Independent men and

women most frequently supported direct diplomatic talks and most often opposed invading with U.S. troops. Among Republicans, both sexes most frequently favored increasing economic sanctions on Iran and opposed invading. In sum, men are more likely than women to have an opinion on how to address Iran's nuclear development. Men and women from all parties show the most opposition for military invasion, but differences in what options are most favored vary slightly by party.

The U.S. relationship with China has always been delicate, and China's increased economic growth, holding of U.S. debt, manipulation of currency, and trade practices have brought this relationship into the spotlight in recent elections. There is no doubt that China's economy is growing, but how that growth will affect the United States is less clear. Opinions on this issue vary slightly by gender. The majority of men (57.1 percent) and women (58.6 percent) believe that China's economic expansion will have a negative effect on the United States, and this pattern holds across political parties. However, significantly more men (24.4 percent) than women (17.1 percent) believe the Chinese effect will be good for the United States. On the other hand, more women (23.7 percent) than men (18.5 percent) believe that China's economic expansion will have no effect on the United States. While the majority of both sexes have a negative view of China's economic growth, both men and women express little fear of China as a military threat. Most men (48.3 percent) and women (50.5 percent) believe that China's military poses only minor threat.

It is clear that there are some important gender differences in how men and women feel about the military and foreign affairs issues, although these differences are not as drastic as the gaps on domestic issues. Men and women are similar in their opinions about the war in Afghanistan; regardless of political party, most voters believe the war has not been worth it and has not reduced the risk of terrorism. Men and women also agree on the threat posed by China's economic expansion, with the majority believing it will have a negative effect on the United States. Both sexes also have similar opinions on the threat posed by Iran, and most oppose military intervention to address the issue.

However, the above analysis does show some gender differences. In general, women are more opposed to military conflict, especially if it is motivated by strategic or economic interests. Women are also more supportive of engaging with other countries for humanitarian reasons and support providing foreign aid. Finally, women are more fearful of a terrorist attack on U.S. soil, and in turn, they are more supportive of government monitoring to prevent an attack. In all, men and women are not drastically different in their opinions on foreign policy and military issues, but the differences that do emerge reflect differing opinions about the role of government and the need for military solutions.

THE IMPORTANCE OF GENDER GROUP IDENTIFICATION AND GENDER-ROLE IDEOLOGY

As previous chapters have demonstrated, not all women view the world the same way, and their level of gender group identification and beliefs about appropriate gender roles are important factors in understanding how women view the political world. For example, the previous analysis of gender differences revealed that women were more supportive of allowing gays and lesbians to adopt children, but this was not all women. In fact, 38.2 percent opposed such a policy. Another example of women's differing opinions is evident with abortion rights. Most women (46.3 percent) believe that abortion should be legal and be a matter of personal choice. On the other hand, 27.1 percent of women believe that abortion should only be allowed in the cases of rape, incest, or danger to the health of the mother. These differences *between* women voters are also important in understanding specific subgroups of women voters who may swing an election. Discovering these groups' unique issue priorities and the motivations behind those beliefs not only aids in our understanding of women voters but also provides insight into how campaigns can reach them through targeted messaging. In order to better understand the nuances of women voters, this section explores the relationships between issue priorities, gender group identification, and gender-role beliefs among women voters.

The issue positions of candidates and the importance of those issues to voters are important factors in deciding which candidate to support. Previous research has found that certain types of issues are considered more important than others. For example, political scientists Leoine Huddy and Nayda Terkildsen discovered in their foundational research that voters believed that military and economic issues were most important when making voting decisions for higher-level offices, such as the U.S. Senate or president.[42] On the other hand, so-called compassion issues—which include issues like health care, education, and assistance to the poor—were considered the least important. This analysis looked at voters as a whole, but when further analyzed by voters' gender, they found that men ranked compassion issues as less important than women ranked these issues.

It is important to note that Huddy and Terkildsen's research was conducted in 1990, and while some more recent research has confirmed that these findings are generally still true today, it is important to explore the relevance of these findings in current contexts and to examine how their research applies to modern women voters. Further, studies on gender identification and consciousness have found commonalities in issue positions among women with a similar sex-role ideology or level of identification.[43] In an effort to bridge this literature, the Women's Political Involvement survey described in this section seeks to reveal which issues women voters find most important in their ideal candidate and if there are differences between women based on gender group identification and sex-role ideology.

Based on Huddy and Terkildsen's research, participants in the Women's Political Involvement Survey were asked to indicate the importance of a variety of issues in their decision to support a candidate. These issues fell into three categories: compassion issues, economic issues, and military/foreign affairs issues. Compassion issues included assisting the poor, gender wage gap, child welfare, education, and children's health care. Economic issues included budget deficit, ability to deal with business leaders, employment, economic crisis, and the cost of living. Military/ foreign affairs issues included military readiness, terrorism, international relations, the war in Afghanistan, and the war in Iraq. Looking at women as a whole, the top 3 of 15 rated issues were economic crisis, education, and employment.

Given that the survey data was collected in 2011 as the economy was recovering from the 2008 recession, it is not surprising that economic issues would be among the most important to voters. The rating of education as one of the most important is more interesting because it likely reflects women's greater prioritization of the issue. The prioritization of issues is further reflected in the ratings of issue categories; women rated economic issues as most important, followed by compassion issues, and military/foreign affairs as least important.[44] These findings run counter to previous research, which has found economic and military issues to be the most important voters; this study's findings indicate that compassion issues are more important in women's vote choice than are military issues.

Next, the influence of gender group identification on women's issue prioritization was examined. Analyses revealed that greater gender group identification was associated with greater importance of economic and compassion issues. In other words, the more a woman identifies with her gender group, the greater importance she places on economic and compassion issues when deciding which candidate to support.[45] To further explore the importance of identification on issue priorities, Identified and Individualist women were examined in detail. First, the type of issues (economic, compassion, military) women prioritize were examined. Both

Identified and Individualist women rated military/foreign affairs issues as the least important category. Additionally, both groups rated economic issues as most important and compassion issues as second most important.[46] This demonstrates an important commonality: women do not consider military/foreign affairs issues as very important in their decision to support a candidate. Candidates looking to win women voters should instead focus on economic and compassion issues.

However, there are some significant differences between women. Among Identified women, child welfare, child health care, education, and economic crisis were rated as the most important issues. On the other hand, Individualist women rated economic crisis, education, and employment as the top three most important issues in their vote choice. Here we see an important difference emerge between groups of women. For those who identify strongly with their gender group, issues related to children are among the most important, but women who do not identify with their gender group place greater emphasis on economic issues. Additionally, Identified women rated economic and compassion issues as significantly more important than did Individualist women; they also rated military/foreign affairs issues higher, but the group difference was not statistically significant.[47] In short, Identified women rate most issues as more important than do Individualist.

This may reflect greater political engagement among Identified women, as discussed in chapter 4. Women who are more engaged in politics will have stronger opinions on issues, and for Identified women, this results in a greater prioritization of a variety of issues. Understanding these differing issue priorities can allow campaigns to better craft their message to address issues their target audience most cares about. Furthermore, the influence of gender identification gives a peek into the psychological and sociological reasons women vote. Gender identity plays an important role for some women in terms of what issues they find most important and why they find those issues important.

In addition to gender group identification, sex-role beliefs influence how women view political issues. Previous research has found that feminist, or more egalitarian, beliefs are associated with more progressive views on a variety of issues. Furthermore, feminism has been associated with more positive feelings toward other women and a sense of women's interdependence. However, as was established in earlier chapters, nonfeminist women can also feel a sense of interdependence and base political opinions on what they think is best for the group. Analysis of women participating in the Women's Political Involvement survey reveals that gender-role beliefs are associated with certain political positions. More

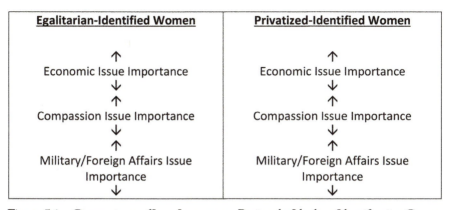

Figure 5.1   Comparisons of Issue Importance Ratings by Ideology-Identification Groups
Note: Items in the same column were tested for significant differences.

traditional gender-role ideologies are associated with higher ratings in the importance of military/foreign affairs issues.[48] On the other hand, more egalitarian beliefs are associated with higher ratings of compassion issues.[49] These findings indicate that women holding more traditional beliefs place greater importance on military/foreign affairs issues, such as terrorism and the war in Afghanistan, than do more egalitarian women. On the other hand, egalitarian women place greater importance on compassion issues, such as the wage gap and child welfare.

To further explore these differences, Egalitarian-Identified and Traditional-Identified women were examined separately to see whether they felt that economic, compassion, or military/foreign affairs issues were most important. Figure 5.1 shows how the comparisons were made; the ratings for each group are reported in Table 5.16. For Egalitarian-Identified women, compassion issues were rated as most important, followed by economic issues and then military/foreign affairs issues, which were rated significantly lower than the other two issue categories.[50] Among Traditional-Identified women, economic issues were rated as significantly more important than compassion or military/foreign affairs issues. They also rated compassion issues as significantly more important than military/foreign affairs issues.[51]

The important difference between women reflected in these findings is that Egalitarian-Identified women consider compassion issues to be the most important in their decision to support a candidate, a finding that sets this group apart from previous research on issue importance and suggests that candidates courting the votes of these women are best served by messaging that focuses on issues such as education, health care, and women's issues. Furthermore, all groups rated military/foreign affairs issues as least

Table 5.16 Issue Category Ratings by Ideology and Identification Group

Egalitarian-Identified Women	Traditional-Identified Women	Individualist Women
1) Compassion issues (M=4.46)	1) Economic issues (M=4.41)	1) Economic issues (M=4.16)
2) Economic issues (M=4.44)	2) Compassion issues (M=4.25)	2) Compassion issues (M=4.06)
3) Military/foreign affairs issues (M=3.96)	3) Military/foreign affairs issues (M=4.05)	3) Military/foreign affairs issues (M=3.89)

important. Previous research has found these issues to be among the most important in races for national office, but this appears to no longer be the case, at least among women.

Examining the ratings of specific issues provides greater insight into the issue priorities of Egalitarian-Identified, Traditional-Identified, and Individualist women. Table 5.17 displays the mean scores for Egalitarian-Identified, Traditional-Identified, and Individualist women's issue and issue category ratings. Egalitarian-Identified women rated education, economic crisis, and employment as the three most important issues. Similarly, Traditional-Identified women rated economic crisis, education, and employment as their top three. In short, group-identified women, regardless of sex-role ideology, place the economy, education, and employment among their three most important issues in deciding for whom they will vote.

There are, however, significant differences between groups of women when they are compared side by side. Egalitarian-Identified and Traditional-Identified women rated both compassion and economic issues as significantly more important than Individualist women, a finding that might reflect the relationship between greater group identification and greater political engagement. [52] Additionally these data show that Egalitarian-Identified women find compassion issues to be more important in their vote choice than do Traditional-Identified and Individualist women, and Traditional-Identified women find compassion issues as more important than Individualist women. In other words, compassion issues are prioritized higher among Identified women than Individualist and more highly among Egalitarian-Identified than Traditional Identified.

Looking at the specific issues, the reasons for these differences become clearer. Egalitarian-Identified women rate each of the compassion issues (wage gap, child welfare, assisting the poor, education, and child health care) as more important than do Traditional-Identified and Individualist

Table 5.17   Issue Importance Rating by Ideology and Identification Group

	Egalitarian-Identified	Traditional-Identified	Individualist
Economic issues	4.44_a	4.41_a	4.16_b
Budget deficit	4.32	4.32	4.13
Deal with business leaders	4.12_a	4.20_a	3.78_b
Employment	4.67_a	4.51_{ab}	4.41_b
Economic crisis	4.71_a	4.64_{ab}	4.47_b
Cost of living	4.36^a	4.36_a	4.03_b
Compassion issues	4.46_a	4.25_b	4.06_c
Wage gap	4.18_a	3.82_b	3.67_b
Child welfare	4.57_a	4.33_b	4.11_b
Assisting the poor	4.33_a	4.10_b	3.92_b
Education	4.75_a	4.57_b	4.41_b
Child health care	4.50_a	4.44_a	4.19_b
Military/foreign affairs issues	3.96_{ab}	4.13_a	3.89_b
Military readiness	3.72_a	4.05_b	3.81_{ab}
Terrorism	3.91_a	4.31_b	4.06_{ab}
International relations	4.53_a	4.33_b	4.12_b
Afghanistan war	3.89	3.97	3.73
Iraq War	3.76	3.98	3.70

Note: Scores are based on a five-point scale, where 1 = very unimportant and 5 = very important. Means in the same row that do not share the subscripts significantly differ at $p < .01$ in the Fisher's LSD comparison.

women. While all three groups of women consider military/foreign affairs issues to be the least important, Traditional-Identified women rated military/foreign affairs issues as significantly more important than did Individualist women, and they rated several specific military/foreign affairs issues higher than Egalitarian-Identified women. Most notably, Traditional-Identified women rated military readiness and terrorism as significantly more important than did Egalitarian-Identified women. This likely reflects a greater fear of terrorism and conflict among this group. Interestingly, the only military/foreign affairs issue Egalitarian-Identified rated higher than the other groups was international relations, a finding that is likely related to the more feminist and diplomatic beliefs of this group.

Further examination suggests three important findings. First, Egalitarian-Identified women rate nearly all of the specific economic and compassion issues higher than the other two groups. For example, Egalitarian-Identified women's ratings of employment, economic crisis, child welfare, and education were all significantly higher than those of Traditional-Identified or Individualist women. Egalitarian-Identified women's higher scores on these issues might exist because Egalitarian-Identified women are also the most politically engaged group, and greater political engagement is related to having stronger opinions on issues. Second, most of the statistically significant differences between groups' ratings on compassion and military/foreign affairs issues show that Traditional-Identified and Individualist women are similar to each other but different from Egalitarian-Identified women. For example, Egalitarian-Identified women rate wage gap, child welfare, assisting the poor, and education significantly higher than both Traditional-Identified and Individualist women. They also rate military readiness and terrorism significantly lower than the other two groups. Finally, when it comes to economic issues, there are fewer differences between groups. In many cases, Egalitarian-Identified women rate specific economic issues, such as employment, higher than Traditional-Identified women, who rate those issues higher than Individualist women.

Knowing which issues women find most important provides context for understanding their evaluations of candidates' ability to handle issues. The candidate a woman feels is best able to handle the issues she finds important is more likely to gain her vote. Importantly, the findings of this study indicate that the issues women find most important vary based on their sex-role ideology and level of gender group identification. A 2011 Gallup poll conducted two weeks prior to data collection for this study provides some insight into the issues the general American population found most important. The poll indicated that the majority of Americans believed the economy was the most important issue facing the country. However, compassion issues—such as health care, ethical decline, and education—followed the economy as the most important issues facing the country.

The Gallup poll findings were mirrored in the ratings of Traditional-Identified and Individualist in this study; both of these groups rated economic issues as most important and compassion issues as second most important in their decision to support a candidate (Privatized-Identified: Economic M = 4.41, Compassion M = 4.25; Individualist: Economic M = 4.16, Compassion M = 4.06). However, in contrast, Egalitarian-Identified women rated compassion issues as most important in deciding to support a candidate, and economic issues were the second most important (Compassion M = 4.46, Economic M = 4.44). Egalitarian-Identified women considered compassion issues as significantly more important than economic issues, and they found compassion issues to be significantly more important than did Traditional-Identified or Individualist women.

Egalitarian-Identified women are unlike the general population in the issues they prioritize; they consider compassion issues to be the most important in their decision to support a candidate. This finding confirms previous research that found egalitarian sex-role beliefs and gender group identification to be associated with support for compassion issues, such as social programs.[53] Furthermore, Egalitarian-Identified women's prioritization of compassion issues may indicate that they might also be more likely to support a female candidate over a male, since previous research has demonstrated that women are considered better able to handle compassion issues because they play to women's stereotypical strengths.[54]

Women find military/foreign affairs issues to be the least important issue category in their decision to support a candidate. Of note, this finding is contrary to previous research that found voters consider these issues to be some of the most important. Additionally, the relative unimportance of military/foreign affairs issues in women's decision to support a candidate suggests candidates courting women's votes in a similar political environment should not focus on these issues; rather, they should focus on compassion or economic issues. Further, in any given political environment, it is important for campaign strategists to examine and address the issues most important to women because they may be different from those men find important and may even vary between groups of women.

Despite the fact that all women rated military/foreign affairs issues as least important, women with traditional sex-role beliefs rated military/foreign affairs issues as more important than those with egalitarian beliefs. There are a few possible explanations for this finding. First, it might be that women with traditional sex-role beliefs simply believe what previous research has found—that candidates need to be able to handle military and foreign affairs issues. Another possible explanation is that militarism is closely tied to traditional sex-role beliefs, as feminist theorists like Cynthia Enloe and Betty Reardon have argued, so women with traditional sex-role beliefs find military issues to be more important than women with egalitarian beliefs.[55] Future research ought to investigate the relationship between traditional sex-role beliefs and the importance of military/foreign affairs issues to better understand how women (and men) with traditional sex-role beliefs evaluate political issues.

CONCLUSION

Women see many issues differently than men, but there are also important differences among women. Women have consistently had a more liberal stance on many issues than their male counterparts. Even accounting for political party, there are gender differences. In general, women are more supportive of government spending for social welfare programs, such as health care, education, and care for the elderly. Women are more supportive of government regulation of businesses and the economy, and they are more supportive of environmental and gun regulations. They are also more likely to believe social inequality is a problem that the government needs to address it, and they are more supportive of rights for LGBTQ persons and immigrants. Women are less supportive of war and military interventions but are more supportive of humanitarian interventions abroad. The gender differences are important in understanding why women choose particular candidates over others and in understanding what types of campaign messaging and appeals are likely to be effective.

It is also extremely important to mention differences among women. Women differ from each other, and many of those differences can be traced back to how connected they feel to their gender group and their beliefs about societal gender roles. Identified women, those with a strong sense of connection to their gender group, tend to find issues more important than Individualist women, likely because Identified women are more politically engaged and interested. Egalitarian-Identified women tend to consider compassion issues as more important than Traditional-Identified women. On the other hand, Traditional-Identified women rated military/foreign affairs issues as slightly more important than did Egalitarian-Identified women. While these differences also reflect partisan differences (Democrats are more supportive of compassion issues and Republicans of military issues), this study indicates that political party affiliation alone does not fully explain these differences. To truly understand women voters, one must consider their level of gender group identification and gender-role beliefs.

CHAPTER 6

The Traits Women Care About

The issue stances of candidates are important factor in voters' decision making, but they are not the only factor. In fact, some research suggests that issues are not even the most important factor in some cases. Voter perception of candidates' personalities and character is an extremely important factor in vote choice. It is common to hear media reports about which candidate voters most want to have a beer with. What this sentiment is really expressing is that voters want to elect someone they like. The qualities that make a candidate likable are difficult to pin down; research has demonstrated some consistencies over time as well as a good deal of variance depending on the specific candidates and the electoral context. The research presented later in this chapter also suggests there are some important differences in how men and women evaluate candidates' traits and that there are also important differences among women.

What qualities does the ideal candidate have? This question has been asked for decades by political researchers. A candidate's image is an important factor in whether or not he or she will persuade voters. An unlikable candidate is going to have a harder time than a likable one, but identifying what makes a candidate likable has been challenging. As political rhetoric scholars Allan Louden and Kristen McCauliff argue in their 2004 essay, "Candidate image is a complex construct that can be conceived as message projection or auditor's reception, composed of discrete judgments or holistic blends, as idiosyncratic or stable tendencies."[1] They define image as "an evaluation negotiated and constructed by candidates, voters, and the media in a cooperative nature."[2] In short, candidate image is not determined by the candidate's actual traits. Rather, it is cocreated through communication and perception by the candidate, media, and voters.

The elements of candidate image have been examined by numerous political science and communication scholars, resulting in a rather expansive list of image qualities. Louden and McCauliff categorize previous image research into four categories: issue stances, personal qualities, competences, and communicative behavior. They then extend this by adding a fifth category: authenticity.[3] The issue-stances category consists of a candidate's ability to talk about the nation's problems and to have solutions or favorable stances as well as the homophily, or similarity, between those stances and the voters' stances. While this element is tied to issues, it is also based on how issue positions are communicated by the candidate and the media as well as on how voters perceive those positions. Judith Trent, professor of communication at the University of Cincinnati, and her colleagues have studied the image qualities voters find most important for over 30 years and consistently found that talking about and having solutions to the nation's problems are some of the most desirable qualities.[4]

The next category, personal qualities, include traits such as character, compassion, calmness, honesty, likability, and personality homophily. Numerous studies have found that honesty and character are among the traits considered most important by voters.[5] For example, Trent et al.'s 2010 study examined the importance of a host of traits over the course of six presidential elections and found honesty to be the most important trait in 2008, 2004, 2000, and 1992 and the second most important in 1996 and 1988.[6]

Competence is seemingly an important quality in electing someone to any office, particularly the presidency. This category includes traits such as intelligence, leadership ability, qualification, experience, and strength. Interestingly, Trent and her colleagues' previous research on the 1988 and 1992 election found that experience in office was not among the most important traits but that having an energetic and aggressive leader was.[7] Additionally, later research found that competence varied in importance from election to election, with competence being more important post-2000 and more important in 1992, 2000, and 2008 than in 1988, 1996, and 2004.[8] This research suggest that demonstrated competence in office has become increasingly important but varies significantly in certain contexts. Candidates' communicative behavior is another important element of their image. This includes ability to communicate, believability, composure, friendliness, humor, and aggressiveness. Trent et al. found that being a forceful public speaker was consistently important and that its importance has increased over time.[9]

Authenticity is trickier to define, because it has traditionally been used by media and pundits without definitional precision. Louden and

McCauliff explain that authenticity is how "true to themselves"[10] candidates are perceived to be. They argue that candidates who are perceived as inauthentic are seen as trying to fake desirable qualities and are assumed to be untrustworthy. On the other hand, candidates who are seen as authentic have much more leeway with their behavior, as long as they are seen as internally consistent. Hillary Clinton provides a good example of a candidate who struggled with authenticity. For example, in 2008, she teared up when answering a media question, and instead of seeming humanized in voters' eyes, many argued that she was faking it. Clinton's gender likely complicated perceptions of her authenticity, and it seemed that no matter what she did, she was viewed as inauthentic and disliked for it.

Similarly, political communication scholars Benjamin Warner and Mary Banwart identify five factors of image: intelligence, leadership, character, benevolence, homophily, and charm.[11] This categorization overlaps some with Louden and McCauliff's, but it also highlights additional factors in image construction. Warner and Banwart's study of the 2012 presidential race found that character was an important element in the decision to vote for Obama and Romney. This is in line with previous research that found honesty and trustworthiness to be among the most important image qualities. Additionally, one of their biggest contributions is the category of homophily. Voters generally want a candidate who is similar to them in key ways, such as sharing their values, understanding people like them, and understanding the problems they face. Warner and Banwart's study of Senate races in three states found that only homophily predicted vote choice on all three races. They also found no support for the belief that people vote for candidates they like over those they think are qualified. Rather, they argue, "This suggests that when voters use candidate image as a heuristic to make important democratic decisions, they are not using shallow personality judgments. Instead, voters appear to decide whether they trust a candidate to represent them and their values."[12]

Numerous studies have also demonstrated that voters' perceptions of candidates' traits shape their overall evaluation of the candidate and ultimately their vote choice.[13] For example, Kim Fridkin and Patrick Kenney, political scientists at Arizona State University, examined 2006 U.S. Senate candidates and found that trait assessments were a significant predictor of vote choice.[14] Their work also examined differences between evaluations of incumbents and challengers and found that leadership was the most important trait in evaluations of incumbents, followed by honesty and caring. For challengers, caring was the most important trait, followed by leadership, honesty, and experience. This is congruent with earlier research, such as political scientist Charles Prysby's study finding that trait assessments were an important factor in the choices to vote for George W. Bush or John Kerry in the 2004 presidential election.

The research on candidate image demonstrates that individuals make voting decisions, at least partly, based on the character traits of candidates and particularly how well a candidate represents their values and interests. Then it follows that people with different values and interests would prefer different candidates. Men and women are socialized differently and have different experiences because of their gender identity, so it makes sense they might prioritize different characteristics in their ideal candidate. Trent et al. examined survey data from 1988 to 2008 and found that both sexes rated honesty most important, compassion second, and talking about the nation's problems third.[15] However, they found differences in how important these and other qualities were to women and men. For example, women considered it more important for candidates to demonstrate competence in office, have compassion about the needs of people, be comfortable discussing national security issues, have solutions to problems facing the country, and be supportive of the needs of children and senior citizens. In fact, this study found that women had higher expectations for candidates and rated more attributes to be of greater importance than men.

Furthermore, as was established in the previous chapter, there are important differences in how men and women view issues, which likely relate to differences in the image qualities they find most desirable. Louden and McCauliff argue that attitudes about issues and traits are interrelated, with issue stances serving as evidence of the type of person the candidate is, and other research has shown that when voters perceive that candidates possess certain character traits, they also perceive them to be able to handle related issues.[16] For example, candidates demonstrating compassion are seen as better able to handle issues like health care and children's welfare, and candidates seen as strong and assertive are seen as better able to handle military and security issues. Surprisingly, though, relatively little research has examined gender differences in the image qualities men and women find most important and the way that they evaluate candidates on those qualities. The next section fills some of this gap by exploring differences in how men and women viewed presidential candidates in the 21st century and the influence it had on their vote.

GENDER AND CANDIDATE IMAGE IN 21ST-CENTURY PRESIDENTIAL ELECTIONS

The 2000 presidential election will go down in history as one of the most controversial and unique. While the Supreme Court ultimately decided the winner of the election, the candidates' images played an important role as well. Al Gore had served as vice president for the previous eight years, but what he had in experience he lacked in charisma. On the other hand, George W. Bush was a candidate voters wanted to "have a beer with" or, in Bush's case, a root beer. The personalities of these two candidates couldn't have been more different. *Saturday Night Live* (*SNL*) did numerous skits during the 2000 election season satirizing the candidates' personalities. In one of the most memorable skits, Gore, played by Darrell Hammond, spoke robotically about his plan for a "lockbox" while Bush, played by Will Ferrell, appeared casual, yet confused.[17]

Analysis of data from the American National Election Study revealed that Bush, who ultimately won the election, was viewed less favorably than Gore on a variety of character traits (see Table 6.1). Many of those traits were reflected in *SNL*'s parodies of Bush. Both men and women rated Bush significantly lower than Gore on intelligence, knowledge, and caring.[18] Women also rated Bush as less moral. However, men rated Bush as a stronger leader than Gore, and ultimately Bush won the male vote. Women's ratings reflected their preference for the Democratic candidate; their ratings of Gore were significantly higher than men's on four of the five traits measured: intelligence, morality, strong leadership, and caring.

This gender difference is reflected in the election results. Bush won male voters 53 percent to 42 percent, and Gore won female voters 54 percent to 43 percent. Further analysis revealed that these traits were significant predictors of overall evaluations of the candidates. After controlling for political party, the higher men and women rated Bush's intelligence, morality, leadership, and caring, the higher they rated his overall favorability.[19] These variables explained 42 percent of the variance (after accounting for political party) in Bush's overall favorability ratings for male voters and 30 percent for female voters. Morality, leadership, and caring were also significant predictors of male and female voters' favorability ratings of Gore, but for women, knowledge was also a significant predictor.[20] For male voters, the aforementioned traits explained 28 percent of the variance in men's overall favorability ratings of Gore and 34 percent for women's overall favorability ratings.

It is worth noting that the explanatory power of these traits in the candidates' favorability ratings varied by candidate and gender. In other words, perceived traits are an important factor in voters' overall evaluations of candidates, but as previous research suggests, this varies based on context. In this case, men who voted for Bush were motivated by their perception of his intelligence, morality, caring, and leadership. Women who voted for Gore were likely to view him as more moral and caring than Bush.

Table 6.1   2000 Presidential Election Trait Ratings

Trait	Candidate (Party)	Males		Females	
		M	SD	M	SD
Intelligence	Gore (D)	3.10	.72	3.11	.73
	Bush (R)	2.82**	.78	2.94**	.78
Knowledge	Gore (D)	3.05	.72	3.10	.72
	Bush (R)	2.76	.81	2.81	.80
Morality	Gore (D)	2.80**	.87	3.02**	.85
	Bush (R)	2.87	.83	2.89	.78
Strong leadership	Gore (D)	2.51**	.88	2.71**	.85
	Bush (R)	2.71	.85	2.72	.85
Care	Gore (D)	2.47**	.91	2.73**	.90
	Bush (R)	2.34	.88	2.37	.93

Note: Items in the same row marked with * are significant at p < .05 and ** at p <. 01.

Public perceptions and comedic parodies of Bush changed little between 2000 and 2004. In 2004, Bush was again rated less favorably, by both men and women, than the Democratic candidate, John Kerry, on the same traits as 2000: intelligence, knowledge, and caring (see Table 6.2). However, he was rated significantly higher than Kerry on leadership by both sexes and on morality by men.[21] So while Bush continued to be perceived less favorably than the Democratic candidate in some areas, he was viewed more positively in others. This difference has more to do with the Democratic candidates than with Bush. In fact, the only area where Bush was viewed significantly more favorably in 2004 than in 2000 was in his leadership, and only men's ratings increased during this time. Views of Bush's intelligence and knowledge actually decreased significantly among both men and women.

Fewer gender differences existed in 2004, but like in 2000, women rated the Democratic candidate significantly higher than men on morality and leadership. Men, on the other hand, rated Bush significantly higher than women did on leadership. The real difference from 2000 to 2004 came in women's ratings of the Democratic candidate. To put it simply, women did not like Kerry as much as Gore. Women viewed Kerry as significantly less knowledgeable, moral, and caring and as a weaker leader than Gore. The Election Day totals demonstrate this difference; Gore won women voters by 11 points, but Kerry won the women vote by only 3 points.

Much of the campaign messaging surrounding the two candidates focused on their image, particularly their leadership ability. Bush emphasized his leadership following the September 11 terrorist attacks and the wars that followed, and Kerry emphasized leadership during his time in

Table 6.2   2004 Presidential Election Trait Ratings

Trait	Candidate (Party)	Males		Females	
		M	SD	M	SD
Intelligence	Kerry (D)	3.09	.69	3.11	.73
	Bush (R)	2.61	.93	2.67	.97
Knowledge	Kerry (D)	2.97	.74	2.97	.73
	Bush (R)	2.61	.93	2.65	.95
Morality	Kerry (D)	2.67*	.84	2.80*	.81
	Bush (R)	2.87	.94	2.87	.97
Strong leadership	Kerry (D)	2.42**	.90	2.57**	.88
	Bush (R)	2.86*	.94	2.73*	1.00
Care	Kerry (D)	2.53	.89	2.63	.91
	Bush (R)	2.33	1.03	2.38	1.08

Note: Items in the same row marked with * are significant at $p < .05$ and ** at $p < .01$.

the military and U.S. Senate. However, Bush was often still portrayed as less intelligent (especially in late-night comedy) and Kerry was portrayed as dishonest in the advertising paid for by the Swift Boat Veterans for Truth. Kerry's robotic speaking style combined with images of him wind surfing made him seem out of touch with everyday Americans.

In 2004, as in 2000, gender differences existed between men and women's perceptions of Bush and Kerry's traits in relation to favorability. The higher men and women rated Bush on knowledge, morality, leadership, and caring, the more favorably they viewed Bush overall. For men, Bush's perceived intelligence also predicted favorability. After accounting for political party, trait ratings explained 62 percent of the variance in men's ratings of Bush and 48 percent of women's.[22] Similarly, the higher ratings of Kerry's intelligence, morality, leadership, and caring, the higher men and women rated his overall favorability. Traits explained 42 percent of men's favorability ratings of Kerry and 41 percent of women's.[23]

What is noteworthy with these findings it that men's perception of Bush's traits were such a strong predictor of their favorability ratings compared to women's ratings of Bush and both sexes' ratings of Kerry. While the outcome of the 2004 election was not as close or controversial as 2000, Bush still won male voters (55 percent to 41 percent), and Kerry won female voters (51 percent to 48 percent). Analysis of men's perceptions of Bush indicate that their perceptions of Bush's knowledge, morality, caring, intelligence, and leadership were driving forces in their decision to vote for him. On the other hand, women voting for Kerry were motivated by their perception of his intelligence, morality, caring, and leadership.

The images of the 2008 presidential candidates could not have been farther apart. On one hand was the young, charismatic, first-term senator from Illinois, Barack Obama, and on the other, a self-proclaimed maverick and four-term senator, John McCain. McCain suffered from being tied to an unpopular sitting president while Obama offered something fresh and hopeful. This was the first presidential election in decades where the majority of men voted for the Democratic candidate, although Obama won the male vote by only 1 point. It was also one of the largest gender gaps of all time, with Obama winning women voters by 13 points. Given the results, it is not all that surprising that there were no significant gender differences in how men and women viewed the 2008 presidential candidates. Obama was viewed by both sexes as a stronger leader and as more intelligent, knowledgeable, moral, and caring than McCain[24] (see Table 6.3).

After accounting for political party, leadership and caring were both significant predictors of men and women's overall favorability ratings of Obama. Interestingly, intelligence was negatively related to Obama's favorability ratings. In other words, the more intelligent men and women perceived Obama to be, the less they liked him.[25] However, trait ratings explained a very small amount of the variance in Obama's favorability ratings, only 6 percent for men and 8 percent for women. This is markedly less than the importance of traits in the previous two elections. This was also the case for McCain; traits explained only 4 percent of women's ratings of McCain and 6 percent of men's. Specifically, women's favorability ratings of McCain were positively related to leadership and caring but negatively related to intelligence. For male voters, caring was positively related to favorability ratings of McCain and knowledge was negatively related.[26]

In 2012, there were significant differences in how men and women rated the candidates' traits (see Table 6.4). One major reason was that the Republican candidate, Mitt Romney, had a woman problem. After several gaffes, including one during the second presidential debate where he referred to the "binders full of women" he had as governor, and the fallout from the words and deeds of down-ballot Republicans, the Republican party was particularly unpopular with women. Women believed Obama to be more intelligent, knowledgeable, moral, caring, and honest and to be a stronger leader than his Republican opponent.[27] In general, women held a more favorable view of Obama than men did in 2012. Women rated Obama significantly higher than men did on all five traits measured in previous elections (intelligence, knowledge, moral, leadership, caring) and higher on a trait measured for the first time in 2012: honesty.

On the other hand, men had a much more favorable view of Romney than women did. Men rated him higher than women on intelligence,

Table 6.3   2008 Presidential Election Trait Ratings

Trait	Candidate (Party)	Males		Females	
		M	SD	M	SD
Intelligence	Obama (D)	1.61	1.75	1.71	1.80
	McCain (R)	1.39	1.56	1.43	1.58
Knowledge	Obama (D)	1.46	1.62	1.56	1.69
	McCain (R)	1.36	1.52	1.41	1.56
Morality	Obama (D)	1.37	1.56	1.47	1.64
	McCain (R)	1.28	1.48	1.29	1.47
Strong leadership	Obama (D)	1.37	1.58	1.48	1.65
	McCain (R)	1.27	1.49	1.26	1.46
Care	Obama (D)	1.37	1.58	1.45	1.64
	McCain (R)	1.05	1.27	1.07	1.28

knowledge, morality, leadership, and honesty. While men rated Romney higher than woman on most traits, they actually rated Obama higher than Romney on several traits: intelligence, knowledge, caring, and honesty.[28] This is particularly noteworthy given that Romney won the majority of male voters. Unlike 2008 but similar to 2000 and 2004, traits played an important role in voters' overall favorability ratings of Obama and Romney. Traits explained 45 percent of men's and 44 percent of women's favorability ratings of Obama, and all six traits were significant predictors.[29] For men, all six traits were significant predictors of Romney's favorability ratings and explained 42 percent of the variance. All traits except intelligence significantly predicted women's favorability ratings of Romney, and traits explained 40 percent of the variance.[30] The effects of gender differences in opinions of the candidates played out on Election Day. Obama won women voters 55 percent to 44 percent, and Romney won male voters 52 percent to 45 percent.

While male and female voters use assessments of candidates' traits in voting decisions, men and women often view candidates differently, and the effect trait assessment has on vote choice and overall favorability ratings of candidates varies. In each of the four elections analyzed, women voted for the candidate they rated as more knowledgeable, intelligent, and caring. For women voters, leadership and caring were significant factors in the overall favorability ratings of the candidate who won their vote. There was far less consistency across elections among male voters. In three of the four elections, men voted for the candidate they saw as the stronger leader and, in half, the candidate they viewed as more moral. Leadership, caring, and intelligence were also significant predictors of candidates' favorability ratings by men in all four elections.

Table 6.4   2012 Presidential Election Trait Ratings

Trait	Candidate (Party)	Males		Females	
		M	SD	M	SD
Intelligence	Obama (D)	3.71**	1.18	3.86**	1.16
	Romney (R)	3.37**	1.18	3.21**	1.25
Honesty	Obama (D)	2.97**	1.43	3.20**	1.43
	Romney (R)	2.54**	1.35	2.42**	1.34
Knowledge	Obama (D)	3.38**	1.29	3.59**	1.25
	Romney (R)	3.08**	1.21	2.92**	1.27
Morality	Obama (D)	3.12**	1.39	3.35**	1.38
	Romney (R)	2.97**	1.36	2.83**	1.39
Strong leadership	Obama (D)	2.88**	1.41	3.17**	1.40
	Romney (R)	2.80**	1.30	2.68**	1.33
Care	Obama (D)	2.97**	1.47	3.22**	1.48
	Romney (R)	2.18	1.25	2.13	1.30

Note: Items in the same row marked with * are significant at p < .05 and ** at p < .01.

It is clear that how men and women view candidates as people—whether they think they are honest, caring, knowledgeable, or strong leaders—plays an important role in how they vote. It is also clear that men and women often have different opinions about the traits candidates possess and that these differences can partially explain the gender gap in vote choices. While political party affiliation certainly plays an important part in voters' decision making, party alone does not explain vote choices or the gender differences in those choices. This analysis examined men and women in the aggregate, which sheds light on gender differences, but further analysis is needed to understand the similarities and differences among women and the reasons behind them. The next section delves deeper into women as voters, the traits they find most important in candidates, and the psychological and sociological explanations for those opinions.

GENDER GROUP IDENTIFICATION, GENDER ROLE IDEOLOGY, AND WOMEN'S TRAIT PRIORITIES

Leadership has traditionally been associated with traits that are also tied to masculinity, such as being assertive, aggressive, and strong. Leonie Huddy and Nayda Terkildsen's research on the relationships between gender, issues, and traits found that instrumental traits, such as those listed above, were more often associated with male candidates and were also seen as more important for national and executive offices, like the presidency.[31] On the other hand, warmth/expressiveness traits tended to be associated with femininity and female candidates; these traits were viewed as less important for candidates serving at all levels of office. Based on the data from the American National Election Studies described in the previous section, both instrumental traits, like strong leadership and intelligence, and warmth/expressiveness traits, like caring and morality, are important in voters' opinions about candidates. However, the ANES data is limited by the number and types of traits included in the survey. The Women's Political Involvement (WPI) survey dived deeper into the relationships between the traits of ideal political candidates and gender.

WPI respondents were asked how important they considered a variety of issues when deciding to vote for a candidate. The list of traits was based on Huddy and Terkildsen's work and consisted of 16 traits.[32] Seven of the traits were warmth/expressiveness traits (warm, emotional, talkative, cautious, sensitive, gentle, feminine), and nine were instrumental traits (assertive, coarse, stern, self-confident, active, rational, aggressive, tough, masculine). Participants rated the importance of each traits on a five-point scale ranging from "not important at all" (1) to "very important" (5).[33]

Consistent with previous research, women in the WIP study rated instrumental traits as significantly more important than warmth/expressive traits.[34] While there was a statistically significant difference between these two types of traits, it was not extremely large, indicating that women view warmth/expressive traits as important but not as important as instrumental traits. However, as has been established, women are not a monolith, and different women may find specific traits more or less desirable. To begin understanding difference among women, those women who identified with their gender group were compared to those who did not, as was done in the examination of issue priorities and engagement in previous chapters.

Several important differences existed between the two groups. First, as shown in Table 6.5, Identified and Individualist women were similar in how important they view many traits. Both groups ranked being rational, self-confident, assertive, active, and tough as the top five most desirable traits in a political candidate. The few differences that did exist are related to Identified women rating certain traits significantly higher than Individualist women (see Table 6.5). For example, women who strongly identify with their gender group find warmth/expressiveness traits in general, and specifically being sensitive and emotional, as significantly more important than do Individualist women. Identified women also rate assertiveness and self-confidence as significantly more important than do Individualist women.

The difference in prioritization of warmth/expressiveness traits is likely tied to Identified women's connection to their gender group. These

Table 6.5   Identified and Individualist Women's Preferred Character
Traits

| | Identified | | Individualist | |
	M	**SD**	**M**	**SD**
Warmth	3.40**	.56	3.17	.70
Warm	3.79	.83	3.58	.92
Emotional	3.02*	.98	2.75	1.13
Talkative	3.37	.99	3.11	1.11
Cautious	3.77	.89	3.63	1.02
Sensitive	3.49*	.93	3.19	1.14
Gentle	3.45	.95	3.22	1.13
Feminine	2.87	.85	2.69	.86
Instrumental	3.82	.52	3.73	.59
Assertive	4.46*	.65	4.23	.87
Coarse	2.78	1.12	2.78	1.0
Stern	3.41	1.10	3.22	1.03
Self-confident	4.55*	.62	4.36	.90
Active	4.24	.83	4.06	.99
Rational	4.62	.63	4.53	.78
Aggressive	3.55	1.06	3.41	1.17
Tough	3.83	.95	3.89	.91
Masculine	2.93	1.00	3.05	1.03

Note: Items marked with * are significant at $p < .05$. Items marked with ** are significant
at $p < .01$.

traits are often tied to women and femininity, and by definition, Identified women are proud to be a member of their gender group and feel it
is central to who they are. This then relates to prioritizing traits associated with that identity. However, they also still value some traditionally
masculine traits associated with political leadership, like self-confidence
and assertiveness. It is also worth noting that, while not always statistically significant, Identified women rated nearly every trait higher than did
Individualist women. This may indicate that the character of a candidate
is more important to Identified women. It may also reflect the greater
political engagement of Identified women outlined in chapter 4. In sum,
candidates appealing to Identified and Individualist women voters should
focus on the traits they both find most important—being rational, self-
confident, assertive, active and tough—but attempts to appeal specifically
to Identified women should also emphasize the sensitive and emotional
side of candidates.

Women's level of group identification is related to the traits they prioritize, but it is not the only factor. Women's feelings about appropriate

gender roles and expectations also relate to the traits they prefer to see in a candidate. The role of gender is especially important in the analysis of traits, since they are often associated with either masculinity or femininity. Egalitarian-Identified and Traditional-Identified women were similar when it came to the traits they found most important. Both groups rated self-confidence, rationality, assertiveness, activeness, and toughness in their top five. These are all instrumental traits, most often associated with masculinity and male candidates.

It seems, then, that even among women, regardless of their gender-role beliefs, stereotypically masculine traits are associated with political leadership. This is not to say that women candidates are doomed, but it does suggest that women candidates, even when courting women voters, must demonstrate that they possess these traits. Furthermore, for both groups of women, the stereotypically feminine traits of warmth and cautiousness came in sixth and seventh respectively. So while instrumental traits are viewed as most important, some warmth/expressiveness traits are also very important to women voters. Candidates courting either of these groups of women would be wise to demonstrate a balance of masculine and feminine traits with particular attention to self-confidence, rationality, assertiveness, toughness, warmth, and cautiousness.

There were also many differences in how Egalitarian-Identified and Traditional-Identified women rated character traits (see Table 6.6). In general, Traditional-Identified women tended to put more importance on the measured traits, both instrumental traits and warmth/expressiveness traits. Specifically, Traditional-Identified women rated being warm, talkative, cautious, feminine, coarse, stern, masculine, active, aggressive, and tough all as significantly more important than did Egalitarian-Identified women. This indicates that Traditional-Identified women value character more in their evaluations of candidates than do their egalitarian counterparts. On the other hand, the only traits that Egalitarian-Identified women rated higher than Traditional-Identified women were being sensitive and rational.

Candidates courting the votes of Traditional-Identified women should pay special attention to their image and the traits they emphasize in their campaign communication. Traditional-Identified women are looking for a candidate who demonstrates a well-rounded personality that includes stereotypically masculine traits like being aggressive and tough while also possessing traits more often associated with femininity, like being warm, talkative, and cautious. On the other hand, Egalitarian-Identified women put less emphasis on candidates' traits, but they are still important. Communication targeting this group of women should focus specifically on candidates' rationality and sensitivity.

Table 6.6 Preferred Candidate Traits by Egalitarian and Traditional Group-Identified Women

	Egalitarian-Identified		Traditional-Identified	
	M	SD	M	SD
Warmth	3.32*	.57	3.51	.54
Warm	3.71*	.88	3.92	.75
Emotional	2.98	.97	3.09	1.00
Talkative	3.22*	.99	3.59	.96
Cautious	3.68*	.93	3.91	.80
Sensitive	3.51	.93	3.47	.94
Gentle	3.41	.98	3.51	.90
Feminine	2.74*	.91	3.05	.74
Instrumental	3.71*	.49	3.98	.52
Assertive	4.46	.64	4.46	.66
Coarse	2.55**	1.14	3.13	1.01
Stern	3.23*	1.06	3.67	1.11
Self-confident	4.54	.57	4.56	.67
Active	4.15*	.88	4.38	.75
Rational	4.70*	.56	4.50	.71
Aggressive	3.41*	1.07	3.76	1.03
Tough	3.73*	.95	3.99	.93
Masculine	2.63**	1.01	3.39	.80

Note: Items marked with * are significant at $p < .05$. Items marked with ** are significant at $p < .01$.

THE RELATIONSHIP BETWEEN TRAITS AND ISSUES

Understanding which traits women find important can help us understand why certain candidates are liked more than others, but traits (and perceptions of them) do not exist in a vacuum. Traits relate to issues; research has shown that certain traits are associated with political figures' ability to handle certain issues.[35] For example, candidates perceived to be more compassionate are seen as better able to handle issues like child welfare or poverty, and those perceived to be tough are seen as better able to address military issues. Statistical correlations were used to examine the relationships between women's trait and issue priorities. Keeping in mind that all women are not the same, these correlations were run for each group of women: Egalitarian-Identified, Traditional-Identified, and Individualist. Correlations are displayed in Tables 6.7 through 6.9.

In relation to the broad issue and trait categories, a few important findings become apparent. For Egalitarian-Identified women, there is a positive correlation between ratings of warmth/expressiveness traits and the

Table 6.7a Egalitarian-Identified Women: Ideal Traits and Economic Issues Correlations

	Economic Issues (Combined)	Budget Deficit	Ability to Deal with Business Leaders	Unemployment	Economic Crisis	Cost of Living
Warmth/expressiveness traits (combined)	.20**	.05	.21**	.03	.05	.29**
Warm	.21*	.03	.23**	.10	.04	.30**
Emotional	.00	-.03	.08	-.15*	-.08	.12
Talkative	.10	-.00	.09	.03	.07	.17*
Cautious	.13	.04	.13	.10	.10	.07
Sensitive	.12	.08	.03	.08	.07	.17*
Gentle	.19*	.08	.20**	.05	.04	.25**
Feminine	.08	.03	.14	-.08	-.01	.13
Instrumental traits (combined)	.33**	.21**	.38**	.01	.23**	.24**
Assertive	.34**	.15	.35**	.19*	.26**	.22**
Coarse	.04	.02	.14	-.11	.00	.03
Stern	.19**	.04	.30**	-.04	.09	.19*
Self-confident	.45**	.32**	.41**	.24**	.31**	.26**
Active	.23**	.19*	.19*	.06	.19*	.17*
Rational	.28**	.23**	.15	.27**	.27**	.12
Aggressive	.16*	.06	.24**	-.03	.12	.13
Tough	.18*	.16*	.22**	-.05	.15	.09
Masculine	.12	.06	.03	-.17*	-.01	.08

Note: Items marked with * are significant at $p < .05$. Items marked with ** are significant at $p < .01$.

Table 6.7b Egalitarian-Identified Women: Ideal Traits and Military and Foreign Policy Issues Correlations

	Military/Foreign Policy Issues (Combined)	Military Readiness	Terrorism	International Relations	Afghanistan War	Iraq War
Warmth/expressiveness traits (combined)	.20**	.06	.13	.13	.19*	.24**
Warm	.10	.04	.08	.08	.04	.14
Emotional	.06	-.04	-.00	.06	.08	.14
Talkative	.07	-.01	.03	.04	.07	.11
Cautious	.26**	.14	.21**	.09	.26**	.25**
Sensitive	.06	-.01	.03	.13	.07	.04
Gentle	.10	.02	.08	.13	.08	.11
Feminine	.20**	.12	.12	.05	.21**	.21**
Instrumental traits (combined)	.47**	.31**	.41**	.23**	.39**	.40**
Assertive	.32**	.23**	.28**	.22**	.22**	.25**
Coarse	.20**	.11	.21**	-.05	.18*	.22**
Stern	.32**	.16*	.23**	.17*	.28**	.34**
Self-confident	.36**	.27**	.30**	.32**	.23**	.27**
Active	.17*	.02	.10	.21**	.19*	.17*
Rational	.16*	.08	.06	.35**	.13	.06
Aggressive	.34**	.22**	.33**	.12	.30**	.29**
Tough	.34**	.28**	.36**	.13	.28**	.20**
Masculine	.18*	.23**	.14	-.07	.13	.16*

Note: Items marked with * are significant at $p < .05$. Items marked with ** are significant at $p < .01$.

Table 6.7c Egalitarian-Identified Women: Ideal Traits and Compassion Issues Correlations

	Compassion Issues (Combined)	Wage gap	Child welfare	Children's Health Care	Assisting the Poor	Education
Warmth/expressiveness traits (combined)	.19*	.19*	.19*	.21**	.12	-.01
Warm	.24**	.20**	.27**	.27**	.09	.14
Emotional	.06	.12	.07	.07	.03	-.13
Talkative	.08	.09	.11	.08	.04	-.02
Cautious	.06	.07	.02	.06	.07	-.03
Sensitive	.21**	.17*	.18*	.19*	.17*	.11
Gentle	.21**	.18*	.16*	.23**	.17*	.02
Feminine	-.05	-.02	.01	-.00	-.07	-.13
Instrumental traits (combined)	-.02	-.02	.02	.02	-.08	-.02
Assertive	.12	.04	.18*	.13	.04	.13
Coarse	-.16	-.14	-.15*	-.06	-.13	-.17*
Stern	.01	.01	.02	.11	-.04	-.06
Self-Confident	.19*	.07	.25**	.14	.09	.28**
Active	.09	.08	.04	.15*	.01	.10
Rational	.17*	.07	.19*	.11	.14	.21**
Aggressive	-.01	.10	.01	-.04	-.07	-.04
Tough	-.11	-.06	-.08	-.10	-.09	-.13
Masculine	-.18*	-.14	-.12	-.19*	-.15*	-.12

Note: Items marked with * are significant at $p < .05$. Items marked with ** are significant at $p < .01$.

importance they place on all three issue categories (economic, military/ foreign affairs, and compassion). In other words, the more important Egalitarian-Identified women think these types of issues are, the more important they think it is for candidates to possess warmth/expressiveness traits. Specifically, warmth/expressiveness traits are correlated with gender wage gap, child welfare, children's health care, dealing with business leaders, cost of living, and wars in Iraq and Afghanistan.

Interestingly, instrumental traits are correlated with economic and military/foreign affairs issues for this group but not compassion issues. Specifically, instrumental traits were correlated with budget deficit, dealing with business leaders, economic crisis, the cost of living, military readiness, terrorism, international relations, and the wars in Iraq and Afghanistan. It is particularly noteworthy that Egalitarian-Identified women generally relate warmth/expressiveness traits to candidates' ability to handle all issues, but they do not relate instrumental traits to candidates' ability to handle compassion issues, such as child welfare or education. It seems that for this group of women, traits often considered feminine are linked to compassion issues, which are also often linked to femininity and caregiving.

The picture is somewhat different for Traditional-Identified women. For this group, instrumental traits correlate with all three issue categories, signaling that this group believes that instrumental traits are important in handling all issues. Specifically, instrumental traits are correlated with international relations, war in Afghanistan, dealing with business leaders, employment, economic crisis, cost of living, children's health care, assisting the poor, and education. Traditional-Identified women's prioritization of warmth/expressiveness traits was also correlated with compassion issues and military/foreign affairs issues. What is noteworthy is that, unlike Egalitarian-Identified women, there was no significant relationship between warmth traits and economic issues for Traditional-Identified women. In fact, cost of living is the only economic issue correlated with warmth/expressiveness traits. This indicates that Traditional-Identified women view economic issues through a lens of instrumentality rather than compassion. However, warmth/expressiveness traits were correlated with issues that tend to have a clear human side, such as the gender wage gap, child welfare, children's health care, assisting the poor, and cost of living.

The differences between Individualist women and the two groups of Identified women are also worth noting. Warmth/expressiveness traits did not correlate with any issue category, and instrumental traits only correlated with economic issues for Individualist women. For Individualist

Table 6.8a Traditional-Identified Women: Ideal Traits and Economic Issues Correlations

	Economic Issues (Combined)	Budget Deficit	Ability to Deal with Business Leaders	Unemployment	Economic Crisis	Cost of Living
Warmth/expressiveness traits (combined)	.18	.09	.17	.15	.05	.23*
Warm	.16	.15	.09	.10	.13	.16
Emotional	.03	.02	.11	-.03	-.13	.13
Talkative	.07	-.03	.15	.07	.02	.06
Cautious	.24**	.15	.18	.26**	.07	.27**
Sensitive	.11	.01	.07	.16	.10	.09
Gentle	.20**	.18*	.08	.18	.13	.22*
Feminine	-.05	-.11	.04	-.12	-.09	.08
Instrumental traits (combined)	.41**	.37**	.25**	.42**	.25**	.30**
Assertive	.46**	.45**	.22*	.50**	.34**	.28**
Coarse	.04	.06	.08	-.04	-.11	.15
Stern	.25	.19*	.20*	.30**	.08	.17
Self-confident	.37**	.31**	.24**	.36**	.31**	.20*
Active	.25**	.24**	.12	.20*	.22*	.21*
Rational	.44**	.42**	.11	.49**	.41**	.30**
Aggressive	.23*	.25**	.07	.25**	.13	.20*
Tough	.29**	.31**	.10	.34**	.19*	.20*
Masculine	.06	-.07	.27**	.01	-.01	-.03

Note: Items marked with * are significant at $p < .05$. Items marked with ** are significant at $p < .01$.

Table 6.8b Traditional-Identified Women: Ideal Traits and Military and Foreign Policy Issues Correlations

	Military/Foreign Policy Issues (Combined)	Military Readiness	Terrorism	International Relations	Afghanistan War	Iraq War
Warmth/expressiveness traits (combined)	.19*	.11	.14	.16	.16	.17
Warm	.15	.02	.16	.11	.13	.16
Emotional	.10	.02	.05	.06	.13	.14
Talkative	.04	.06	.03	-.08	.04	.08
Cautious	.13	.14	.11	.20*	.05	.02
Sensitive	.13	.13	.07	.15	.05	.08
Gentle	.18	.05	.15	.24**	.15	.12
Feminine	.09	.02	.04	.01	.12	.14
Instrumental traits (combined)	.30**	.22*	.37**	.25**	.20*	.16
Assertive	.37**	.33**	.42**	.32**	.22*	.19*
Coarse	.09	.01	.09	-.04	.14	.13
Stern	.15	.08	.27**	.08	.11	.07
Self-confident	.33	.19*	.34**	.29**	.26**	.22*
Active	.11	.07	.11	.25**	.00	-.00
Rational	.36**	.33**	.35**	.38**	.18	.18
Aggressive	.20	.14	.26**	.11	.16	.11
Tough	.26**	.22*	.29**	.25**	.12	.15
Masculine	-.11	-.10	-.02	-.09	-.08	-.14

Note: Items marked with * are significant at *p* < .05. Items marked with ** are significant at *p* < .01.

Table 6.8c Traditional-Identified Women: Ideal Traits and Compassion Issues Correlations

	Compassion Issues (Combined)	Wage Gap	Child Welfare	Children's Health Care	Assisting the Poor	Education
Warmth/expressiveness traits (combined)	.30**	.27**	.25**	.35**	.22*	.11
Warm	.22	.20*	.17	.28**	.11	.13
Emotional	.11	.18*	.09	.13	.12	-.08
Talkative	-.02	-.10	.03	.03	-.02	-.01
Cautious	.35**	.32**	.30**	.28**	.32**	.16
Sensitive	.02*	.15	.19*	.25**	.14	.10
Gentle	.35**	.30**	.27**	.38**	.20*	.25**
Feminine	.08	.12	.00	.17	.10	-.07
Instrumental traits (combined)	.34**	.20*	.38**	.26**	.25**	.28**
Assertive	.44**	.32**	.47**	.35**	.24**	.43**
Coarse	.07	.10	.10	.01	.13	-.06
Stern	.17	.08	.24**	.10	.21*	.02
Self-confident	.38**	.24**	.37**	.37**	.22*	.36**
Active	.20*	.15	.23*	.17	.09	.19*
Rational	.39**	.23*	.43**	.33**	.20*	.41**
Aggressive	.17	.05	.19*	.12	.13	.20*
Tough	.26**	.14	.28**	.18*	.23*	.23*
Masculine	-.08	-.12	-.07	-.02	-.05	-.06

Note: Items marked with * are significant at $p < .05$. Items marked with ** are significant at $p < .01$.

women, there is nearly no correlation between how important they rate trait and issue categories. However, at the level of individual issues, there are some correlations for Individualist women. Warmth/expressiveness traits are correlated with their prioritization of economic crisis and cost of living, and instrumental traits are correlated with terrorism, Iraq War, education, children's health care, economic crisis, and the cost of living. When specific traits are examined, more interesting findings emerge. Individualist women considered being rational and self-confident as the two most important traits in a candidate, and these traits are significantly correlated with these women's prioritization of most of the issues examined. In fact, rationality is correlated with 11 of 15 issues, and self-confidence is correlated with 9.

Rationality, self-confidence, and assertiveness were also rated as the most important candidate traits by Egalitarian-Identified and Traditional-Identified women. Not surprisingly, these traits are also correlated with the most issues for both groups. The higher Egalitarian-Identified women rated rationality as a desired trait, the higher they rated six issues (budget deficit, unemployment, economic crisis, child welfare, education, and international relations), indicating that Egalitarian-Identified women associate handling these issues with a candidate's rationality. Traditional-Identified women's ratings of rationality was correlated with 10 of the 15 issues measured: budget deficit, unemployment, economic crisis, cost of living, military readiness, terrorism, gender wage gap, child welfare, children's health care, and assisting the poor.

While the two groups of women overlap in their prioritization of rationality, there are also some notable differences. The relationship between rationality and international relations and education existed only for Egalitarian-Identified women. On the other hand, being rational correlated with military readiness, terrorism, wage gap, children's health care, assisting the poor, and cost of living only for Traditional-Identified women. In sum, rationality is an important trait and is associated with many issues for both Egalitarian and Traditional-Identified women, although the importance of that trait varies some based on specific issues.

Self-confidence was significantly correlated with all 15 issues for Traditional-Identified women. In other words, the higher these women rated all issues measured, the higher they rated self-confidence, indicating that Traditional-Identified women consider self-confidence a necessary trait for candidates to be able to handle issues. Similarly, self-confidence was correlated with most of the issues for Egalitarian-Identified women; the exceptions were unemployment, education, and economic crisis. This indicates that self-confidence is an important trait for these women, too,

Table 6.9a Individualist Women: Ideal Traits and Economic Issues Correlations

	Economic Issues (Combined)	Budget Deficit	Ability to Deal with Business Leaders	Unemployment	Economic Crisis	Cost of Living
Warmth/expressiveness traits (combined)	.20	.10	.00	.19	.27*	.26*
Warm	.20	.20	.08	.06	.18	.28*
Emotional	.06	.01	.03	.07	.05	.08
Talkative	-.13	-.19	-.21	-.08	-.04	.04
Cautious	.14	-.03	-.10	.21	.29*	.27*
Sensitive	.23	.12	.05	.29*	.28*	.22
Gentle	.22	.16	.03	.18	.28*	.24
Feminine	.25	.28*	.19	.13	.23	.11
Instrumental traits (combined)	.28*	.10	.11	.16	.33**	.43**
Assertive	.36**	.24	.23	.19	.41**	.37**
Coarse	-.13	-.12	-.21	-.16	-.09	.07
Stern	-.03	-.12	-.11	-.05	-.03	.24
Self-confident	.39**	.26*	.29*	.20	.46**	.33**
Active	.23	.17	.14	.12	.19	.31*
Rational	.50**	.33**	.25	.41**	.53**	.46**
Aggressive	.01	-.14	-.04	.07	.06	.12
Tough	.32*	.13	.15	.24	.34**	.44**
Masculine	.06	-.05	.06	-.00	.09	.13

Note: Items marked with * are significant at $p < .05$. Items marked with ** are significant at $p < .01$.

Table 6.9b Individualist-Identified Women: Ideal Traits and Military and Foreign Policy Issues Correlations

	Military/Foreign Policy Issues (Combined)	Military Readiness	Terrorism	International Relations	Afghanistan War	Iraq War
Warmth/expressiveness traits (combined)	.09	.03	.09	-.02	.09	.16
Warm	.07	.04	.14	-.03	-.03	.14
Emotional	-.08	-.06	-.11	-.19	.05	.00
Talkative	-.20	-.23	-.12	-.33**	-.14	.05
Cautious	.17	.13	.15	.08	.12	.16
Sensitive	.19	.10	.08	.25*	.22	.09
Gentle	.18	.11	.19	.06	.10	.22
Feminine	.12	.07	.08	.12	.09	.08
Instrumental traits (combined)	.22	.18	.27*	.03	.07	.26*
Assertive	.29	.27*	.39**	.16	.06	.18
Coarse	-.14*	-.18	-.16	-.29*	-.04	.11
Stern	.06	-.03	.11	-.19	.13	.19
Self-confident	.35**	.33**	.37**	.11	.19	.31*
Active	.08	.08	.19	.07	-.10	.07
Rational	.32*	.30*	.30*	.33**	.07	.22
Aggressive	.02	.02	.06	-.11	-.05	.14
Tough	.31*	.32**	.37**	.07	.13	.28*
Masculine	.04	.01	.01	.16	.02	-.04

Note: Items marked with * are significant at $p < .05$. Items marked with ** are significant at $p < .01$.

Table 6.9c Individualist-Identified Women: Ideal Traits and Compassion Issues Correlations

	Compassion Issues (Combined)	Wage Gap	Child Welfare	Children's Health Care	Assisting the Poor	Education
Warmth/expressiveness traits (combined)	.22	.17	.14	.22	.16	.18
Warm	.14	-.03	.19	.15	.09	.17
Emotional	-.08	.18	-.05	.06	-.02	.02
Talkative	.00	-.08	.05	.10	-.06	.00
Cautious	.27*	.05	.19	.26*	.33**	.26*
Sensitive	.28*	.30*	.15	.18	.31*	.15
Gentle	.22	.17	.18	.20	.11	.21
Feminine	.04	.20	-.09	.04	-.03	.02
Instrumental traits (combined)	.21	-.11	.21	.34**	.09	.35**
Assertive	.17	-.21	.23	.24	.09	.37**
Coarse	.06	.05	-.04	.18	-.02	.07
Stern	.08	-.11	.10	.17	.11	.05
Self-confident	.21	-.07	.21	.28*	.11	.31*
Active	.29*	-.01	.30*	.39**	.18	.30*
Rational	.36**	.12	.32*	.30*	.20	.51**
Aggressive	.11	-.12	.14	.19	.05	.20
Tough	.09	-.17	.12	.20	-.07	.29*
Masculine	-.13	-.07	-.18	-.08	-.10	-.09

Note: Items marked with * are significant at $p < .05$. Items marked with ** are significant at $p < .01$.

but it may not be the most important trait in their consideration of a candidate's ability to handle unemployment, education, and economic crisis.

Assertiveness was also correlated with all 15 issues for Traditional-Identified women, indicating that assertiveness is a very important trait to this group of women. Egalitarian-Identified women also considered assertiveness important, but it was not correlated with budget deficit, wage gap, assisting the poor, education, and children's health care. This is noteworthy because all but one of these are compassion issues. This suggests that while Egalitarian-Identified women consider assertiveness to be an important trait for candidates handling many issues, it may not be as important in their consideration of how well a candidate can handle compassion issues. Rather, these issues seem to be more related to the more feminine traits of warmth and sensitivity.

Another way to look at these correlations is by examining which traits correlate with the issues women find most important, particularly the traits that are tied to multiple important issues. As noted in chapter 5, both Egalitarian-Identified and Traditional-Identified women rated education, employment, and economic crisis as the issues they found most important for a candidate to be able to handle. For Egalitarian-Identified women, all three of these issues were related to self-confidence and rationality. Assertiveness was also correlated with economic crisis and employment for this group. For Traditional-Identified women, those three issues were correlated with assertiveness, self-confidence, activeness, and toughness. Rationality was correlated with economic crisis and employment, and aggressive was correlated with both education and employment.

In other words, candidates courting the votes of Egalitarian-Identified women should emphasize their self-confidence and rationality in relation to their handling of education, employment, and economic crisis, and they should also demonstrate their assertiveness in handling the latter two traits. Candidates targeting Traditional-Identified women should stress being assertive, active, self-confident, and tough in relation to their ability to handle economic crisis and employment issues.

CONCLUSION

Gender matters when it comes to perceptions of political candidates and vote choices. As the analysis of four presidential elections demonstrate, men and women do not always view candidates the same. Furthermore, the traits that seem to matter most and to drive voting decisions differ based on the voters' gender as well as the specific candidate and electoral context. Both men and women use their assessment of candidates' traits in determining their overall opinion and vote choice. Women, at least in the 21st century, tended to vote for the presidential candidate they viewed as more intelligent, knowledgeable, and caring. Men tended to vote for the candidate they viewed as the stronger leader.

There are more similarities than differences among women when it comes to the traits they want in a candidate. Whether women identified with their gender group or not and whether they had traditional or egalitarian gender-role beliefs, the traits they rated as most important were rationality, self-confidence, assertiveness, toughness, and activeness. However, women who identified with their gender group were more likely to consider warmth/expressiveness traits in general and being sensitive and emotional as important traits for a candidate to have.

There were also many similarities and some differences among Identified women in how they related candidates' traits to important issues. Regardless of gender-role ideology, Identified women considered rationality, self-confidence, and assertiveness to be important traits when it came to handling the three issues they found most important (education, economy, and employment). However, among Egalitarian-Identified women, candidates' ability to handle all three broad issue categories (compassion, military/foreign affairs, and economic) was correlated with possessing warmth and expressiveness traits, but only military/foreign affairs and economic issues were associated with instrumental traits. For Traditional-Identified women, instrumental traits were associated with the three issue categories, and warmth/expressiveness traits were associated only with compassion and military/foreign affairs issues. In sum, both groups find similar traits important when it comes to handling a variety of political issues; however, warmth/expressiveness traits are related to more issues for Egalitarian-Identified women, and instrumental traits are related to more issues for Traditional-Identified women.

CHAPTER 7

Do Women Voters Prefer Women Candidates?

After Hillary Clinton lost the 2008 Democratic presidential nomination, the political pundits on cable news began speculating about what this would mean for women voters in the general election. Some argued that the women who supported Clinton were so angered by her loss that they would not vote in the general election, and some went so far as to argue that they would vote Republican. This debate was fueled by John McCain's announcement that Sarah Palin would be his running mate. The talking heads on cable news began debating whether or not women voters who had supported Clinton were so desperate to elect a woman that they would cross party lines and vote for McCain-Palin. Of course, this did not happen. Women voted overwhelmingly for Obama in 2008. However, the 2008 election raised an important question: do women voters prefer women candidates?

Using data collected in the Women's Political Involvement Survey, which included an experiment testing the theory of gender affinity, this chapter explores the idea of gender affinity in vote choices and evaluations of political candidates. The gender affinity effect is defined as a preference for a particular gender group and, in this case, women voters' preference for women candidates. The first section of this chapter explores the existing research and literature on women voters and gender affinity. Next, I examine survey data to determine if women, and which women, feel female candidates represent them better. Last, using experimental data, I explore how women voters view male and female candidates in a low-information mock election and the influence of gender group identification in those views.

GENDER AFFINITY IN VOTING

The idea that women voters prefer women candidates has some support in political science and communication research. As was discussed
in chapter 2, high levels of group identification are associated with a preference for the in-group, so women who feel strongly connected to their
gender group will (in some cases) prefer a member of that group to represent them in government. Kathleen Dolan, political science professor
at the University of Wisconsin-Milwaukee, examined National Election
Study data from 1990 to 2000 with a focus on U.S. House races including
a female candidate. Dolan found that women were more engaged in political campaigns when a woman was running for office and that women
voters rated female Democratic candidates more favorably than male candidates. However, female Republican candidates were not viewed more
favorably than men. Dolan also found that higher affect translated into
votes; in other words, women voters liked Democratic women candidates
more and were more likely to vote for them.[1]

Dolan's study highlights an important caveat to claims that women prefer voting for women: political party matters. For example, a study of voters
in the 1992 election, often referred to as "The Year of the Woman," found
that women were more likely to vote for women candidates, and this was
true in both parties. However, gender group identification competed with
party identification as a cue for voting decisions, and Democratic female
candidates who were seen as more feminist benefited the most from a
gender affinity effect in voting.[2] In a related study, political scientist Craig
Leonard Brians examined U.S. House races from 1990 to 2002 and found
that women show a slight preference for female candidates, whereas men
are equally split, and in open-seat races, both Republican and Democratic women show a stronger preference for female candidates of their
own party. Most noteworthy are Brians's results about the willingness to
cross party lines to vote for a female candidate. He found that Republican
women and men were more likely than Democrats to do this, and Republican women in particular were the most likely to cross party lines when a
Democratic woman faced a Republican man.[3]

Additional support for the gender affinity effect can be found in
research relate to Campbell and Wolbrecht's role model theory. The
role model theory argues that the presence of viable female candidates
increases women's political involvement and interest.[4] Related to this
theory, Atkeson's contextual cue theory posits that women's engagement
is increased when there is a viable female candidate on the ballot.[5] This
happens because the female candidate's presence sends a cue to women

that they are part of the political system and that the system is responsive to their concerns. Both of these theories indicate that the presence of women in campaigns has an influence on female voters and provides support for the idea of a gender affinity effect.

However, it is important to note that the mere presence of a female candidate is not enough to increase women's interest or engagement; the women need to be viable and visible. In races where a candidate is not highly visible, female voters are unlikely to be aware of the female candidate, so there is little chance of increased involvement.[6] If the candidate is not viable, meaning that chances of winning are very low, then female voters behave similar to those in a race with no female candidate on the ballot.[7] In areas where there is a visible and competitive female candidate, women's political involvement is often influenced. Numerous studies have found that women show higher levels of interest and efficacy in elections that include a viable female candidate.[8] Women also demonstrate greater political knowledge and are more likely to discuss politics and attempt to persuade others when a woman is on the ballot.

GENDER AFFINITY EFFECT AND GROUP IDENTIFICATION

Gender affinity likely happens when women voters feel that they are best represented by other women because they share a common group identity. Previous research has found that political party plays an important part, as does whether or not a female candidate is viewed to be feminist. To better understand the relationships between gender group identification, gender role beliefs, and gender affinity, women completing the Women's Political Involvement survey were asked to indicate their level of agreement regarding their feelings about women candidates. The scale is grounded in homophily research, which has found that voters prefer candidates they view as similar to themselves, but in this case, I measured gender homophily of candidates in the abstract to see if women prefer women candidate generally

Participants were asked to indicate their level of agreement ranging from "strongly disagree" (1) to "strongly agree" (5) on the following items: "candidates of my gender group see the world like me"; "candidate of my gender group are concerned with issues that are important to me"; "candidates of my gender group share my value"; "candidates of my gender group are in touch with my problems"; and "candidates of my gender group have had experiences similar to my own." This scale had high reliability with a Cronbach's alpha of .90. To directly test for gender affinity in vote choice, participants were also asked to indicate their agreement to the statement "I prefer to vote for candidates of my gender group when they are of the same party as me."

Regression analysis revealed that gender group identification and sex-role beliefs were significant predictors of gender homophily.[9] Together, these variables explained 30 percent of the variance in gender homophily scores. The variables were also significant predictors of agreement with the statement "I prefer to vote for candidates of my gender group when they are of the same party as me," explaining 18 percent of the variance.[10] These findings indicate that the more a woman identified with her gender group, the more likely she is to see female candidates as similar to herself and the more likely she is to vote for female candidates. Interestingly, more egalitarian gender views were associated with gender homophily, indicating a feeling of commonality, but more traditional views were associated with explicit preference for a female candidate.

To delve deeper into these relationships, differences and similarities between Egalitarian-Identified, Traditional-Identified, and Individualist women were examined. The mean scores for gender homophily and gender affinity are displayed in Table 7.1.[11] Not surprisingly, Individualist women, who by definition feel less connected to their gender group, scored significantly lower on gender-candidate homophily and were significantly less likely to prefer a candidate of their own gender. What is most noteworthy is that traditional views about gender roles is associated with greater feelings of gender-candidate homophily. Traditional-Identified women scored significantly higher than Egalitarian-Identified women on the scale as a whole and were specifically more likely to feel that women candidates were concerned with issues important to them, share their values, and in touch with their problems.

Earlier research on gender group identification and political action found that feminist consciousness, or connection to a feminist identity, was a strong predictor of voting behavior and preference for female candidates.[12] While Egalitarian-Identified women in this study were more likely than Individualist women to feel a sense of homophily with female candidates, women with more traditional views on gender feel the strongest connection to women candidates. However, Egalitarian-Identified and Traditional-Identified women were statistically similar in their preference for a female candidate, and both scored significantly higher on this measure than did Individualist women.

These findings provide some insights for female candidates courting female voters. In general, a successful strategy for women candidates courting women voters would be to focus campaign messaging on shared

Table 7.1 Gender-Candidate Homophily

Scale	Egalitarian-Identified	Traditional-Identified	Individualist
Mean gender-candidate homophily	4.49_a	4.80_b	3.73_c
Sees the world like me	4.31_a	4.49_a	3.50_b
Concerned with issues important to me	4.68_a	4.97_b	3.86_c
Shares my values	4.50_a	4.89_b	3.63_c
In touch with my problems	4.42_a	4.82_b	3.67_c
Experiences similar to my own	4.55_a	4.82_a	4.02_b
Prefer candidate of my gender when of my party	4.57_a	4.34_a	3.52_b

Note: Items in the same row with different subscripts are significant at $p < .05$.

values and experiences. Women with a strong sense of gender group identification will likely be persuaded to vote for these women over a male opponent, especially if they are of the same political party. Republican women candidates may particularly benefit from this strategy. Women with traditional views on gender more often identify as Republican, and the findings of this study indicate they are particularly likely to feel a sense of commonality with female candidates of their own party.

GENDER AND CANDIDATE EVALUATIONS

The candidate-gender-homophily measure above asked women voters about female candidates in the abstract. To get a better idea of whether or not women voters prefer women candidates, it is necessary to see how they evaluate real candidates. A good deal of research has examined how male and female candidates are generally perceived by voters, but less research looks at differences between men and women voters or the nuances of women's evaluations of candidates. The following sections explore the existing research and report results of an experiment testing women's perceptions of male and female candidates.

It is necessary to first explore the existing research on how women candidates are viewed and the challenges their gender creates. Beliefs about sex-roles vary, and a woman's sex-role ideology may influence how she evaluates the traits and competency of female political candidates. Traditional gender-role stereotypes have made a division of the sexes seem natural. These assumptions make women's primary place the private sphere of the home and men's place the public sphere of government or business. This division between the public and private spheres has been one of the primary barriers to women's entrance in politics.[13] With the division of roles come beliefs about the personalities and abilities of men and women, with women being constructed as nurturing and compassionate caretakers and men constructed as ambitious, tough, breadwinners. These beliefs about appropriate gender roles make it especially difficult for a woman to ascend to the presidency, because women are thought to have a primary responsibility to their families and because their stereotypical traits are assumed to make them unable to handle the requirements of office.

In an attempt to explain the challenges faced by female leaders, Alice Eagly and Steven Karau proposed the role congruity theory in 2002.[14] This theory posits that traditional gender roles create a double bind for female leaders; women are seen as unfit for leadership positions, or women who are strong leaders are evaluated as too unfeminine and hence unacceptable. Eagly and Karau propose that gender roles have both descriptive and prescriptive norms. Descriptive norms tell us how a group is perceived to be; women are perceived to be gentle, warm, and nurturing, and men are perceived as strong, assertive, and independent. Prescriptive norms tell us how people *should* behave.

When these norms are violated, the violator is viewed less favorably. For example, an assertive, ambitious female is violating her prescribed gender role and may be viewed negatively. This puts female leaders in a precarious position. Potential women leaders are viewed as less qualified because good leadership traits and assumed female traits are incongruent, so people view them as less able to perform in a leadership role.[15] On the other hand, women who are in leadership positions and demonstrate strong leadership traits are viewed as too masculine, and they are evaluated negatively because they have failed to meet the prescribed gender-role expectations.

Role congruity theory can help us explain some of the barriers faced by female candidates. Research has supported role congruity theory in relation to candidates. Generally, female candidates are seen as possessing stereotypical feminine traits, such as being more warm, compassionate, emotional, passive, and honest; male candidates are believed to possess more stereotypical masculine traits, such as assertiveness, ambition, strength, and decisiveness.[16] Role congruity theory is further confirmed by Leoine Huddy and Nadya Terkildsen's work exploring trait desirability and level of political office.[17] They found that holders of all levels of office were expected to possess more masculine than feminine traits, and while local officeholders were not expected to be as extreme in masculine traits, possession of feminine traits did not advantage candidates running for those offices. On the other hand, possession of masculine traits did advantage candidates running for national offices. This work supports role congruity theory, demonstrating that women are not only assumed to have certain traits that are different from men but also that those feminine traits are not the traits voters look for in a political leader.

Gender-role expectations not only influence voters' evaluation of a candidate's traits but also affect perceptions of the candidate's ability to handle various issues. Huddy and Terkildsen found a relationship between perceived traits and issue competencies, specifically that women were believed to be better able to handle compassion issues, such as elder care, aid to the poor, health care, and education.[18] This is likely because these issues are related to the perceived traits held by women; successful handling of these issues would arguably require a gentle, compassionate, maternal approach. Men, on the other hand, were perceived to be more competent at issues related to their perceived traits; these issues included the military, national security, and crime. Numerous studies have supported this research, consistently finding that there are certain issue women are thought to be better able to handle and other issues that men are assumed to be better fit to address.[19] Assumptions about issue competencies have a real effect on female candidates, because the issues deemed most important for national office, including the presidency, are the issues men are assumed to be more capable of handling.

With an increasing number of women running for and winning political offices at the local, state, and national level, one cannot claim that gender-role expectations always translate into women being perceived as incapable of handling the duties of office. There are factors that limit or enhance gender cues in an election. Research has found that gender cues are most influential in low-information elections, so when voters know little about the candidates, gender stereotypes fill in some of the gaps and assist in decision making.[20] Deborah Alexander and Kristi Anderson of Syracuse University also found in 1993 that incumbency was the most influential variable in favorability ratings, and since more information is usually known about incumbents, gender cues are less influential.[21] Conversely, political scientist Jeffery Koch found a gender effect in competitive races but not in noncompetitive races; he suggests that in noncompetitive races, political party serves as enough information.[22]

Political party is another variable that interacts with gender cues. A good deal of research tells us that female candidates are perceived as more liberal than their male counterparts regardless of party and as more liberal than they actually are.[23] This may be particularly detrimental to female

Democrats, but it may help female Republicans in a general election. Because Democrats are seen as more liberal than Republicans and female Democrats are believed to be even more liberal than male Democrats, this pushes female Democrats farther away from the center (toward the liberal extreme) of the conservative-to-liberal spectrum. Since most Americans consider themselves to be toward the middle of the political spectrum, female Democrats are perceived to be less ideologically similar to most voters.

However, the female Republican is believed to be more liberal than male Republicans, but this puts her closer to the center of the spectrum. Research examining evaluations of male and female Republicans by each party (Republicans, Democrats, and Independents) found that all groups rated the female Republican as more trustworthy and more likely to share their concerns than the male.[24] Additionally, for Democrats and Independents, the Republican female scored higher on trust, empathy and leadership skills than the male Republican. This seems to indicate that a female Republican has a greater chance than a male Republican of winning some Independent and Democratic ballots. This scenario of course assumes the female Republican makes it through the primary to the general election, and this might be the greatest hurdle for her.

Republican women seem to face the greatest difficulty in winning votes from their own party. One experimental study tested preference for female or male candidates based on voter party and found that while Democrats were more likely to choose the female candidate than the male, Republicans were more likely to choose the male candidate.[25] Additionally, Republican women do not benefit from the stereotyped issue competencies within their party and are viewed by their own party as less able to handle crime and more likely to be pro-choice, a negative for many Republican voters.[26] Republican women may face an especially difficult time winning a primary, but if they are able to win, they are more likely than male Republicans to win votes from outside the party. Democratic women face a different challenge; Democrat women tend to have an easier time winning within their party, but since they are seen as more liberal than a male Democrat, they may find it difficult to win ballots from Independents or Republicans in a general election.

The news is not all bad for female candidates. Recent trends in attitudes toward women in politics demonstrate that people are generally reporting more modern and egalitarian attitudes about gender, which is good for women aspiring to offices historically held by men.[27] In some cases, women can benefit from gender stereotypes. For example, one study found that emphasizing compassion issues can sometimes be a successful strategy for female candidates.[28] In their 2009 work, Kim Fridkin and Patrick Kenney, professors at Arizona State University, found that female Senate candidates in 2006 were viewed as more honest and caring and as stronger leaders than men, and they were evaluated as more competent at handling health care and the economy.[29]

This indicates that certain stereotypes still exist but that women are now being seen as possessing some of the traits and skills more often associated with men. Most importantly, these trait and issue perceptions lead to an increased favorability rating among female candidates. Fridkin and Kenney are careful to note that the 2006 election, while providing some good news, may be an anomaly due to the amount of scandal at the time. Research also shows that certain groups show a preference for female candidates. While women have been found to stereotype female candidates more than male voters, these are usually beneficial stereotypes,[30] and women prefer female candidates more than men prefer male candidates.[31] This project further explores women's beliefs and attitudes about female candidates to determine if a woman's gender-role ideology and level of gender identification, in part, explain her evaluations of political candidates. This knowledge may not only explain elements of voting behavior but also assist female candidates in constructing successful campaign messages.

A GENDER AFFINITY EXPERIMENT

This experiment tested whether or not women voters perceived a female candidate as better able to handle important issues and as possessing more desirable leadership traits than a male candidate. As part of the Women's Political Involvement Survey, participants rated what issues (discussed in chapter 5) and traits (discussed in chapter 6) they felt were most important in a political candidate. Later they viewed a series of political advertisements from a previous election. Participants were told that the candidates were considering running for Senate in a future election and asked to evaluate each candidate in the second part. Each participant viewed three ads from a female candidate (Kristi Noem of South Dakota) and three ads from a male candidate (John Thune of South Dakota). The candidates' political party was not revealed in the advertisements, and to further guard against the influence of political party, participants viewed a matchup between two Republican candidates. Furthermore, the content of the ads was similar and focused on general economic issues.

After watching the advertisements, participants rated each candidate on issues and traits. The issues had three dimensions: compassion issues (e.g., health care, assisting the poor); military/foreign affairs issues (e.g., military crisis, terrorism); and economic issues (e.g., federal budget deficit, economic crisis).[32] A total of 16 traits were measured; 7 were warmth/expressiveness traits, such as being warm, talkative, and gentle, and the remaining 9 were instrumental traits such as being assertive, stern, and self-confident.[33]

Issues

Analysis of the experimental data indicated that women as a whole rated the female candidates as most able to handle economic issues, followed by compassion issues and then military/foreign affairs issues.[34] Ratings of the male candidate were similar. He was rated as best able to handle economic issues, second most able to handle compassion issues, and least able to handle military/foreign affairs issues. Since the content of the advertisements focused on economic issues, it is not surprising that both candidates were viewed as best able to handle economic issues.[35] What is noteworthy is that they were seen as significantly better able to handle compassion issues than military/foreign affairs issues, despite the fact that these issues were not discussed in the advertisements. Perhaps women voters associated the ability to handle economic issues with competence in handling compassion issues. Since many compassion issues deal with government spending, such as education and health care, there is a logical link between these two issue categories.

Next, ratings of the male and female candidates were compared to see if women voters rated their ability to handle each issue category differently, and they did. The male candidate was rated as significantly better able to handle economic and military/foreign affairs issues than the female. However, the female candidate was rated as significantly better able to handle compassion issues than the male candidate. These findings are consistent with previous research; in low-information elections, gender can serve as an important cue, and women are often perceived as better able to handle compassion issues and men better able to handle economic and military issues.[36]

This analysis is enlightening, but looking at women as a single group does not provide a complete picture. As has been made clear in previous chapters, women's political opinions vary based on their level of gender group identification and their gender-role beliefs. To understand the effect of these variables on evaluations of male and female candidates, Egalitarian-Identified, Traditional-Identified, and Individualist women were examined separately and compared to each other. Tables 7.2 , 7.3, and 7.4 display the means for ratings in each issue category and each individual issue. Analysis of this data reveal that in most cases the male and female candidates are evaluated similarly but each sex does have some advantages.

Somewhat surprisingly, Egalitarian-Identified women rated the candidates most similar to their gender-stereotyped strengths. These women rated the male candidate as better able to deal with business leaders, unemployment, and terrorism, all stereotypical male strengths. On the other hand, Egalitarian-Identified women rated the female candidate significantly higher on feminine/compassion issues generally and child welfare, children's health care, and education specifically. Traditional-Identified women only gave an advantage to the male candidate on the masculine issues of military readiness, terrorism, international relations, and the war in Iraq, but they did not give the female candidate any advantage with the stereotypically feminine issues. Individualist women also rated the male candidate higher in the masculine areas of economic issues in general, cost of living, military/foreign affairs issues generally, and the war in Iraq.

First and foremost, these findings indicate that women did not perceive many differences in how well an unknown male and female candidate

Table 7.2   Egalitarian-Identified Women's Evaluation of Candidates on Issues

Issues	Male Candidate	Female Candidate
Economic issues	3.54	3.44
Economic crisis	3.40	3.34
Budget deficit	3.55	3.55
Dealing with business leaders	3.76**	3.59
Unemployment	3.55*	3.39
Cost of living	3.43	3.35
Compassion issues	3.25*	3.36
Child welfare	3.32*	3.47
Children's health care	3.20*	3.34
Wage gap	3.22	3.25
Assisting the poor	3.24	3.33
Education	3.27*	3.42
Military/foreign affairs issues	2.97	2.93
Military readiness	3.10	3.01
Terrorism	3.01**	2.87
International relations	2.88	2.95
War in Afghanistan	2.94	2.90
War in Iraq	2.91	2.91

Note: Items marked with * are significant at $p < .05$. Items marked with ** are significant at $p < .01$.

Table 7.3   Traditional-Identified Women's Evaluation of Candidates on Issues

	Male Candidate	Female Candidate
Economic issues	3.78	3.70
Economic crisis	3.74	3.65
Budget deficit	3.79	3.67
Dealing with business leaders	3.77	3.71
Unemployment	3.77	3.75
Cost of living	3.84	3.73
Compassion issues	3.60	3.69
Child welfare	3.64	3.76
Children's health care	3.55	3.68
Wage gap	3.55	3.52
Assisting the poor	3.59	3.68
Education	3.66	3.80
Military/foreign affairs issues	3.17	3.07
Military readiness	3.21*	3.03
Terrorism	3.23**	3.03
International relations	3.13*	3.32
War in Afghanistan	3.13	3.0
War in Iraq	3.14*	2.97

Note: Items marked with * are significant at $p < .05$. Items marked with ** are significant at $p < .01$.

would handle issues. For most issues and issue categories, women's ratings of the candidates were statistically similar. However, there were some notable differences. This study indicates that women, even feminist women, still associate certain issues with masculinity. As Huddy and Terkildsen found in 1993, these "masculine" issues, such as economic and military issues, tend to be the ones considered most important, particularly in higher-level races like the presidency. However, that was not the case for all women in this study. Looking back to chapter 5, this study found that Traditional-Identified and Individualist women did rate economic issues as most important, but military/foreign affairs issues were considered the least important issue category by all three groups of women. Traditional-Identified women did rate the male candidate as better able to handle several military/foreign affairs issues, but these issues were least important in their decision to support a candidate. This group also rated the male and female candidates similarly in the issues they viewed as most important, indicating that neither sex has a strong advantage on issues with Traditional-Identified women.

Additionally, this study supports the idea that some women voters have a preference for female candidates.[37] Egalitarian-Identified women rated

Table 7.4 Individualist Women's Evaluation of Candidates on Issues

Issues	Male Candidate	Female Candidate
Economic issues	3.48*	3.32
Economic crisis	3.45	3.28
Budget deficit	3.41	3.41
Dealing with business leaders	3.58	3.34
Unemployment	3.41	3.25
Cost of living	3.58*	3.30
Compassion issues	3.22	3.24
Child welfare	3.28	3.41
Children's health care	3.17	3.28
Wage gap	3.13	3.11
Assisting the poor	3.19	3.09
Education	3.34	3.30
Military/foreign affairs issues	2.98*	2.81
Military readiness	2.98	2.88
Terrorism	2.95	2.80
International relations	2.86	2.75
War in Afghanistan	3.05	2.83
War in Iraq	3.09*	2.80

Note: Items marked with * are significant at $p < .05$. Items marked with ** are significant at $p < .01$.

compassion issues as most important in their decision to support a candidate, and this group also rated the female candidate as better able to handle these issues. The perception that women are better able to handle compassion issues had been found in several studies[38] but in this case, it may also be evidence of a gender affinity in vote choice among Egalitarian-Identified women because of the issues they find most important and the person they believe is better equipped to handle those issues. Additionally, Egalitarian-Identified women exhibit findings of previous research on female voters, a positive stereotyping of female candidates[39] and belief that female candidates are more likely to share their concerns.[40]

However, Individualist women's ratings of the male candidate are consistent with previous research indicating voters stereotype candidates' ability to handle issues based on gender.[41] This group rated economic issues as most important to their vote, and they perceived the male candidate as better able to handle these issues. While it was the least important issue category for them, Individualist women rated the male candidate higher on military/foreign affairs issues. However, contrary to previous research, they did not stereotype the female candidate as better at compassion issues. Male candidates may actually have an advantage with Individualist women because they may be perceived as better able to handle two issue categories.

It is also worth noting that Traditional-Identified women rated both candidates' ability to handle the issues higher than did Egalitarian-Identified and Individualist women. In other words, women with traditional sex-role beliefs and high gender-group identification considered both candidates as equally able to handle the issues, and they thought that the candidates were more capable than other women thought them to be. The reasons for these findings warrant further investigation, but one possible explanation might be the political party of the candidates featured in the advertising stimulus. Both of the candidates were Republican, and more Traditional-Identified women reported being Republican (42 percent) than Democrat (31.9 percent) or Independent/Other (26.1 percent). On the other hand, Egalitarian-Identified women were largely Democrats (50 percent).

The political party of the candidates was not explicitly stated in the advertisements, but it is possible that women picked up on subtle party cues, influencing their ratings of the candidates. For example, both candidates' advertisements emphasized cutting taxes and government spending, and called for change. Since those issues are generally tied to Republicans and Democrats controlled the Presidency and Congress at the time the ads aired, viewers may have assumed that both candidates were Republican. This may have led the Republican women to feel that both candidates were competent and evaluate their ability to handle issues highly. On the other hand, Democrats may have not particularly liked either candidate because of a difference in political party, but as previous research has found, they preferred the female Republican to the male Republican.[42] Another possible explanation for higher issue-ability ratings among Traditional-Identified women might be varying levels of political cynicism between groups of women. It is possible that this group simply had more positive views of political candidates in general. This study did not measure levels of political cynicism among women, but future research should explore if Traditional-Identified women report lower cynicism than other women and if low cynicism is associated with higher ratings of candidates' ability to handle issues among Traditional-Identified women.

The findings of this study do support a possible gender affinity among some women when it comes to their perceptions of candidates' abilities to handle issues. Furthermore, even when a gender affinity effect isn't supported, group identified women in general seemed to view the candidates similarly on most issue categories, particularly the ones they found most important. However, a candidate's ability to handle issues is only one factor in voters' decision to support or not support. The person, or voters' perception of the person, is also an extremely important factor. The next section explores how women view the traits of candidates in a mixed-gender race.

Traits

The whole sample of women was examined to determine whether male and female candidates were rated higher in warmth/expressiveness traits, often considered "feminine" traits, or instrumental traits, often labeled "masculine" traits. Women rated the female candidate significantly higher on warmth/expressiveness traits than on instrumental traits.[43] This is consistent with previous research that has found female candidates are often viewed as having more so-called feminine traits.[44] Also consistent with this line of research, women rated the male candidate significantly higher on instrumental traits than on warmth/expressiveness traits.[45] However, as has been noted earlier, all women are not the same, so we must delve deeper.

Further examination of Egalitarian-Identified, Traditional-Identified, and Individualist women yielded interesting results. Both groups of Identified women rated the female candidate higher on warmth/expressiveness traits than on instrumental traits, but there was no statistical difference in their ratings of the male candidate's trait categories.[46] However, Individualist women's ratings fell along stereotypical lines; they rated the female higher on warmth/expressiveness traits than instrumental, and they rated the male higher on instrumental traits than warmth/expressiveness.[47] Individualist women's ratings reiterate the findings in previous research; candidates are perceived to have traits stereotypically associated with their gender, but Identified women only perceived female candidates in stereotypical ways. To understand the implications of these differences, it is necessary to compare how each group of women rated the candidates. Specifically, did women rate the male or the female higher on desired traits?

As shown in Table 7.5, Egalitarian-Identified women rated the female higher than the male candidate on warmth/expressiveness traits in general, but they actually rated the male candidate significantly higher on the specific traits of warmth and cautiousness.[48] They also rated the female candidate significantly higher on four instrumental traits: coarseness, sternness, aggressiveness, and toughness.[49] These differences are noteworthy for a few reasons. First, Egalitarian-Identified women flipped gender stereotypes in several cases by rating the male candidate higher on warmth and cautiousness and the female higher on four instrumental traits. Second, Egalitarian-Identified women rated instrumental traits as

Table 7.5   Egalitarian-Identified Women's Evaluation of Candidates on Traits

Traits	Male Candidate	Female Candidate
Warmth/expressiveness traits	3.31**	3.46
Warm	4.01*	3.85
Emotional	3.03*	3.22
Talkative	3.52	3.44
Cautious	3.26**	3.03
Sensitive	3.49	3.50
Gentle	3.56	3.44
Feminine	2.30**	3.75
Instrumental traits	3.40	3.34
Assertive	3.68	3.78
Coarse	2.44*	2.59
Stern	2.86**	3.18
Self-confident	4.05	4.09
Active	3.83	3.82
Rational	3.66	3.68
Aggressive	3.03*	3.22
Tough	3.14*	3.30
Masculine	3.89**	2.43

Note: Items marked with * are significant at $p < .05$. Items marked with ** are significant at $p < .01$.

most important in their decision to support a candidate, and they rated the female significantly higher on four of those traits, with toughness being among the top five most important traits to this group.

Why this group rated the female candidate higher on these traits is unclear from this study, but the fact they attributed these "masculine" traits more to the female in a situation where little was known about the candidate is important, because it contradicts previous research and stereotypes. Perhaps this group of women voters believed that a woman running for office must be particularly tough, aggressive, stern, and coarse. On the other hand, the male candidate was rated significantly higher on only three traits, none of which were among the top five most important to Egalitarian-Identified women. Again, it is unknown why the male candidate was rated higher on the "feminine" traits of warmth and cautiousness. This could have something to do with the content of the ad. Or it could be that participants viewed the male in contrast to the female, and since they felt the female was more tough, they also felt that made her less warm. This experiment can only tell us what voters' perceptions of these candidates were, but future research needs to explore why voters perceive candidates in certain ways, particularly when it violates gender stereotypes.

Table 7.6   Traditional-Identified Women's Evaluation of Candidates on Traits

Traits	Male Candidate	Female Candidate
Warmth/expressiveness traits	3.51**	3.74
Warm	3.98	3.85
Emotional	3.49	3.64
Talkative	3.66	3.67
Cautious	3.50	3.41
Sensitive	3.61	3.69
Gentle	3.78	3.84
Feminine	2.54**	4.06
Instrumental traits	3.55	3.50
Assertive	3.78	3.78
Coarse	2.88	2.92
Stern	3.27*	3.45
Self-confident	3.99	4.09
Active	3.89	3.90
Rational	3.76	3.78
Aggressive	3.25	3.39
Tough	3.31	3.45
Masculine	3.84**	2.69

Note: Items marked with * are significant at $p < .05$. Items marked with ** are significant at $p < .01$.

Traditional-Identified women rated the female candidate higher on warmth/expressiveness traits in general and specifically on the trait of being feminine (see Table 7.6).[50] They also rated the female candidate higher on the instrumental trait of being stern. Traditional-Identified women rated the male candidate significantly higher than the female on only one trait: being masculine. As was noted in chapter 6, this group of women found instrumental traits to be the most important in making their decision to support a candidate, and neither the male or female candidate had an advantage on this issue category in the experiment, indicating that Traditional-Identified women viewed the two sexes similarly in desired traits. However, this group also rated the female candidate higher on the "feminine" category of warmth/expressiveness, but these were not the traits they found most important. In fact, not one warmth/expressiveness trait made the top five most important traits for Identified women. Additionally, counter to previous research, Traditional-Identified women rated the female candidate higher on the stereotypically masculine trait of being stern. The reasons for this are unknown. It could have something to do with the content of the advertisement stimuli, or it could be that the

Table 7.7   Individualist Women's Evaluation of Candidates on Traits

Traits	Male Candidate	Female Candidate
Warmth/expressiveness traits	3.26**	3.60
Warm	3.94	3.91
Emotional	3.05*	3.33
Talkative	3.36	3.48
Cautious	3.34	3.23
Sensitive	3.38	3.56
Gentle	3.48	3.66
Feminine	2.25**	4.03
Instrumental traits	3.46*	3.28*
Assertive	3.77	3.58
Coarse	2.67	2.67
Stern	2.92	3.08
Self-confident	3.98	4.00
Active	3.73	3.77
Rational	3.77	3.77
Aggressive	3.20	3.20
Tough	3.22	3.17
Masculine	3.91**	2.34

Note: Items marked with * are significant at $p < .05$. Items marked with ** are significant at $p < .01$.

female candidate's sternness stood out because it violated expectations of femininity.

Like both groups of Identified women, Individualist women rated the female candidate higher on warmth/expressiveness traits in general (see Table 7.7); they also rated her higher on femininity.[51] This group also rated the male candidate higher in instrumental traits generally and specifically on masculinity. Individualist women are most like voters in previous research; they rated the female candidate as having more stereotypically feminine traits and the male candidate as having more stereotypically masculine traits. This group also rated instrumental traits as more important in their decision to support a candidate. However, this group rated the male higher only in masculinity, which was among the least important traits. In short, this group did give the male candidate the advantage on the trait category they found most important, but the ratings of the two candidates were statistically similar on the individual traits they found most important.

CONCLUSION

This chapter set out to explore whether there is a gender affinity effect in vote choice among women. The findings of this study suggest that there is gender affinity among some women, but the strength and importance of that affinity varies based on women's identification with their gender group and beliefs about gender roles. Support for a gender affinity effect was found in Identified women's assessment of gender-candidate homophily. Women who felt strongly connected to their gender group were more likely to believe that female candidates were more in touch with their problems, shared their worldview, and had similar life experiences. Furthermore, group-identified women, particularly those with traditional gender-role beliefs, were more likely to say that they prefer voting for a female candidate if she is of their own political party.

The question of gender affinity was less clear when it came to perceptions of candidates' ability to handle important issues. Among Egalitarian-Identified women, a gender affinity effect was found. This group rated the female candidate as significantly better able to handle compassion issues, the issue category they considered most important in deciding to support a candidate. Traditional-Identified women viewed the male and female candidate similarly on three issue categories and only rated the male higher on four military/foreign affairs issues, which were issues they considered least important. On the other hand, Individualist women tended to replicate findings in previous studies about gender stereotypes and perceptions of candidates.

Many earlier studies have found that voters perceive male candidates as better able to handle economic issues and military/foreign affairs issues, and these issues tend to be those considered most important for candidates running for higher office. Individualist women rated the male candidate as significantly more able to handle these issue categories, and this group had previously rated economic issues as most important in their decision to support a candidate. However, unlike previous research, this group did not rate the female candidate as better able to handle compassion issues; they rated the male and female statistically similarly on this category. These findings suggest that among Individualist women, male candidates may still have an advantage. It also demonstrates the importance of gender group identification in perceptions of candidates' strengths.

Finally, with regard to candidates' traits, this research suggests that there may be a gender affinity effect for some women but not others. All three groups of women rated instrumental traits as most important, and Individualist women rated the male candidate higher on this trait category. Traditional-Identified women did not give the male candidate the advantage with these traits, and Egalitarian-Identified women gave the advantage to the female candidate on several specific instrumental traits. This suggests that a gender affinity effect may exist for Egalitarian-Identified women. In a low-information mock election, this group drew conclusions about the two candidates that violated many gender stereotypes, and they perceived the female candidate as having significantly more of the traits they look for in a candidate.

Traditional-Identified women landed more in the middle. They saw the female candidate as possessing more warmth/expressiveness traits, their stereotypical strength, but this category was not the most important in their decision to support a candidate. They also rated the male candidate slightly higher on two instrumental traits, but they were also not among the most important. Neither sex seems to have a strong advantage with Traditional-Identified women when it comes to traits; rather, this group views them as very similar. On the other hand, Individualist women affirmed previous research by rating the female candidate higher on stereotypical "feminine" issues and the male candidate higher on "masculine" issues. This suggests that female candidates might have the hardest time with Individualist women, but male candidates may find it easier to convince them have the necessary personality traits to lead.

In sum, this study provides evidence of a small but significant gender affinity effect among women who strongly identify with their gender group. These women tend to feel that female candidates have more in common with them and, in turn, better represent their interests. Given the choice, they tend to prefer a female candidate of their own party over a male, and this is particularly true among women with more traditional gender-role beliefs. There is also evidence that some women believe that a female candidate is best able to handle the issues they find most important and possess more of the desired personality traits. Women who feel strongly connected to their gender group are the most likely to demonstrate a gender affinity in candidate choice, but they largely view the two sexes as equal. However, women who do not feel connected to their gender group are the most likely to evaluate candidates in stereotypical ways and to see a male candidate as more qualified.

CHAPTER 8

What Does It All Mean?

Women are the same; women are different. Those are the two seemingly contradictory lessons of this book. Decades of research show clear and consistent differences in how men and women vote and what issues they care about. On the other hand, election results demonstrate that not all women are the same; if they were, 100 percent would vote for the same candidate. This book has explored two questions: how are women different from men, and how are women different from each other? In this final chapter, I summarize the major findings as they relate to each of these questions and demonstrate how these ideas and findings apply to real-world elections.

WOMEN ARE DIFFERENT THAN MEN

Since 1980, women have voted in higher numbers than men, and they have been more likely to identify as Democrats. In every presidential election since 1980, a greater proportion of women than men have supported the Democratic candidate, and in every presidential election since 1996, the majority of women voted for the Democratic candidate. Male voters have varied slightly more; a greater proportion supported the Republican presidential candidate in 1980, 1984, 1988, 1996, 2000, 2004, 2012, and 2016, but a higher percentage supported the Democratic candidate in 1992 and 2008. Having said that, the male vote was nearly evenly split in 1992 and 2008, with a difference of only 3 percent in 1992 and 1 percent in 2008. Furthermore, women are more likely to identify as Democrats; since 2000, the party gap in women voters has averaged 12.25 percent, meaning that on average 12.25 percent more women identified as Democrats than Republicans. On the other hand, men have been more likely to identify as Republicans but by a much smaller margin; since 2000, the male party gap has averaged only 3.25 percent.[1] Furthermore, women vote in higher numbers and proportions than men. Since 2000, an average of 63.7 percent of eligible women have voted compared to 60.14 percent of eligible men.[2] While that percentage may seem small, in real numbers, that average represents a difference of 9.2 million votes.

These differences were clearly illustrated in 2016. According to the Pew Research Center, 56 percent of women identified as Democrats and 49 percent of men identified as Republicans in 2016.[3] The 2016 election also tied the record for the largest gender gap in history of 11 percent, with 54 percent of women supporting Democrat Hillary Clinton and 52 percent of men supporting Republican Donald Trump. Additionally, nearly 10 million more women voted than men in 2016. While the Electoral College ultimately decided the 2016 election making Donald Trump the 45th president of the United States, the majority of women voted for Clinton, and had only women voted, Clinton would have won the presidency. According to CNN exit polls, had only women voted, Clinton would have won several states she lost to Trump, including Alabama, Florida, Georgia, Iowa, Michigan, Ohio, Pennsylvania, Texas, and Wisconsin.[4]

Women vote differently than men because they have different issue positions and priorities. Women are more likely to believe in a larger, active government. They, in general, are more supportive of government regulation of the economy, particularly as it relates to income inequality. They are also more likely to support government spending on social services, such as aid to the poor, education, childcare, and assistance to the elderly. Women are also more concerned with issues of inequality and are more supportive of government action to address inequalities related to gender, race, and sexual orientation. While women are more supportive of government action and spending in these areas, they are less supportive than men on issues related to military spending and intervention. Differences do exist based on political party, but even taking those differences into account, women tend to want a larger, more active government, while men tend to believe the less government the better.

Consistent with previous elections, the issues men and women considered important differed in 2016. According to the Pew Research Center, men and women both considered the economy and terrorism to be the two most important issues. While health care, gun policy, and foreign policy rounded out the top five most important issues for both sexes, women considered health care and gun policy as considerably more important than men, and male voters rated foreign policy as more important than did female voters.[5] Furthermore, women were more concerned with several issues: 17 percent more women than men rated "treatment of gay, lesbian, and transgender" people as very important to their vote; 13 percent more women rated "treatment of racial, ethnic minorities" as very important; 14 percent more women rated abortion as very important; and 10 percent more women rated the environment as very important. On the other hand, 10 percent more men than women rated trade policy as very important.[6]

These differences in issue priorities are noteworthy for two reasons. First, they confirm a clear and consistent difference in men's and women's issue priorities and positions since 2000. Second, they reflect the difference in vote choice and party identification. Hillary Clinton made many of the issues women considered more important a central part of her 2016 campaign. For example, in a speech given eight days before the election, Clinton said, "The future of our economy is at stake, of our education system is at stake. Fighting climate change and clean, renewable-energy jobs are at stake. LGBT equality is at stake. Equal pay for women is at stake. Actually, in the end, the American dream itself is at stake. So I want you to think about how you will feel on November 9."[7] This is not to say Clinton didn't talk about the top issues, the economy, and terrorism; she did. However, she also spoke to the issues where women and men differed.

On the other hand, Trump's 2016 message focused on the economy and specifically trade issues, which men considered to be more important. Trump dedicated an entire speech in June 2016 to trade policy, where he spoke generally about trade issues, saying, "We allowed foreign countries to subsidize their goods, devalue their currencies, violate their agreements, and cheat in every way imaginable, and our politicians did nothing about it. Trillions of our dollars and millions of our jobs flowed overseas as a result." Later in the same speech, he focused on specific trade issues: "First, the North American Free Trade Agreement, or the disaster called NAFTA. Second, China's entry into the World Trade Organization. NAFTA was the worst trade deal in the history—it's like—the history of this country. And China's entrance into the World Trade Organization has enabled the greatest job theft in the history of our country."[8]

Again, this is not to say that Trump spoke only about trade policy. He spoke about many issues, including Obamacare and immigration, but he also made issues men cared about more a central part of his campaign. As was noted in chapter 1, Trump had a problem with women voters for many reasons, ranging from his political party affiliation to his disparaging comments to and about women. Trump did not target women voters. He made the choice to ignore many of the issues that women considered more important than men, and in some cases, like immigration, he took positions in direct opposition to the positions of many women.

Women also want different traits in their political leaders, and they have historically had different perceptions of candidates. Women want candidates who demonstrate that they care, are a strong leader, and are intelligent. Men have varied more, but they generally have supported candidates they see as moral, intelligent, and strong leaders. The list of traits is similar, but men care more about morality and women more about compassion. Additionally, men and women often see candidates differently.

In 2000, women rated Al Gore as a stronger leader and more caring than did men. In 2004, men rated George W. Bush as a stronger leader than women did. In 2012, men rated Mitt Romney as more moral and as a stronger leader than women did, and women rated Obama as more caring and a stronger leader than did men. While not part of the data analyzed in this book, the 2016 election was similar. A Pew study found that 53 percent of women and 42 percent of men said that Clinton "understands the needs of people like you well." On the other hand, 44 percent of men and only 29 percent of women said the same about Trump.[9] Even among voters who supported Clinton, there were gender differences. Compared to male Clinton supporters, women supporters rated her as more inspiring, moral, and honest and as a stronger leader and good role model. Male supporters rated her as more "hard to like" and more reckless than female supporters.[10]

It should be clear that, in general, women voters are different than men, and since women vote in higher numbers than men, candidates are smart to target women voters. In order to win an election, candidates, particularly presidential candidates, must speak to the issues women care about, and must display the personality traits women want to see in their leaders. As 2016 demonstrates, winning the majority of women voters does not necessarily translate into winning the election, but it makes it a lot easier.

Political party certainly plays a role in this; women identify more with the Democratic Party, but there are also lessons to be learned for Republican candidates. Speaking about issues women care about and avoiding issues that will push women away are just two of these lessons. These gender differences might be even more important in primary elections. Since political party is not a factor in these elections, it is important for candidates to know what issues and traits the women in their party care about, and as was explained in chapter 7, female candidates might have a slight advantage with female primary voters.

It is important to make clear that women are not a monolithic voting bloc. The numbers and percentages showing gender differences speak to women and men in the aggregate and do not mean that all women, or all men, see the world the same way. As has been explained throughout this book, women have many similarities as a group, but there are also very important differences between women.

WOMEN ARE DIFFERENT

Women's life experiences—be it through socialization, discrimination, motherhood, or a host of other occurrences—mean that women as a group have some things in common. This sometimes leads women to see things differently than men. However, women are not all the same. The research reported in this book demonstrates that women's sense of identification with their gender group, the level of connection they feel to other women, is extremely important in understanding the motivations and opinions of women voters. Furthermore, women have differing ideas about gender roles and norms in our society, and these differences also influence women's political behavior. Together these factors create distinct groups of women.

The large majority of women studied here indicate a high level of identification with their gender group, expressing feelings of shared experiences and group attachment. One useful way of looking at women voters is by splitting them based on their level of identification with other women, which creates two groups: Identified and Individualist women. Identified women report higher levels of political engagement, more confidence in their interpersonal communication about politics, and an overall greater concern about a variety of issues, particularly those related to children. Identified women are also more likely than Individualist women to find warmth/expressiveness traits to be important for a candidate to demonstrate, but they also rate assertiveness and self-confidence as more important than Individualist women. They are also more likely to believe that female candidates better represent them and to vote for a female candidate over a male when they are of the same party. Individualist women are more likely to view candidates in stereotypical terms—attributing traits to candidates based on gender stereotypes. This group is more likely to give the advantage to a male candidate based on those stereotypes.

Women who feel connected to their gender group may have different feelings about what it means to be a woman and how their gender identity is related or should relate to politics. A great deal of academic research has examined the relationship between group identification among feminist women and political behavior, but as this book should make clear, nonfeminist women—those with traditional gender-role beliefs—can also feel connected to their gender group and make political decisions based on that identity. In many ways, Identified women, regardless of whether they hold egalitarian or traditional gender-role beliefs, see the world similarly. They believe their gender is a central part of their identity and make political decisions, at least partially, based on what they believe is best for the group or fits within their view of gender.

However, there are some noteworthy differences. Egalitarian-Identified women rate compassion issues, such as health care and child welfare, as the most important issue categories. This group of women also rate compassion issues as significantly more important than do Traditional-Identified women, and they express a greater desire for candidates to have warmth/expressiveness traits. Last, Egalitarian-Identified women are the group most likely to have a gender affinity in voting; they prefer candidates of their own gender and, in a low-information situation, rated the female candidate as better able to handle issues they cared about and possess important traits.

On the other hand, Traditional-Identified women find compassion issues less important than Egalitarian-Identified women; rather, they rate economic issues as the most important. Like Egalitarian-Identified women, they rate military/foreign affairs issues as the least important, but they do consider these issues to be more important than Egalitarian-Identified women do. Traditional-Identified women also put greater priority on a variety of leadership traits, indicating that the character of the candidate is uniquely important in their voting decisions. While still showing some preference for female candidates, Traditional-Identified women seem to view the sexes relatively equally in their ability to handle issues and possess certain traits.

The categories are useful in understanding women voters and provide a more nuanced understanding than political party affiliation and gender alone. The categories—Identified, Individualist, Egalitarian, and Traditional—cross party lines. Egalitarian-Identified women are most likely to identify as Democrats (50 percent), but 26 percent identify as Republican and 24 percent as Independents. Traditional-Identified women are more likely to be Republican (42 percent), but 32 percent identify as Democrats and 26 percent as Independents. Among Individualist women, 48 percent are Republican, but about one-quarter are Democrats and another quarter Independents. Furthermore, there is no clear trend in level of education for these groups. Each group includes women with education ranging from high school diplomas to graduate degrees. The point here is that understanding the psychological and sociological motivations behind women's political beliefs and behavior provide a richer understanding than simply carving women voters into demographic groups.

Again, the 2016 election provides a good example of how scholars and media attempt to understand or report on women voters. This election is particularly valuable because it included the first major-party female candidate and a hypermasculine male candidate. While the majority of women voted for Hillary Clinton, not all did, and the media were quick with headlines like "White Women Helped Elect Donald Trump"[11] and "Why So Many Women Abandoned Hillary Clinton."[12] It is true that 52 percent of White women voted for Trump, but 94 percent of Black women and 65 percent of Latina women voted for Clinton.

There are countless ways to break up women by demographics, and each only tells a part of the story. For example, Clinton won Democratic women (91 percent), Independent women (47 percent), unmarried women (55 percent), and White women with college degrees (51 percent).[13] Demographics are easy to analyze and easy for the news media to report, but they don't tell us *why* these women voted for Clinton and others for Trump. They also don't tell us what those who voted for Clinton have in common with each other. The study reported in this book did not look at 2016 voters, but it does raise some questions about the 2016 results and our analysis of election data in the future.

We know that Individualist women are more likely to rely on gender stereotypes in their evaluations of candidates, to prefer a male candidate, and to see themselves as an individual rather than a member of a (gender) group. Perhaps women who supported Trump fell into this category. This would explain why women were not alienated by Trump's comments about women and why Trump was perceived as a stronger and better leader than Clinton. We also know that Identified women are more likely to support a female candidate and that Egalitarian-Identified women are more likely to believe that a female candidate can best address the issues they find most important, which tend to be compassion issues. Perhaps women who supported Clinton had stronger gender-group identification, and it's likely that many also had more egalitarian gender-role beliefs.

Of course, this analysis of the role of gender group identification in the 2016 election is speculation, but it is speculation based in research. If scholars, media, and candidates are to have a real understanding of women voters, then they need to look closer than mere demographics. Delving into the psychological and sociological motivations for women's political behavior and the differences between women makes it possible for candidates to target their messaging to winnable voters and for scholars to understand why a candidate was or was not successful in courting specific groups of women voters. Nearly 40 years of elections and research have demonstrated that women voters in the aggregate are different than men. It is past time to take our understanding of women voters a step further than their sex and beyond catchy sound bites like "soccer moms" and "Beyoncé voters." To understand the "women's vote," we must understand what being part of the group "women" means to women voters and how that influences their political behavior.

Notes

SERIES FOREWORD

1. Risman, Barbara. "Gender As a Social Structure: Theory Wrestling with Activism." *Gender & Society* 18 (2004): 429–50.

2. See, for example, McCall, Leslie. "The Complexity of Intersectionality." *Signs* 30 (2005): 1771–800.

CHAPTER 1

1. Silver, Nate. "'Gender Gap' Near Historic Highs." *New York Times*, October 21, 2012, accessed May 29, 2016, http://fivethirtyeight.blogs.nytimes .com/2012/10/21/gender-gap-near-historic-highs/?_r=0.

2. "Carrie Chapman Catt (1859–1947)." Carrie Chapman Catt Center for Women in Politics, accessed July 20, 2018, https://awpc.cattcenter.iastate .edu/directory/carrie-chapman-catt/.

3. The Census Bureau did not track voter turnout by sex until 1964. Available data is based on voter turnout tracked in Chicago in 1920 and estimates made by social scientists. See Allen, Jodie T. "Reluctant Suffragettes: When Women Questioned Their Right to Vote." *Pew Research Center*, March 18, 2009, accessed November 19, 2015, http://www.pewresearch.org/2009/03/18 /reluctant-suffragettes-when-women-questioned-their-right-to-vote/.

4. Seltzer, Richard A., Jody Newman, and Melissa Voorhees Leighton. *Sex as a Political Variable: Women as Candidates & Voters in U.S. Elections*. Boulder, CO: Lynne Rienner Publishers, 1997.

5. Shapiro, Robert Y., and Harpreet Mahajan. "Gender Differences in Party Preferences: A Summary of Trends from the 1960s to the 1980s." *The Public Opinion Quarterly* 50, no. 1 (1986): 42–61.

6. Norrander, Barbara. "The Interparty Gender Gap: Differences between Male and Female Voters in the 1980–2000 Presidential Primaries." *PS: Political Science and Politics* 36, no. 2 (2003): 181–86.

7. "Gender Differences in Voter Turnout." Center for American Women and Politics, Eagleton Institute of Politics, Rutgers University, 2015, accessed November 18, 2015, http://www.cawp.rutgers.edu/sites/default/files/resources/genderdiff.pdf.

8. "The Gender Gap: Attitudes on Public Policy Issues." Center for American Women and Politics, Eagleton Institute of Politics, Rutgers University, 2012, accessed September 13, 2015, http://www.cawp.rutgers.edu/sites/default/files/resources/gg_issuesattitudes-2012.pdf.

9. Burrell, Barbara C. "Gender, Presidential Elections, and Public Policy: Making Women's Votes Matter." *Journal of Women, Politics, & Policy* 27, no. 1 (2005): 31–50.

10. "The Gender Gap: Voting Choices in Presidential Elections." Center for American Women and Politics, Eagleton Institute of Politics, Rutgers University, 2017, accessed May 1, 2018, http://www.cawp.rutgers.edu/sites/default/files/resources/ggpresvote.pdf.

11. Burrell, "Gender, Presidential Elections, and Public Policy," 31–50.

12. "Party Identification and Presidential Performance Ratings." Center for American Women and Politics, Eagleton Institute of Politics, Rutgers University, 2014, accessed September 17, 2015, http://www.cawp.rutgers.edu/sites/default/files/resources/ggprtyid.pdf.

13. Kaufmann, Karen M., and John R. Petrocik. "The Changing Politics of American Men: Understanding the Sources of the Gender Gap." *American Journal of Political Science* 43, no. 3 (1999): 864–887.

14. Percentage computed using data from "The Gender Gap: Voting Choices in Presidential Elections."

15. Kaufmann and Petrocik, "The Changing Politics of American Men," 864–887.

16. Eagly, Alice H., Amanda B. Diekman, Mary C. Johannesen-Schmidt, and Anne M. Koening. "Gender Gaps in Sociopolitical Attitudes: A Social Psychological Analysis." *Journal of Personality and Social Psychology* 87, no. 6 (2004): 796–816.

17. Kaufmann, Karen M. "Culture Wars, Secular Realignment, and the Gender Gap in Party Identification." *Political Behavior* 24, no. 3 (2002): 288–89.

18. Norrander, Barbara, and Clyde Wilcox. "The Gender Gap in Ideology." *Political Behavior* 30 (2008): 503–23.

19. Howell, Susan E., and Christine L. Day. "Complexities of the Gender Gap." *The Journal of Politics* 62, no. 3 (2000): 858–74.

20. Ibid.

21. Eagly et al., "Gender Gaps in Sociopolitical Attitudes," 796–815.

22. Kaufmann and Petrocik, "The Changing Politics of American Men," 864–887.

23. Seltzer, Newman, and Leighton, *Sex as a Political Variable*, 11–30.

24. Condon, Meghan, and Amber Wichowsky. "Same Blueprint, Different Bricks: Reexamining the Sources of the Gender Gap in Political Ideology." *Politics, Groups, and Identities* 3, no. 1 (2014): 4–20.

25. Kaufmann and Petrocik, "The Changing Politics of American Men," 864–887.

26. Moore, David W. "Gender Gap Varies on Support for War." *Gallup*, November 19, 2002, accessed February 26, 2016, http://www.gallup.com/poll/7243 /gender-gap-varies-support-war.aspx.

27. Brooks, Deborah Jordan, and Benjamin A. Valentino. "The War of One's Own: Understanding the Gender Gap in Support for War." *Public Opinion Quarterly* 75, no. 2 (2011): 270–86.

28. Seltzer, Newman, and Leighton, *Sex as a Political Variable*, 11–30.

29. Ibid.

30. Thomas, Clarence. "Statement before the Senate Judiciary Committee." American Rhetoric, October 11, 1991, accessed November 14, 2015, http://www .americanrhetoric.com/speeches/clarencethomashightechlynching.htm.

31. Greenberger, Marcia D. "What Anita Hill Did for America." *CNN*, October 22, 2010, accessed February 24, 2016, http://www.cnn.com/2010/OPINION/10/21 /greenberger.anita.hill/.

32. Carroll, Susan J. "The Disempowerment of the Gender Gap: Soccer Moms in the 1996 Elections." *PS: Political Science and Politics* 32, no. 1 (1999): 7–11.

33. Kaufmann and Petrocik, "The Changing Politics of American Men," 864–887.

34. MacFarquhar, Neil. "What's a Soccer Mom Anyway?" *New York Times*, October 20, 1996, accessed November 18, 2015, http://www.nytimes.com/1996/10/20 /weekinreview/what-s-a-soccer-mom-anyway.html.

35. Dionne, E. J. "Clinton Swipes the GOP's Lyrics; the Democrat as Liberal Republican." *Washington Post*, July 21, 1996.

36. Carroll, "The Disempowerment of the Gender Gap," 7–11.

37. Burrell, "Gender, Presidential Elections, and Public Policy," 31–50.

38. Carroll, "The Disempowerment of the Gender Gap," 7–11.

39. Mannies, Jo. "Undecided Women May Hold Key to the Election." *St. Louis Post-Dispatch*, September 24, 2000.

40. Mann, Judy. "Mobilizing the Family Planning Vote." *Washington Post*, October 11, 2000.

41. Seelye, Katharine Q. "The Rallying Cry; 'Working Families' Becomes a Theme Meant to Attract Female Voters." *New York Times*, August 22, 2000.

42. Babington, Charles. "Strength among Women Is the Atlas of Gore's Campaign." *Washington Post*, September 24, 2000.

43. Butler, Kevin. "Even Softening GOP's Tough Image Isn't Helping Bush Bridge Gender Gap." *Investor's Business Daily*, September 19, 2000.

44. Ibid.; Keen, Judy. "Bush Working to Win Back Women's Supporters." *USA Today*, September 15, 2000.

45. Burrell, "Gender, Presidential Elections, and Public Policy," 31–50.

46. Wells, Matthew. "Soccer Moms Are Security Moms Now." *Guardian*, October 12, 2004.

47. Goodman, Ellen. "Presidential Race May Hinge on Undecided 'Security Moms.'" *Deseret Morning News (Salt Lake City)*, October 8, 2004; Baker, Gerard. "Security Moms: Bush's Secret Election Weapon." *Times (London)*, September 30, 2004.

48. Burrell, "Gender, Presidential Elections, and Public Policy," 31–50; Carroll, Susan J. "Security Moms and Presidential Politics: Women Voters in the 2004 Election." In *Voting the Gender Gap*, edited by Lois Duke Whitaker, 75–90. Urbana: University of Illinois Press, 2008.

49. Anderson, Karrin Vasby, and Jessie Stewart. "Politics and the Single Woman: The 'Sex and the City Voter' in Campaign 2004." *Rhetoric & Public Affairs* 8, no. 4 (2005): 595–616.

50. Burrell, "Gender, Presidential Elections, and Public Policy," 31–50.

51. Elder, Laurel, and Steven Greene. "The Myth of 'Security Moms' and 'NASCAR Dads': Parenthood, Political Stereotypes, and the 2004 Election." *Social Science Quarterly* 88, no. 1 (2007): 1–19.

52. Burrell, "Gender, Presidential Elections, and Public Policy," 31–50.

53. Elder and Greene, "The Myth of 'Security Moms' and 'NASCAR Dads,'" 1–19.

54. Kaufmann, Karen M. "The Gender Gap." *PS: Political Science and Politics*, no. 3 (2006): 447–53.

55. Elder and Greene, "The Myth of 'Security Moms' and 'NASCAR Dads,'" 1–19.

56. Clark, Cal, and Janet M. Clark. "The Reemergence of the Gender Gap in 2004." In *Voting the Gender Gap*, 50–74.

57. Lopez, Mark Hugo, and Paul Taylor. "Dissecting the 2008 Electorate: Most Diverse in U.S. History." *PEW Research Center*, accessed October 2, 2015, http://www.pewhispanic.org/2009/04/30/dissecting-the-2008-electorate-most-diverse-in-us-history/.

58. Newport, Frank, and Joseph Carroll. "Who Likes Hillary Clinton, and Who Doesn't." *Gallup*, October 1, 2007, accessed July 12, 2018, http://www.gallup.com/poll/28834/Who-Likes-Hillary-Clinton-Who-Doesnt.aspx.

59. "Young Women Propel Clinton's Lead in '08 Test." *Pew Research Center*, October 31, 2007, accessed January 4, 2016, http://www.people-press.org/files/legacy-pdf/366.pdf.

60. Newport, Frank, and Lydia Saad. "Education and Gender Help Predict Democratic Preferences." *Gallup*, February 9, 2008, accessed January 4, 2016, http://www.gallup.com/poll/104263/Education-Gender-Help-Predict-Democratic-Preferences.aspx.

61. Newport, Frank, and Jeffery M. Jones. "Hillary Clinton's Gender Advantage over Obama Narrows." *Gallup*, February 1, 2008, accessed January 4, 2016, http://www.gallup.com/poll/104104/Hillary-Clintons-Gender-Advantage-Over-Obama-Narrows.aspx.

62. Carroll, S. J. "Voting Choices: The Politics of the Gender Gap." In *Gender and Elections: Shaping the Future of American Politics* (2nd Edition), edited by S. J. Carroll and R. L. Fox, 117–43. New York: Cambridge University Press, 2010.

63. "Palin Press Coverage: Fair and Important." *Pew Research Center*, September 10, 2008, accessed January 22, 2016, http://www.people-press.org/files/legacy-pdf/449.pdf.

64. Brians, C. L. "Women for Women? Gender and Party Bias in Voting for Female Candidates." *American Politics Research* 33, no. 3 (2005): 357–75; Rosenthal, Cindy Simon. "The Role of Gender in Descriptive Representation." *Political Research Quarterly* 48, no. 3 (1995): 599–611.

65. Steinhauser, Paul. "Poll: Women and Men Don't See Eye-to-Eye on Palin." *CNN Political Ticker Blogs*, September 9, 2008, accessed January 4, 2016, http://politicalticker.blogs.cnn.com/2008/09/09/poll-women-and-men-dont-see-eye-to-eye-on-palin/.

66. Cohen, Jon, and Jennifer Agiesta. "Perceptions of Palin Grow Increasingly Negative, Poll Says." *Washington Post*, October 24, 2008, accessed January 4, 2016, http://www.washingtonpost.com/wp-dyn/content/article/2008/10/24/AR2008102402698.html.

67. "The Gender Gap: Voting Choices in Presidential Elections." Center for American Women and Politics.

68. "The Campaign against Women." *New York Times*, May 20, 2012, accessed January 4, 2016, http://www.nytimes.com/2012/05/20/opinion/sunday/the-attack-on-women-is-real.html?_r=1.

69. Cary, Mary Kate. "Five Myths about the So Called 'Republican War on Women.'" *USA Today*, August 22, 2012, accessed January 4, 2016, http://www.usnews.com/opinion/articles/ 2012/08/29/five-myths-about-the-so-called-republican-war-on-women.

70. Seltzer, Sarah, and Lauren Kelley. "Eight Staggering GOP Comments on Rape and Women." *Salon.com*, August 22, 2012, accessed January 4, 2016, http://www.salon.com/2012/08/22/eight_staggering_gop_comments_on_rape_and_women/.

71. Ibid.

72. Wilner, Elizabeth. "Romney and Republicans Outspent Obama, but Couldn't Out-Advertise Him." *Ad Age*, November 9, 2012, accessed January 4, 2016, http://adage.com/article/campaign-trail/romney-outspent-obama-advertise/238241/.

73. Fowler, Erika Franklin, and Travis N. Ridout. "Negative, Angry, and Ubiquitous: Political Advertising in 2012." *The Forum* 10, no. 4 (2004): 51–61.

74. Winfrey, Kelly L., Mary C. Banwart, and Benjamin R. Warner. "Communicating with Voters 30 Seconds at a Time: Presidential Campaign Advertising 2012." In *Alienation: The Divide and Conquer Election of 2012*, edited by Mary C. Banwart, Mitchell S. McKinney, and Dianne G. Bystrom, 48–67. New York: Peter Lang Publishing, 2014.

75. "October 16, 2012 Debate Transcript." Commission on Presidential Debates, 2012, accessed January 4, 2016, http://www.debates.org/index.php?page= october-16-2012-the-second-obama-romney-presidential-debate.

76. "Women Seen as the Key to November Victory." *Dayton Daily News (Ohio)*, September 23, 2012; Leslie, Katie. "Election 2012 Examining the Gender Gap;

Women Hold Balance of Power." *The Atlanta Journal-Constitution*, October 28, 2012; "It's the Women, Stupid; Romney Repels Female Voters." *Daily Record & Sunday Mail*, August 26, 2012; "Did Debate Woo or Irk Women?" *Palm Beach Post*, October 18, 2012; Angyal, Chloe. "Why American Women's Votes Matter More Than Ever in This Election." *Guardian*, September 19, 2012.

77. Reinhard, Beth. "Romney, Obama Fates Hinge on Shrinking Sliver of Undecideds." *National Journal*, August 15, 2012, accessed January 4, 2016, http://news.yahoo.com/romney-obama-fates-hinge-shrinking-sliver-undecideds -060006850.html.

78. "The Undecided Voter: Just Like the Unicorn?" *NPR*, October 15, 2012, accessed May 19, 2013, http://www.npr.org/2012/10/20/163309696/the -undecided-voter-justlike-the-unicorn.

79. Rettig, Jessica. "Walmart Moms Could Swing 2011 Elections." *US News and World Report*, November 2, 2012, accessed January 4, 2016, http:// www.usnews.com/news/blogs/ken-walshs-washington/2011/11/02/walmart -moms-could-swing-2012-elections.

80. Adams, Paul. "Walmart Moms: America's Next Big Voting Bloc." *BBC News*, December 29, 2011, accessed January 4, 2016, http://www.bbc.com/news /world-us-canada-16340126.

81. Negrin, Matt. "Put a Ring on It: Obama Wins Women, but Not the Married Kind." *ABC News*, April 3, 2012, accessed January 4, 2016.

82. Dugan, Andrew. "Women in Swing States Have Gender-Specific Priorities." *Gallup*, October 17, 2012, accessed January 4, 2016, http://www.gallup .com/poll/158069/women-swing-states-gender-specific-priorities.aspx.

83. "Presidential Election Results," *NBC News online*, accessed July 12, 2018, http://elections.nbcnews.com/ns/politics/2012/all/president/

84. Omero, Margie, and Tara McGuinness. "How Women Changed the Outcome of the Election." Center for American Progress, last modified December 12, 2012, https://www.americanprogress.org/issues/women/report/2012/12/12/47916 /how-women-changed-the-outcome-of-the-election/.

85. Clinton, Hillary Rodham. "Official Campaign Launch—June 13, 2015." Carrie Chapman Catt Center for Women and Politics Archive of Women's Political Communication, accessed July 12, 2018, https://awpc.cattcenter.iastate .edu/2017/03/09/official-campaign-launch-june-13-2015/.

86. Ibid.

87. Ibid.

88. Clinton, Hillary Rodham. "Rejecting Trump's Vision for America—May 23, 2016." Carrie Chapman Catt Center for Women and Politics Archive of Women's Political Communication, accessed July 12, 2018, https://awpc.cattcenter .iastate.edu/2017/03/21/remarks-rejecting-trumps-vision-for-america-may-23-2016.

89. Clinton, Hillary Rodham. "Mirrors—Sep. 23, 2016." Carrie Chapman Catt Center for Women and Politics Archive of Women's Political Communication, accessed July 12, 2018. https://awpc.cattcenter.iastate.edu/2017/03/21 /mirrors-sep-23-2016/.

90. Yan, Holly. "Donald Trump's 'Blood' Comment about Megyn Kelly Draws Outrage." *CNN Politics*, last modified August 8, 2015, https://www.cnn.com/2015/08/08/politics/donald-trump-cnn-megyn-kelly-comment/index.html.

91. Stetler, Brian. "Trump Insults Fiorina in Rolling Stone: 'Look at That Face!'" *CNN*, last modified July 9, 2015, http://money.cnn.com/2015/09/09/media/donald-trump-rolling-stone-carly-fiorina/index.html.

92. Fahrenthold, David A. "Trump Recorded Having Extremely Lewd Conversation about Women in 2005." *Washington Post*, last modified October 8, 2016, https://www.washingtonpost.com/politics/trump-recorded-having-extremely-lewd-conversation-about-women-in-2005/2016/10/07/3b9ce776-8cb4-11e6-bf8a-3d26847eeed4_story.html?noredirect=on&utm_term=.5edeae0e103d.

93. Ibid.

94. Cooney, Samantha. "These Are the Women Who Have Accused President Trump of Sexual Misconduct." *Time*, December 13, 2017, http://time.com/5058646/donald-trump-accusers/.

95. Nelson, Libby. "Hostility toward Women Is One of the Strongest Predictors of Trump Support." *Vox*, last modified November 1, 2016, https://www.vox.com/2016/11/1/13480416/trump-supporters-sexism.

96. Ripley, Amanda. "What It Will Take for Women to Win." *Politico*, last modified June 12, 2017, https://www.politico.com/interactives/2017/women-rule-politics/.

CHAPTER 2

1. Tajfel, Henri, and John C. Turner. "The Social Identity Theory of Intergroup Behavior." In *Psychology of Intergroup Relations*, edited by Stephen Worchel and William G. Austin, 7–24. Chicago, IL: Nelson-Hall, 1986; Tajfel, Henri. *Human Groups and Social Categories*. Cambridge: Cambridge University Press, 1981; Tajfel, Henri. *Differentiation between Social Groups*. New York: Academic Press, 1978.

2. Gurin, Patricia, Arthur H. Miller, and Gerald Gurin. "Stratum Identification and Consciousness." *Social Psychology Quarterly* 43, no. 1 (1980): 30.

3. Rinehart, Sue Tolleson. *Gender Consciousness and Politics*. New York: Routledge, 1992.

4. Conover, Pamela Johnston. "The Influence of Group Identifications on Political Perception and Evaluation." *The Journal of Politics* 46, no. 3 (1984): 760–85.

5. Conover, Pamela Johnston. "The Role of Social Groups in Political Thinking." *British Journal of Political Science* 18, no. 1 (1988): 58.

6. Carroll, S. J. "Voting Choices: The Politics of the Gender Gap." In *Gender and Elections: Shaping the Future of American Politics (2nd Edition)*, edited by S. J. Carroll and R. L. Fox, 117–43. New York: Cambridge University Press, 2010.

7. Rinehart, *Gender Consciousness and Politics*, 33–34.

8. Miller, Arthur H., Patricia Gurin, Gerald Gurin, and Oksana Malanchuk. "Group Consciousness and Political Participation." *American Journal of Political Science* 25, no. 3 (1981): 494–511.

9. Koch, Jeffery. "Candidate Gender and Women's Psychological Engagement in Politics." *American Politics Quarterly* 25, no. 1 (1997): 118–33.

10. Banwart, Mary C., and Kelly Winfrey. "Leadership, Gender, and Politics: Political Perceptions and Participation of Young Female Voters in a Presidential Primary." *Educational Considerations* 37, no. 1 (2009): 40–52; Reingold, Beth, and Jessica Harrell. "The Impact of Descriptive Representation on Women's Political Engagement." *Political Research Quarterly* 63, no. 2 (2010): 280–94.

11. Atkeson, Lonna Rae. "Not All Cues Are Created Equal: The Conditional Impact of Female Candidates on Political Engagement." *The Journal of Politics* 65, no. 4 (2003): 1040–61.

12. Hansen, Susan B. "Talking about Politics: Gender and Contextual Effects on Political Proselytizing." *The Journal of Politics* 59, no. 1 (1997): 73–103.

13. Dolan, Kathleen. "Symbolic Mobilization? The Impact of Candidate Sex in American Elections." *American Politics Research* 34, no. 6 (2006): 687–704.

14. Brians, Craig Leonard. "Women for Women? Gender and Party Bias in Voting for Female Candidates." *American Politics Research* 33, no. 3 (2005): 357–75.

15. Dolan, Kathleen. "Is There a 'Gender Affinity Effect' in American Politics? Information, Affect, and Candidate Sex in U.S. House Elections." *Political Research Quarterly* 61, no. 1 (2008): 79–89.

16. Anderson, Peter A., and William R. Todd de Mancillas. "Scales for the Measurement of Homophily with Public Figures." *Southern Speech Communication Journal* 43, no. 2 (1978): 169–79.

17. Allen, Jerry L., and Daniel J. Post. "Source Valence in Assessing Candidate Image." *Communication Research Reports* 21, no. 2 (2009): 174–87; Anderson, Peter A., and Robert J. Kibler. "Candidate Valence as a Predictor of Voter Preference." *Human Communication Research* 5, no. 1 (1978): 4–14; Kendall, Kathleen E., and June Ock Yum. "Persuading the Blue-Collar Voter: Issues, Images, and Homophily." *Communication Yearbook* 8, no. 1 (1984): 702–22.

18. Rosenthal, Cindy Simon. "The Role of Gender in Descriptive Representation." *Political Research Quarterly* 48, no. 3 (1995): 599–611.

19. Participants for this study consisted of 359 women ranging in age from 18 to 85 years ($M = 33.38$, $SD = 16.15$) who completed an online survey between November 21, 2011 and December 26, 2011. Women were recruited in three ways. First, women enrolled in a communication course at a major Midwestern university received class credit for their participation in the study (45.7%). Second, non-student women were recruited through student referral (30.1%). Finally, women were recruited through outreach efforts to various businesses and organizations such as Chambers of Commerce and Parent Teacher Organizations (24%). Participants' race was reported as 87.5% White/Caucasian, 5.3% Black/African American, 3.3% Asian American, 1.1% Hispanic/Latin American, 1.1% American Indian, 1.7% Other/Not Reported. The large majority of women (80.8%) said they were registered to vote, and these voters came from 31 different states. Political party affiliation was 40.1% Democrat, 35.4% Republican, and 24.5% Independent/Other. Participants completed a two-part online survey. Part

1 contained measures of gender identification, gender consciousness, sex-role ideology/sexism, political efficacy, political engagement, political interpersonal communication competence, candidate trait importance, and issue importance. Participants were then exposed to a stimulus consisting of six political advertisements and were then asked to complete Part 2 of the survey, which consisted of evaluating the two candidates featured in the advertisements on perceived traits and ability to handle issues.

20. Mael, Fred A., and Lois E. Tetrick. "Identifying Organizational Identification." *Educational and Psychological Measurement* 52 (1992): 813–24.

21. Tajfel, *Differentiation between Social Groups*.

22. Mael and Tetrick, "Identifying Organizational Identification," 814.

23. Ibid., 816.

24. Ibid.

25. Ibid.

26. Greene, Steven. "Social Identity Theory and Party Identification." *Social Science Quarterly* 85, no. 1 (2004): 136–53.

27. Brewer, Marilynn B., and Michael D. Silver. "Group Distinctiveness, Social Identification, and Collective Mobilization." In *Self, Identity, and Social Movements*, edited by Sheldon Stryker, Timothy J. Owens and Robert W. White, 152–71. Minneapolis: University of Minnesota Press, 2000.

28. Mael and Tetrick, "Identifying Organizational Identification," 813–824.

29. Schmitt, Michael T., Nyla R. Branscombe, Diane Kobrynowicz, and Susan Owen. "Perceiving Discrimination against One's Gender Group Has Different Implications for Well-Being in Women and Men." *Personality and Social Psychology Bulletin* 28, no. 2 (2002): 197–210.

30. For IDPG, $F(2, 356) = 4.07$. For Gender Attachment, $F(2, 356) = .40$.

31. Rinehart, *Gender Consciousness and Politics*; Cook, Elizabeth Adell. "Measuring Feminist Consciousness." *Women & Politics* 9, no. 3 (1989): 71–88.

32. Gurin, Miller, and Gurin, "Stratum Identification and Consciousness," 30–47.

33. Rinehart, *Gender Consciousness and Politics*, 32.

34. Conover, "The Role of Social Groups in Political Thinking," 51–76.

35. Miller et al., "Group Consciousness and Political Participation," 494–511.

36. Ibid.; Gurin, Patricia. "Women's Gender Consciousness." *The Public Opinion Quarterly* 49, no. 2 (1985): 143–62.

37. Conover, "The Role of Social Groups in Political Thinking," 51–76.

38. "The ANES Guide to Public Opinion and Electoral Behavior." The American National Election Studies, accessed September 4, 2011, http://www.electionstudies.org/nesguide/toptable/tab7a_2.htm.

39. Ibid.; Duncan, Lauren E. "Motivation for Collective Action: Group Consciousness as Mediator of Personality, Life Experiences, and Women's Right Activism." *Political Psychology* 20, no. 3 (1999): 611–35.

40. $F(2,256) = 1.05$.

41. Henderson-King, Donna H., and Abigail J. Stewart. "Women or Feminists? Assessing Women's Group Consciousness." *Sex Roles* 31, no. 9/10 (1994): 505–16.

42. Cook, "Measuring Feminist Consciousness," 71–88.

43. Reid, Anne, and Nuala Purcell. "Pathways to Feminist Identification." *Sex Roles* 50, no. 11/12 (2004): 759–69.

44. Cook, "Measuring Feminist Consciousness," 71–88.

45. Duncan, Lauren E. "Motivation for Collective Action: Group Consciousness as Mediator of Personality, Life Experiences, and Women's Right Activism." *Political Psychology* 20, no. 3 (1999): 611–35.

46. Cook, Elizabeth Adell. "Feminist Consciousness and Candidate Preference among American Women, 1972–1988." *Political Behavior* 15, no. 3 (1993): 227–46.

47. Conover, Patricia J. "Feminists and the Gender Gap." *The Journal of Politics* 50, no. 4 (1988): 985–1010.

48. Cook, "Feminist Consciousness and Candidate Preference among American Women," 227–246.

49. Ibid.

50. Rinehart, *Gender Consciousness and Politics*, 45.

CHAPTER 3

1. Rinehart, Sue Tolleson. *Gender Consciousness and Politics*. New York: Routledge, 1992.

2. Ibid., 42–43.

3. Macmanus, S. A. "Voter Participation and Turnout: Female Star Power Attracts Women Voters." In *Gender and Elections: Shaping the Future of American Politics*, edited by Susan J. Carroll and Richard L. Fox, 78–116. New York: Cambridge University Press, 2010.

4. Denton, Robert E. "Identity Politics and the 2008 Presidential Campaign." In *The 2008 Presidential Campaign: A Communication Perspective*, edited by Robert E. Denton, 99–126. Lanham, MD: Rowman & Littlefield Publishers, 2009.

5. Barker-Plummer, Bernadette. "Reading Sarah Palin." *Flow*, last modified October 2008, http://flowtv.org/2008/10/reading-sarah-palin-bernadette-barker-plummer-university-of-san-francisco/.

6. Gallagher, Maggie. "Sarah Palin's Pioneering Streak." *RealClearPolitics*, last modified September 3, 2008, http://www.realclearpolitics.com/articles/2008/09/sarah_palins_pioneering_streak.html.

7. Clinton, Hillary " Innovation and Economy—May 31, 2007." Carrie Chapman Catt Center for Women and Politics Archive of Women's Political Communication, accessed July 18, 2018, https://awpc.cattcenter.iastate.edu/2017/03/21/innovation-and-economy-may-31-2007/.

8. Clinton, Hillary. "Speech at the Democratic National Convention." *NPR*, last modified August 28, 2008, http://www.npr.org/templates/story/story.php?storyId=94003143.

9. Palin, Sarah. "Announced as Vice President—August 29, 2008." Carrie Chapman Catt Center for Women and Politics Archive of Women's Political

Communication, accessed July 18, 2018, https://awpc.cattcenter.iastate.edu /2017/03/09/announced-as-vice-president-at-dayton-ohio-rally-aug-29-2008/.

10. Palin, Sarah. "Speech at the Republican National Convention." *Huffington Post*, last modified September 3, 2008, http://www.huffingtonpost .com/2008/09/03/sarah-palin-rnc-conventio_n_123703.html.

11. Clinton, Hillary. "Paygap—November 3, 2015." Carrie Chapman Catt Center for Women and Politics Archive of Women's Political Communication, accessed July 18, 2018, https://awpc.cattcenter.iastate.edu/2017/03/10/paygap-nov-3-2015/.

12. Glick, Peter, and Susan T. Fiske. "The Ambivalent Sexism Inventory: Differentiating Hostile and Benevolent Sexism." *Journal of Personality and Social Psychology* 70, no. 3 (1996): 491–512.

13. Ibid., 491.

14. Glick and Fiske, "The Ambivalent Sexism Inventory," 491–512; Masser, Barbara, and Dominic Abrams. "Contemporary Sexism: The Relationships among Hostility, Benevolence, and Neosexism." *Psychology of Women Quarterly* 23, no. 503–517 (1999): 503.

15. Becker, Julia C. "Why Do Women Endorse Hostile and Benevolent Sexism? The Role of Salient Female Subtypes and Internalization of Sexist Contents." *Sex Roles* 62 (2010): 453–467; Christopher, Andrew N., and Mark R. Wojda. "Social Dominance Orientation, Right-Win Authoritarianism, Sexism, and Prejudice toward Women in the Workforce." *Psychology of Women Quarterly* 32 (2008): 65–73; Glick, Peter, and Susan T. Fiske. "An Ambivalent Alliance." *American Psychologist* 56, no. 2 (2001): 109–18.

16. Fields, Alice M., Suzanne Swan, and Bret Kloos. "'What It Means to Be a Woman': Ambivalent Sexism in Female College Students' Experiences and Attitudes." *Sex Roles* 62, no. 554–567 (2010): 554; Glick, Peter, Jeffrey Diebold, Barbara Bailey-Werner, and Lin Zhu. "The Two Faces of Adam: Ambivalent Sexism and Polarized Attitudes toward Women." *Personality & Social Psychology Bulletin* 23, no. 12 (1997): 1323–235; Glick and Fiske, "The Ambivalent Sexism Inventory," 491–512.

17. The independent variables in this analysis were age and education; the dependent variable was the ASI composite score. Multiple regression revealed that education was significant predictor of the ASI (β = −.44, R^2 = .20, $F(1,179)$ = 22.15, p < .01), but education did not explain any additional variance.

18. Reid, Anne, and Nuala Purcell. "Pathways to Feminist Identification." *Sex Roles* 50, no. 11/12 (2004): 759–69.

19. Rinehart, *Gender Consciousness and Politics*, 67–110.

20. The independent variable in this analysis was placement on the liberal-conservative ideology scale; the dependent variable was the ASI composite score. Regression analysis revealed that the ideology score was a significant predictor of ASI (β = .39, R^2 = .25, $F(1,357)$ = 63.99, p < .01).

21. Rinehart, *Gender Consciousness and Politics*, 67–110.

22. For Identified women, n = 296. For Individualist women, n = 64.

23. Independent sample t-tests revealed that no significant differences emerged between Identified and Individualist women on the ASI (Identified M = 3.23,

Individualist M = 3.10), $t(357)$ = −1.43, p = .26; HS (Identified M = 3.13, Individualist M = 3.14), $t(357)$ = .054, p = .80; or BS (Identified M = 3.34, Individualist M = 3.05), $t(357)$ = −2.52, p = .46.

24. For collective orientation, $t(357)$ = −5.07, p < .01. For polar affect, $t(357)$ = −3.12, p < .01.

25. Cook, Elizabeth Adell. "Feminist Consciousness and Candidate Preference among American Women, 1972–1988." *Political Behavior* 15, no. 3 (1993): 227–46; Conover, Patricia J. "Feminists and the Gender Gap." *The Journal of Politics* 50, no. 4 (1988): 985–1010; Miller, Arthur H., Patricia Gurin, Gerald Gurin, and Oksana Malanchuk. "Group Consciousness and Political Participation." *American Journal of Political Science* 25, no. 3 (1981): 494–511.

26. Rinehart, *Gender Consciousness and Politics*, 67–110.

27. Bryant, Alyssa N. "Changes in Attitudes toward Women's Roles: Predicting Gender-Role Traditionalism among College Students." *Sex Roles* 38, no. 3/4 (2003): 131–42.

28. A one-way MANOVA was conducted to determine the effect of ideology-identification group (Egalitarian-Identified, Traditional-Identified, Individualist) on sexism scores (ASI, Benevolent ASI, Hostile ASI). Significant differences were found among the three groups, Wilkes's λ = .56, $F(2, 710)$ = 58.78, p < .00, η^2 = .25. One-way ANOVAs were conducted as follow-up tests on the dependent variables (ASI, BS, HS), and the Bonferroni method was used to control for family-wise error. The ANOVAs revealed significant differences between the three groups on the ASI $F(2,356)$ = 131.25, p < .001; HS, $F(2,356)$ = 80.80, p < .001; and BS, $F(2,356)$ = 93.62, p < .001.

29. Cook, Elizabeth Adell. "Measuring Feminist Consciousness." *Women & Politics* 9, no. 3 (1989): 71–88; Gurin, Patricia. "Women's Gender Consciousness." *The Public Opinion Quarterly* 49, no. 2 (1985): 143–62; Gurin, Patricia, Arthur H. Miller, and Gerald Gurin, "Stratum Identification and Consciousness." *Social Psychology Quarterly* 43, no. 1 (1980): 30; Miller et al., "Group Consciousness and Political Participation," 494–511.

30. Glick and Fiske, "The Ambivalent Sexism Inventory," 49–513; Masser and Abrams, "Contemporary Sexism: The Relationships among Hostility, Benevolence, and Neosexism," 503–512.

31. Becker, "Why Do Women Endorse Hostile and Benevolent Sexism?" 453–467.

32. Glick, Peter, and Susan T. Fiske. "Hostile and Benevolent Sexism: Measuring Ambivalent Sexist Attitudes toward Women." *Psychology of Women Quarterly* 21 (1997): 119–135.

33. Conover, "Feminists and the Gender Gap," 985–1010; Cook, "Feminist Consciousness and Candidate Preference among American Women, 1972–1988," 227–246.

34. Deckman, Melissa. *Tea Party Women: Mama Grizzlies, Grassroots Leaders, and the Changing Face of the American Right*. New York: New York University Press, 2016, 118–122.

CHAPTER 4

1. "1776 Abigail Adams Urges Husband to 'Remember the Ladies.'" *History Channel*, accessed June 8, 2016, http://www.history.com/this-day-in-history /abigail-adams-urges-husband-to-remember-the-ladies.

2. Sherr, Lynn. *Failure Is Impossible: Susan B. Anthony in Her Own Words.* New York: Times Books, 1995, 134.

3. Banwart, Mary C. "Gender and Young Voters in 2004: Influence of Perceived Knowledge and Interest." *American Behavioral Scientist* 50, no. 9 (2007): 1152–68; Karp, Jeffrey A., and Susan A. Banducci. "When Politics Is Not Just a Man's Game: Women's Representation and Political Engagement." *Electoral Studies* 27 (2008): 105–15; Verba, Sidney, Nancy Burns, and Kay Lehman Scholzman. "Knowing and Caring about Politics: Gender and Political Engagement." *The Journal of Politics* 59, no. 4 (1997): 1051–72.

4. Verba, Burns, and Scholzman, "Knowing and Caring about Politics," 1051–1072.

5. Burns, N. "Gender in the Aggregate, Gender in the Individual, Gender and Political Action." In *Political Women and American Democracy*, edited by C. Wolbrecht, K. Beckwith, and L. Baldez, 55. Cambridge: Cambridge University Press, 2008.

6. Eagly, Alice H., and Linda L. Carli. *Through the Labyrinth: The Truth about How Women Become Leaders.* Boston: Harvard Business School Press, 2007.

7. Lawless, Jennifer L., and Richard L. Fox. "Girls Just Wanna Not Run: The Gender Gap in Young American's Political Ambition." American University School of Public Affairs, accessed August 31, 2014, https://www.american.edu /spa/wpi/upload/Girls-Just-Wanna-Not-Run_Policy-Report.pdf.

8. The interest question was not asked in 2006 or 2010; the reported percentage uses data from 2000, 2002, 2004, 2008, and 2012.

9. For men, $M = 3.53$, $SD = .63$; for women, $M = 3.21$, $SD = 1.10$, $p < .01$, $t = 11.11$.

10. For men, $M = 2.49$, $SD = 2.45$; for women, $M = 2.33$, $SD = 2.48$, $p < .01$, $t = 3.16$.

11. Campbell, David E., and Christina Wolbrecht. "See Jane Run: Women Politicians as Role Models for Adolescents." *The Journal of Politics* 68, no. 2 (2006): 233–47; Wolbrecht, Christina, and David E. Campbell. "Leading by Example: Female Members of Parliament as Political Role Models." *American Journal of Political Science* 51, no. 4 (2007): 921–39.

12. Atkeson, Lonna Rae. "Not All Cues Are Created Equal: The Conditional Impact of Female Candidates on Political Engagement." *The Journal of Politics* 65, no. 4 (2003): 1040–61.

13. Campbell and Wolbrecht, "See Jane Run."

14. Atkeson, "Not All Cues Are Created Equal," 1040–1061.

15. Ibid.

16. Reingold, Beth, and Jessica Harrell. "The Impact of Descriptive Representation on Women's Political Engagement." *Political Research Quarterly* 63, no. 2 (2010): 280–94.

17. Banwart, Mary Christine, and Kelly Winfrey. "Leadership, Gender, and Politics: Political Perceptions and Participation of Young Female Voters in a Presidential Primary." *Educational Considerations* 37, no. 1 (2009): 40–52; Hansen, Susan B. "Talking about Politics: Gender and Contextual Effects on Political Proselytizing." *The Journal of Politics* 59, no. 1 (1997): 73–103; Sapiro, Virginia, and Pamela Johnston Conover. "The Variable Gender Bias of Electoral Politics: Gender and Context in the 1992 U.S. Election." *British Journal of Political Science* 27, no. 4 (1997): 497–523.

18. Dolan, Kathleen. "Symbolic Mobilization? The Impact of Candidate Sex in American Elections." *American Politics Research* 34, no. 6 (2006): 687–704.

19. Atkeson, Lonna Rae, and Nancy Carrillo. "More Is Better: The Influence of Collective Female Descriptive Representation on External Efficacy." *Politics & Gender* 3 (2007): 79–101.

20. Verba, Burns, and Scholzman, "Knowing and Caring about Politics."

21. Lawless, Jennifer L. "Politics of Presence? Congresswomen and Symbolic Representation." *Political Research Quarterly* 57, no. 1 (2004): 81–99.

22. Karp, Jeffery A., and Susan A. Banducci. "When Politics Is Not Just a Man's Game: Women's Representation and Political Engagement." *Electoral Studies* 27 (2008): 105–15; Reingold and Harrell, "The Impact of Descriptive Representation," 280–294.

23. Rinehart, Sue Tolleson. *Gender Consciousness and Politics*. New York: Routledge, 1992.

24. For political interest, α = .93. For political discussion, α = .89.

25. A one-way ANOVA was conducted across the three subgroups, revealing that ideology identification had a significant effect on political interest, $F(2,356)$ = 10.00, $p < .01$, and political discussion $F(2, 356)$ = 13.80, $p < .01$. Post hoc analysis used Fisher's LSD.

26. Stepwise multiple regression revealed that sexism (ASI) was a significant predictor of political interest, β =−.38, R^2 = .15, $F(1,357)$ = 61.017, $p < .01$. The model including group identification (IDPG) did not predict significantly more political discussion than did sexism alone.

27. Stepwise multiple regression revealed that sexism (ASI) was a significant predictor of political discussion, β =−.37, R^2 = .14, $F(1,357)$ = 65.08, $p < .01$. The model including group identification (IDPG) did not predict significantly more political discussion than did sexism alone.

28. Delli Carpini, Michael X., and Scott Keeter. "Stability and Change in the U.S. Public's Knowledge of Politics." *The Public Opinion Quarterly* 55, no. 4 (1991): 583–612; Verba, Burns, and Scholzman, "Knowing and Caring about Politics," 1051-1072.

29. Mondak, Jeffery J., and Mary R. Anderson. "The Knowledge Gap: A Reexamination of Gender-Based Differences in Political Knowledge." *The Journal of Politics* 66, no. 2 (2004): 492–512.

30. Banwart, Mary C. "The Political Interpersonal Communication Index: Developing a Measure of Understanding Why We Talk about Politics." National Communication Association Conference. Chicago, IL, 2007.

31. PIC α = .85.

32. Independent sample t-tests revealed significant differences in PIC (Egalitarian-Identified M = 3.45, SD = .60; Traditional-Identified M = 3.08, SD = .47, p < .01, t = 5.67), cognitive engagement (Egalitarian-Identified M = 3.63, SD = .91; Traditional-Identified M = 3.15, SD = .85, p < .01, t = 4.48), and perceived relevance (Egalitarian-Identified M = 4.05, SD = .65; Traditional-Identified M = 3.53, SD = .65, p < .01, t = 6.79). Perceived knowledge was not significant (Egalitarian-Identified M = 2.17, SD = .76; Traditional-Identified M = 2.28, SD = .81, p = .25, t = 1.15).

33. Stepwise multiple regression revealed that sexism (ASI), β =−.44 and group identification (IDPG), β = .13 were significant predictors of PIC, R^2 = .19, $F(1,357)$ = 44.14, p < .01.

34. Kaid, Lynda Lee, Mitchell S. McKinney, and John C. Tedesco. *Civic Dialogue in the 1996 Presidential Campaign: Candidate, Media, and Public Voices.* Cresskill, NJ: Hampton, 2000; Kaid, Lynda Lee, Mitchell S. McKinney, and John C. Tedesco. "Information Efficacy and Young Voters." National Communication Association Conference. Chicago, 2004.

35. Hansen, "Talking about Politics," 73–103; Atkeson and Carrillo, "More Is Better," 79–101.

36. Rinehart, *Gender Consciousness and Politics,* 132–139.

37. For external efficacy, α = .63. For internal efficacy, α = .87.

38. Independent sample t-tests revealed a difference approaching statistical significance in internal efficacy (Egalitarian-Identified M = 3.56, SD = .92; Traditional-Identified M = 3.19, SD = .77, p = .056, t = 3.58).

39. Independent sample t-tests revealed a difference approaching statistical significance in internal efficacy (Identified M = 2.95, SD = .77; Individualist M = 2.74, SD = .87, p < .05, t =−1.90).

40. Independent sample t-tests revealed a significant difference in internal efficacy (Egalitarian-Identified M = 2.87, SD = .87; Traditional-Identified M = 3.06, SD = .57, p < .05, t =−2.11).

41. Stepwise multiple regression revealed that sexism (ASI), β =−.39 and group identification (IDPG), β = .17 were significant predictors of internal efficacy, R^2 = .16, $F(1,356)$ = 34.79, p < .01.

42. Stepwise multiple regression revealed that sexism (ASI) was a significant predictor of political discussion, β = .10, R^2 = .01, $F(1,357)$ = 3.91, p < .05. The model including group identification (IDPG) did not predict significantly more political discussion than did sexism alone.

43. Rinehart, *Gender Consciousness and Politics,* 111–144.

CHAPTER 5

1. "Party Identification and Presidential Performance Ratings." Center for American Women and Politics, Eagleton Institute of Politics, Rutgers University, 2014, accessed September 17, 2015, http://www.cawp.rutgers.edu/sites/default /files/resources/ggprtyid.pdf.

2. "A Deep Dive into Party Affiliation." *Pew Research Center*, 2015, accessed June 3, 2016, http://www.people-press.org/2015/04/07/a-deep-dive-into-party -affiliation/.

3. "User's Guide and Codebook for the ANES 2012 Time Series Study." American National Election Study, 2015, accessed January 8, 2016, http://www .electionstudies.org/studypages/anes_timeseries_2012/anes_timeseries_2012 _userguidecodebook.pdf.

4. Cross-tabs analysis conducted of 2012 ANES data revealed a significant difference at $p < .05$.

5. Cross-tabs analysis conducted of 2012 ANES data revealed that among Republicans, 80.1 percent of men and 74.6 percent of women believed that Republicans best handled the economy, and 22.1 percent of women and 17.7 percent of men said there was not much difference. The gender difference was significant for both of these comparisons at $p < .05$.

6. Participants responded on a 5-point scale, with 5 indicating that they strongly agreed with the statement "the government should take measures to reduce differences in income levels." Independent t-tests revealed a significant difference between men ($M = 2.6$, $SD = 1.36$) and women ($M = 2.78$, $SD = 1.28$), $p < .01$. A significant difference was also found among Republican men ($M = 1.79$, $SD = 1.12$) and Republican women ($M = 2.05$, $SD = 1.20$), $p < .01$.

7. Independent sample t-tests revealed a significant difference between men, $M = 2.27$ $SD = 1.88$, and women, $M = 2.05$, $SD = 1.66$, $p < .01$. A gender difference was also found between Republican men, $M = 3.22$ $SD = 2.14$, and women, $M = 2.89$ $SD = 2.01$, and between Independent men, $M = .29$ $SD = 1.85$, and women, $M = 2.07$ $SD = 1.63$, $p < .01$.

8. Luckwaldt, Jen Hubley. "Women Are More Likely to Be Underemployed Than Men." *PayScale Career News*, 2016, accessed June 30, 2016, http://www .payscale.com/career-news/2016/06/underemployed-women.

9. Independent samples t-test revealed that men, $M = 4.18$ $SD = .95$, think reducing the deficit is more important than women, $M = 4.12$ $SD = .95$, $p < .05$.

10. Seltzer, Richard A., Jody Newman, and Melissa Voorhees Leighton. *Sex as a Political Variable: Women as Candidates & Voters in U.S. Elections*. Boulder, CO: Lynne Rienner Publishers, 1997.

11. Saad, Lydia. "Economy Is Dominant Issue for Americans as Election Nears." *Gallup*, 2012, accessed June 30, 2016, http://www.gallup.com/poll/158267 /economy-dominant-issue-americans-election-nears.aspx; Chaturvedi, Richa. "A Closer Look at the Gender Gap in Presidential Voting." *Pew Research Center*, July 28, 2016, accessed August 2, 2016, http://www.pewresearch.org /fact-tank/2016/07/28/a-closer-look-at-the-gender-gap-in-presidential-voting/.

12. Ibid.

13. Analysis of ANES 2012 data on approval of president's handling of health care (on a 5-point scale) using independent sample t-tests revealed that women, $M = 2.66$ $SD = 1.35$, approved more strongly than men, $M = 2.49$ $SD = 1.32$, $p < .01$. Cross-tab analysis found no significant difference in the percentage of

men and women who thought that the Affordable Care Act improved, worsened, or had not effect on the quality of health care and the number of insured.

14. Saad, "Economy Is Dominant Issue."

15. Chaturvedi, "A Closer Look."

16. Agiesta, Jennifer, and Tom LoBianco. "Poll: Gun Control Support Spikes after Shooting." *CNN*, June 20, 2016, accessed July 14, 2016, http://www.cnn.com/2016/06/20/politics/cnn-gun-poll/; Kennedy, Brain. "Public Support for Environmental Regulation Varies by State." *Pew Research Center*, February 25, 2016, accessed July 14, 2016, http://www.pewresearch.org/fact-tank/2016/02/25/public-support-for-environmental-regulations-varies-by-state/.

17. "Gun Rights Proponents More Politically Active: In Gun Control Debate, Several Options Draw Majority Support." *Pew Research Center*, 2013, accessed June 30, 2016, http://www.people-press.org/files/legacy-pdf/01-14-13%20Gun%20Policy%20Release.pdf.

18. "2016 Data Point: The Gun Control Gender Gap." American Enterprise Institute, July 11, 2016, accessed August 2, 2016, https://www.aei.org/multimedia/2016-data-point-the-gun-control-gender-gap/.

19. Seltzer, Newman, and Leighton, *Sex as a Political Variable*, 11–30.

20. "2016 Data Point: Marijuana on the Ballot." American Enterprise Institute, August 11, 2016, accessed August 14, 2016, https://www.aei.org/multimedia/2016-data-point-marijuana-on-the-ballot/.

21. Ibid.; Kaufmann, Karen M. "Culture Wars, Secular Realignment, and the Gender Gap in Party Identification." *Political Behavior* 24, no. 3 (2002): 283–307.

22. Chaturvedi, "A Closer Look."

23. Cross-tabulation of ANES 2012 data found a significant difference between men at women at $p < .05$.

24. Analysis of ANES 2012 data using independent sample t-tests revealed men, $M = 3.61$ $SD = 1.60$, supporting significantly less environmental regulation than women, $M = 3.83$ $SD = 1.75$, $p < .05$.

25. "User's Guide and Codebook for the ANES 2012 Time Series Study." The equality measure consisted of six items and had a reliability of $\alpha = .78$.

26. Independent sample t-tests revealed that Democratic women, $M = 3.85$ $SD = .68$, had significantly greater concern for equality than did Democratic men, $M = 3.78$ $SD = .74$, $p < .05$. Republican women, $M = 2.93$ $SD = .76$, also reported greater concern for equality than Republican men, $M = 2.81$ $SD = .76$, $p < .01$.

27. Independent sample t-tests of 2012 ANES data revealed that women had significantly greater support for affirmative action in universities and workplaces. For universities, men $M = 3.06$ $SD = 1.88$, women $M = 3.16$ $SD = 1.85$. For workplaces, men $M = 2.92$ $SD = 1.84$, women $M = 3.07$ $SD = 1.86$.

28. Chaturvedi, "A Closer Look."

29. Independent sample t-tests of 2012 ANES data revealed that women believe men have more opportunities (women $M = 2.60$ $SD = 1.32$; men $M = 3.13$ $SD = 1.38$, $p < .01$) and that the media should pay more attention

to discrimination against women (women M = 3.22 SD = 1.52; men M = 3.61 SD = 1.58, p < .01).

30. Independent samples t-tests of 2000 to 2012 ANES data revealed that women, M =1.85 SD = 1.48, had significantly more equal beliefs than did men, M = 2.03 SD = 1.54, p < .01.

31. Independent sample t-tests of 2012 ANES data revealed that men were more likely to believe that it is harder for a working mother to bond with her child (women M = 5.13 SD = 1.30; men M = 5.42 SD = .79, p < .01), and that it is better for men to work and women to stay home (women M = 3.00 SD = 1.43; men M = 2.88 SD = 1.43, p < .01).

32. Seltzer, Newman, and Leighton, *Sex as a Political Variable*.

33. This data is from analysis of the 2012 ANES Time Series Study.

34. Dugan, Andrew. "Women in Swing States Have Gender-Specific Priorities." *Gallup*, October 17, 2012, accessed July 14, 2016, http://www.gallup.com/poll/158069/women-swing-states-gender-specific-priorities.aspx; Chaturvedi, "A Closer Look."

35. Curry, Tom. "The 'Evolution' of Obama's Stance on Gay Marriage." *NBC Politics*, May 9, 2012, accessed July 17, 2016, http://nbcpolitics.nbcnews.com/_news/2012/05/09/11623172-the-evolution-of-obamas-stance-on-gay-marriage?lite.

36. Eggen, Dan. "Obama's Gay Marriage Announcement Followed by Flood of Campaign Donations." *Washington Post*, May 10, 2012, accessed July 17, 2016, https://www.washingtonpost.com/politics/obamas-gay-marriage-announcement-followed-by-flood-of-campaign-donations/2012/05/10/gIQA2ntCGU_story.html.

37. Chaturvedi, "A Closer Look."

38. Independent samples t-test of 2000 to 2012 ANES data showed that Democratic women, M = 3.72 SD = 1.72, felt more strongly than Democratic men, M = 3.44 SD = 1.82, p < .01. Republican women, M = 3.57 SD = 1.57, felt more strongly than Republican men, M = 3.28 SD = 1.60, p < .01.

39. Independent samples t-tests showed the following results: Democratic women, M = 4.05 SD = 1.51; Democratic men, M = 3.71 SD = 1.71; Republican women, M = 3.96 SD =1.42; Republican men, M = 3.57 SD = 1.58; Independent women, M = 4.22 SD = 11.29; Independent men, M = 3.87 SD = 1.46. Gender differences within party were all significant at p < .01.

40. Seltzer, Newman, and Leighton, *Sex as a Political Variable*, 11–30.

41. Brooks, Deborah Jordan, and Benjamin A. Valentino. "A War of One's Own: Understanding the Gender Gap in Support for War." *Public Opinion Quarterly* 75, no. 2 (2011): 270–86.

42. Huddy, Leonie, and Nayda Terkildsen. "The Consequences of Gender Stereotypes for Women Candidates at Different Levels and Types of Office." *Political Research Quarterly* 46, no. 3 (1993): 503–25; Huddy, Leonie, and Nayda Terkildsen. "Gender Stereotypes and the Perception of Male and Female Candidates." *American Journal of Political Science* 37, no. 1 (1993): 119–47.

43. Conover, Patricia J. "Feminists and the Gender Gap." *The Journal of Politics* 50, no. 4 (1988): 985–1010; Rinehart, Sue Tolleson. *Gender Consciousness and Politics*. New York: Routledge, 1992.

44. A repeated measure ANOVA was conducted; the type of issue was the within-subjects factor, and the importance rating served as the dependent variable, Wilkes's Λ = .719, $F(2,357)$ = 69.76, $p < .01$, multivariate η^2 = .28. Follow-up analysis using paired sample t-tests revealed that women rated economic issues significantly higher than military/foreign affairs issues, $t(358)$ = 11.74, $p < .01$, and economic issues higher than compassion issues $t(358)$ = 1.96, p = .05. Additionally, women rated compassion issues significantly higher than military /foreign affairs issues, $t(358)$ = −7.53, $p < .01$.

45. A stepwise multiple regression revealed that gender group identification was a significant predictor of the importance of economic issues accounting for approximately 4 percent of the variance, β = .20, R^2 = .04, $F(1,357)$ = 15.55, $p < .01$. Regression analysis revealed that identification was a significant predictor of compassion issue ratings, β = .24, R^2 = .058, $F(1,357)$ = 22.16, $p < .01$.

46. ANOVA demonstrated a significant issue effect, Wilkes's Λ = .82, $F(2,62)$ = 6.95, $p < .01$, multivariate η^2 = .18. Paired sample t-tests revealed that Individualist women rated economic issues as significantly more important than military /foreign affairs issues, $t(63)$ = 3.50, $p < .01$.

47. A MANOVA revealed significant group differences, Wilkes's $\Lambda -$ = .96, $F(3, 355)$ = 5.29, $p < .00$, η^2 = .04. Follow-up analysis revealed that Identified women rated both compassion, $F(1,357)$ = 13.73, $p < .01$, and economic issues, $F(1,357)$ = 10.52, $p < .01$, as significantly more important than did Individualist women.

48. Regression analysis revealed that traditional gender-role beliefs were associated with higher ratings of military/foreign affairs issues, β = .18, R^2 = .03 $F(1,357)$ = 12.75, $p < .01$.

49. Regression analysis revealed a relationship between ASI scores and compassion issue ratings, β = −.20, R^2 = .04 $F(1,357)$ = 16.13, $p < .01$.

50. ANOVA for Egalitarian-Identified women revealed a significant issue effect, Wilkes's Λ = .63, $F(2,174)$ = 52.18, $p < .01$, multivariate η^2 = .38. Paired sample t-tests revealed that military/foreign affairs issues were rated significantly less important than both compassion issues, $t(175)$ = −7.86, $p < .01$, and economic issues, $t(175)$ = 10.25, $p < .01$.

51. Repeated measure ANOVA revealed a significant issue effect, Wilkes's Λ = .78, $F(2,117)$ = 16.19, $p < .01$, multivariate η^2 = .28. Paired sample t-tests revealed that economic issues were ranked significantly higher than compassion issues, $t(118)$ = 3.56, $p < .01$, and economic issues were rated significantly higher than military/foreign affairs issues, $t(118)$ = 5.51, $p < .01$. Privatized-Identified women also ranked compassion issues as significantly more important than military/foreign affairs issues, $t(118)$ = 2.34, $p < .05$.

52. MANOVA analysis revealed significant differences between groups, Wilkes's Λ = .91, $F(6,708)$ = 5.66, $p < .00$, η^2 = .05. Follow-up tests using the Bonferroni method revealed significant differences between the three groups on

the importance of economic issues, $F(2,356) = 5.35$, $p < .01$, and the importance of compassion issues, $F(2,356) = 11.20$, $p < .01$.

53. Conover, "Feminists and the Gender Gap," 985–1010.

54. Dolan, Kathleen. "How the Public Views Women Candidates." In *Women and Elective Office: Past, Present, and Future*, edited by Sue Thomas and Clyde Wilcox, 41–59. New York: Oxford University Press, 2005; Dolan, Kathleen. "Is There a 'Gender Affinity Effect' in American Politics? Information, Affect, and Candidate Sex in U.S. House Elections." *Political Research Quarterly* 61, no. 1 (2008): 79–89; Hernson, Paul S., J. Celeste Lay, and Atiya Kai Stokes. "Women Running 'as Women': Candidate Gender, Campaign Issues, and Voter-Targeting Strategies." *The Journal of Politics* 65, no. 1 (2003): 244–55; Matland, Richard E., and David C. King. "Women as Candidates in Congressional Elections." In *Women Transforming Congress*, edited by Cindy Simon Rosenthal, 119–42. Norman: University of Oklahoma Press, 2002; Sanbonmatsu, Kira, and Kathleen Dolan. "Do Gender Stereotypes Transcend Party?" *Political Research Quarterly* 62, no. 3 (2009): 485–94; Thomas, Sue, and Jean Reith Schroedel. "The Significance of Social and Institutional Expectations." In *Rethinking Madam President: Are We Ready for a Women in the White House?* edited by Lori Cox Han and Caroline Heldman, 43–68. Boulder, CO: Lynne Rienner Publishers, 2007.

55. Enloe, Cynthia. *Globalization and Militarism: Feminists Make the Link*. Lanham, MD: Rowman and Littlefield Publishers, 2007; Reardon, Betty. *Sexism and the War System*. Syracuse, NY: Syracuse University Press, 1996.

CHAPTER 6

1. Louden, Allan, and Kristen McCauliff. "The 'Authentic Candidate': Extending Candidate Image Assessment." In *Presidential Candidate Images*, edited by Kenneth L. Hacker, 85–104. Lanhan, MD: Rowman & Littlefield Publishers, 2004.

2. Ibid., 85.

3. Ibid.

4. Trent, Judith S., Paul A. Mongeau, Jimmie D. Trent, Kathleen E. Kendall, and Ronald B. Cushing. "The Ideal Candidate: A Study of the Desired Attributes of the Public and the Media Across Two Presidential Campaigns." *American Behavioral Scientist* 37, no. 2 (1993): 225–39; Trent, Judith S., Cady Short-Thompson, Paul A. Mongeau, Maribeth S. Metzler, Amber K. Erickson, and Jimmie D. Trent. "Cracked and Shattered Ceilings: Gender, Race, Religion, Age, and the Ideal Candidate." *American Behavioral Scientist* 54, no. 3 (2010): 163–83.

5. Trent et al., "The Ideal Candidate," 225–239; Trent, Short-Thompson, Mongeau, Metzler, Erickson, and Trent. "Cracked and Shattered Ceilings"; Warner, Benjamin R., and Mary C. Banwart. "A Multifactor Approach to Candidate Image." *Communication Studies* 67, no. 3 (2016): 163–83.

6. Trent et al., "Cracked and Shattered," 163–183.

7. Trent et al., "The Ideal Candidate," 225–239.

8. Trent et al., "Cracked and Shattered," 163-183.

9. Ibid.

10. Louden and McCauliff, "The 'Authentic Candidate,'" 96.

11. Warner and Banwart. "A Multifactor Approach."

12. Ibid.

13. Bartles, Larry M. "The Impact of Candidate Traits in American Presidential Elections." In *Leaders' Personalities and the Outcomes of Democratic Elections*, edited by Anthony King, 44–70. New York: Oxford University Press, 2002; Funk, Carolyn L. "The Impact of Scandal on Candidate Evaluations: An Experimental Test of the Role of Candidate Traits." *Political Behavior* 18 (1996): 1–24; Markus, Gregory. "Political Attitudes During an Election Year: A Report on the 1980 NES Panel Study." *American Political Science Review* 76 (1982): 538–60.

14. Fridkin, Kim L., and Patrick J. Kenney. "The Role of Candidate Traits in Campaigns." *The Journal of Politics* 73, no. 1 (2011): 61–73.

15. Trent et al., "Cracked and Shattered," 163–183.

16. See, for example, Huddy, Leonie, and Nayda Terkildsen. "Gender Stereotypes and the Perception of Male and Female Candidates." *American Journal of Political Science* 37, no. 1 (1993): 119–47.

17. *Saturday Night Live.* "First Presidential Debate: Al Gore and George W. Bush." Season 26, 2000, accessed July 19, 2018, http://www.nbc.com /saturday-night-live/video/cold-opening-gore--bush-first-debate/n11360?snl=1.

18. Men rated Bush significantly lower than Gore on intelligence ($t(747) = 7.19$, $p < .01$), knowledge ($t(747) = 6.96$, $p < .01$), and caring ($t(724) = 2.67$, $p < .01$), and they rated him significantly higher on leadership ($t(720) = 3.96$, $p < .01$). Women rated Bush significantly lower on intelligence($t(935) = 4.96$, $p < .01$), knowledge($t(934) = 7.81$, $p < .01$), caring ($t(895) = 7.50$, $p < .01$), and morals ($t(857) = 2.76$, $p < .01$).

19. A stepwise multiple regression was conducted with political party in model one and intelligence, knowledge, moral, strong leadership, and caring in model two for all election years and candidates. Male voters' ratings of Bush in 2000 were the following: model one, $R^2 = .05$, $F(1,402) = 20.34$, $p < .01$; model two, R^2 change = .42, $F(6,402) = 57.18$, $p < .0$. Female voters' ratings were the following: model one, $R^2 = .08$, $F(1,531) = 42.30$, $p < .01$; model two, R^2 change = .30, $F(6,531) = 52.38$, $p < .01$.

20. Male voters' ratings of Gore were the following: model one, $R^2 = .23$, $F(1,424) = 124.13$, $p < .01$; model two, R^2 change = .28, $F(6,424) = 70.09$, $p < .01$. Female voters' ratings of Gore were the following: model one, $R^2 = .18$, $F(1,583) = 131.53$, $p < .01$; model two, R^2 change = .34, $F(6,583) =107.74$, $p < .01$.

21. Men rated Bush as less intelligent ($t(547) = 9.09$, $p < .01$), knowledgeable ($t(547) = 6.19$, $p < .01$), and caring ($t(533) = 2.69$, $p < .01$); they rated him as more moral ($t(523) = 3.26$, $p < .01$) and as a stronger leader ($t(539) = 6.60$, $p < .01$). Women rated Bush as less intelligent ($t(610) = 7.99$, $p < .01$), knowledgeable ($t(606) = 5.80$, $p < .01$), and caring ($t(601) = 3.57$, $p < .01$) and as a stronger leader ($t(587) = 2.31$, $p < .05$).

22. Male voters' ratings of Bush in 2004 were the following: model one, R^2 = .07, $F(1,352)$ = 25.40, $p < .01$; model two, R^2 change = .62, $F(6,352)$ = 125.09, $p < .01$. Female voters' ratings of Bush in 2004 were the following: model one, R^2 = .12, $F(1,409)$ = 56.21, $p < .01$; model two, R^2 change = .48, $F(6,409)$ = 99.88, $p < .01$.

23. Male voters' ratings of Kerry in 2004 were the following: model one, R^2 = .17, $F(1,337)$ = 68.06, $p < .01$; model two, R^2 change = .42, $F(6,337)$ = 79.48, $p < .0$. Female voters' ratings of Kerry were the following: model one, R^2 = .14, $F(1,369)$ = 61.78, $p < .01$; model two, R^2 change = .41, $F(6,369)$ = 74.58, $p < .01$.

24. Men rated Obama higher on leadership ($t(984)$ = 2.96, $p < .01$), intelligence ($t(988)$ = 8.37, $p < .01$), knowledge ($t(988)$ = 3.83, $p < .01$), morality ($t(970)$ = 3.26, $p < .01$), and caring ($t(979)$ = 9.28, $p < .01$). Women rated Obama higher on leadership ($t(1286)$ = 7.10 , $p < .01$), intelligence ($t(1303)$ = 12.28, $p < .01$), knowledge ($t(1300)$ = 5.73, $p < .01$), morality ($t(1269)$ = 6.66, $p < .01$), and caring ($t(1283)$ = 11.86, $p < .01$).

25. Male voters' ratings of Obama in 2008 were the following: model one, R^2 = .13, $F(1,716)$ = 107.82, $p < .01$; model two, R^2 change = .06, $F(6,716)$ = 27.17, $p < .0$. Female voters' ratings of Obama in 2008 were the following: model one, R^2 = .10, $F(1,974)$ = 105.41, $p < .01$; model two, R^2 change = .08, $F(6,974)$ = 34.90, $p < .01$.

26. Male voters' ratings of McCain in 2008 were the following: model one, R^2 = .07, $F(1,714)$ = 51.42, $p < .01$; model two, R^2 change = .06, $F(6,714)$ = 17.03, $p < .01$. Female voters' ratings of McCain were the following: model one, R^2 = .09, $F(1,954)$ = 92.23, $p < .01$; model two, R^2 change = .04, $F(6,954)$ = 23.70, $p < .01$.

27. Women rated Obama higher on intelligence ($t(3068)$ = 10.93, $p < .01$), knowledge ($t(3068)$ = 10.56, $p < .01$), morality ($t(3068)$ = 6.22, $p < .01$), caring ($t(3068)$ = 16.15, $p < .01$), honesty ($t(3068)$ = 9.97, $p < .01$), and they rated him as a stronger leader ($t(3068)$ = 4.26, $p < .01$).

28. Men rated Obama higher on intelligence ($t(2844)$ = 6.41, $p < .01$), knowledge ($t(2844)$ = 5.31, $p < .01$), caring ($t(2844)$ = 13.87, $p < .01$), and honesty ($t(2844)$ = 5.75, $p < .01$).

29. Male voters' ratings of Obama in 2012 were the following: model one, R^2 = .34, $F(1,2790)$ = 1434.74, $p < .01$; model two, R^2 change = .45, $F(7,2790)$ = 1462.27, $p < .0$. Female voters' ratings of Obama in 2012 were the following: model one, R^2 = .35, $F(1,2974)$ = 1623.58, $p < .01$; model two, R^2 change = .44, $F(7,2974)$ = 1605.63, $p < .01$.

30. Male voters' ratings of Romney in 2012 were the following: model one, R^2 = .25, $F(1,2731)$ = 915.66, $p < .01$; model two, R^2 change = .42, $F(7,2731)$ = 782.70, $p < .01$. Female voters' ratings of Romney were the following: model one, R^2 = .29, $F(1,2867)$ = 1183.95, $p < .01$; model two, R^2 change = .40, $F(7,2867)$ = 906.10, $p < .01$.

31. Huddy, Leonie, and Nayda Terkildsen. "The Consequences of Gender Stereotypes for Women Candidates at Different Levels and Types of Office." *Political Research Quarterly* 46, no. 3 (1993): 503–25.

32. Ibid.

33. The Cronbach's alpha for instrumental traits was .74, and for warmth/expressiveness traits, it was .72.

34. Paired sample t-tests revealed that instrumental traits (M = 3.80, SD = .53) were rated as significantly more important than warmth/expressiveness traits (M = 3.35, SD = .59), $t(38) = 14.78, p < .01$.

35. See, for example, Huddy and Terkildsen. "Gender Stereotypes and the Perception," 119–147.

CHAPTER 7

1. Dolan, Kathleen. "Is There a 'Gender Affinity Effect' in American Politics? Information, Affect, and Candidate Sex in U.S. House Elections." *Political Research Quarterly* 61, no. 1 (2008): 79–89.

2. Plutzer, Eric, and John F. Zipp. "Identity Politics, Partisanship, and Voting for Women Candidates." *The Public Opinion Quarterly* 60, no. 1 (1996): 30–57.

3. Brians, Craig Leonard. "Women for Women? Gender and Party Bias in Voting for Female Candidates." *American Politics Research* 33, no. 3 (2005): 357–75.

4. Campbell, David E., and Christina Wolbrecht. "See Jane Run: Women Politicians as Role Models for Adolescents." *The Journal of Politics* 68, no. 2 (2006): 233–47; Wolbrecht, Christina, and David E. Campbell. "Leading by Example: Female Members of Parliament as Political Role Models." *American Journal of Political Science* 51, no. 4 (2007): 921–39.

5. Atkeson, Lonna Rae. "Not All Cues Are Created Equal: The Conditional Impact of Female Candidates on Political Engagement." *The Journal of Politics* 65, no. 4 (2003): 1040–61.

6. Campbell and Wolbrecht, "See Jane Run," 233–247.

7. Atkeson, "Not All Cues," 1040–1061.

8. Ibid.; Banwart, Mary C., and Kelly Winfrey. "Leadership, Gender, and Politics: Political Perceptions and Participation of Young Female Voters in a Presidential Primary." *Educational Considerations* 37, no. 1 (2009): 40–52; Hansen, Susan B. "Talking about Politics: Gender and Contextual Effects on Political Proselytizing." *The Journal of Politics* 59, no. 1 (1997): 73–103; Reingold, Beth, and Jessica Harrell. "The Impact of Descriptive Representation on Women's Political Engagement." *Political Research Quarterly* 63, no. 2 (2010): 280–94; Sapiro, Virginia, and Pamela Johnston Conover. "The Variable Gender Bias of Electoral Politics: Gender and Context in the 1992 U.S. Election." *British Journal of Political Science* 27, no. 4 (1997): 497–523; Verba, Sidney, Nancy Burns, and Kay Lehman Scholzman. "Knowing and Caring about Politics: Gender and Political Engagement." *The Journal of Politics* 59, no. 4 (1997): 1051–72.

9. Stepwise multiple regression revealed that both gender group identification and sex-role beliefs were significant predictors of gender homophily. Model one tested gender group identification ($\beta = -.50, R^2 = .25, F(1,358) = 118.877, p < .01$),

and model two tested group identification (β =−.48) and sex-role beliefs (β = .16, R^2 = .28, $F(1, 358)$ = 67.99, p < .01, R^2 change = .03).

10. Stepwise multiple regression revealed that both gender group identification and sex-role beliefs were significant predictors of preferring a same-sex candidate. Model one tested gender group identification (β = .38, R^2 = .25, $F(1,358)$ = 58.44, p < .01), and model two tested group identification (β =−.39) and sex-role beliefs ((β =−.20, R^2 = .18, $F(1, 358)$ = 38.81, p < .01, R^2 change = .04).

11. A one-way MANOVA was conducted to determine the effect of ideology-identification group on gender-candidate homophily scores and preference for same-sex candidates. Significant differences were found among the three groups, Wilkes's λ = .82, $F(2, 702)$ = 6.16, p < .00, η^2 = .10. One-way ANOVAs were conducted as follow-up tests on the dependent variables, and the LSD method was used to control for family-wise error. The ANOVAs revealed significant differences between the three groups on the mean gender-candidate homophily $F(2,356)$ = 27.25, p < .001; "see the world" $F(2,356)$ = 16.65, p < .001; "concerned with issues" $F(2,356)$ = 21.15, p < .001; "share my vales" $F(2,356)$ = 29.74, p < .001; "in touch with my problems" $F(2,356)$ = 21.25, p < .001; "had experiences similar" $F(2,356)$ = 9.68, p < .001; "vote for candidates of my gender group" $F(2,356)$ = 12.30, p < .001.

12. Conover, Patricia J. "Feminists and the Gender Gap." *The Journal of Politics* 50, no. 4 (1988): 985–1010; Manza, Jeff, and Clem Brooks. "The Gender Gap in U.S. Presidential Elections: When? Why? Implications?" *The American Journal of Sociology* 103, no. 5 (1998): 1235–66; Rosenthal, Cindy Simon. "The Role of Gender in Descriptive Representation." *Political Research Quarterly* 48, no. 3 (1995): 599–611.

13. Thomas, Sue, and Jean Reith Schroedel. "The Significance of Social and Institutional Expectations." In *Rethinking Madam President: Are We Ready for a Women in the White House?* edited by Lori Cox Han and Caroline Heldman, 43–67. Boulder, CO: Lynne Rienner Publishers, 2007.

14. Eagly, Alice H., and Steven J. Karau. "Role Congruity Theory of Prejudice toward Female Leaders." *Psychological Review* 109, no. 3 (2002): 573–95.

15. Ibid.; Garcia-Retamero, Rocio, and Esther Lopez-Zafra. "Prejudice against Women in Male-Congenial Environments: Perceptions of Gender Role Congruity in Leadership." *Sex Roles* 55 (2006): 51–61; Ritter, Barbara A., and Janice D. Yoder. "Gender Differences in Leader Emergence Persist Even for Dominant Women: An Updated Confirmation of Role Congruity Theory." *Psychology of Women Quarterly* 28 (2004): 187–93.

16. Alexander, Deborah, and Kristi Anderson. "Gender as a Factor in the Attribution of Leadership Traits." *Political Research Quarterly* 46, no. 3 (1993): 527–45; Dolan, Kathleen. "How the Public Views Women Candidates." In *Women and Elective Office: Past, Present, and Future*, edited by Sue Thomas and Clyde Wilcox, 41–59. New York: Oxford University Press, 2005; Fridkin, Kim L., and Patrick J. Kenney. "The Role of Gender Stereotypes in U.S. Senate Campaigns." *Politics & Gender* 5, no. 3 (2009): 301–24; Huddy, Leonie, and Nayda Terkildsen. "Gender Stereotypes and the Perception of Male and Female Candidates." *American*

Journal of Political Science 37, no. 1 (1993): 119–47; Kahn, Kim Fridkin. "Does Gender Make a Difference? An Experimental Examination of Sex Stereotypes and Press Patterns in Statewide Campaigns." *American Journal of Political Science* 38, no. 1 (1994): 162–195.

17. Huddy, Leonie, and Nayda Terkildsen. "The Consequences of Gender Stereotypes for Women Candidates at Different Levels and Types of Office." *Political Research Quarterly* 46, no. 3 (1993): 503–25.

18. Huddy and Terkildsen, "Gender Stereotypes and the Perception," 119–147.

19. Alexander and Anderson, "Gender as a Factor," 527–545; Dolan, "How the Public Views Women," 41–59; Kahn, "Does Gender Make a Difference," 162–196; Matland, Richard E., and David C. King. "Women as Candidates in Congressional Elections." In *Women Transforming Congress*, edited by Cindy Simon Rosenthal, 119–42. Norman: University of Oklahoma Press, 2002; Sanbonmatsu, Kira, and Kathleen Dolan. "Do Gender Stereotypes Transcend Party?" *Political Research Quarterly* 62, no. 3 (2009): 485–94; Thomas and Schroedel, "The Significance of Social," 43–67.

20. McDermott, Monika L. "Race and Gender Cues in Low-Information Elections." *Political Research Quarterly* 51, no. 4 (1998): 898–918.

21. Alexander and Anderson, "Gender as a Factor," 527–545.

22. Koch, Jeffery W. "Do Citizens Apply Gender Stereotypes to Infer Candidates' Ideological Orientations?" *The Journal of Politics* 62, no. 2 (2000): 414–29.

23. Dolan, "How the Public Views Women," 41–59; Dolan, Kathleen. "Women as Candidates in American Politics: The Continuing Impact of Sex and Gender." In *Political Women and American Democracy*, edited by Carol Wolbrecht, Karen Beckwith, and L. Baldez, 110–27. Cambridge: Cambridge University Press, 2008; Huddy and Terkildsen, "Gender Stereotypes and the Perception," 119–147; Sanbonmatsu and Dolan, "Do Gender Stereotypes Transcend Party?" 485–494.

24. Matland and King, "Women as Candidates," 119–142; King, David C., and Richard E. Matland. "Sex and the Grand Old Party: An Experimental Investigation of the Effect of Candidate Sex on Support for a Republican Candidate." *American Politics Research* 31, no. 6 (2003): 595–612.

25. McDermott, "Race and Gender Cues," 898–918.

26. Sanbonmatsu and Dolan, "Do Gender Stereotypes Transcend Party?" 485–494.

27. Matland and King, "Women as Candidates," 119–142.

28. Hernson, Paul S., J. Celeste Lay, and Atiya Kai Stokes. "Women Running 'as Women': Candidate Gender, Campaign Issues, and Voter-Targeting Strategies." *The Journal of Politics* 65, no. 1 (2003): 244–55.

29. Fridkin and Kenney, "The Role of Gender Stereotypes," 3013324.

30. Kahn, "Does Gender Make a Difference?" 162–196.

31. Dolan, "How the Public Views Women," 41459; Dolan, "Is There a 'Gender Affinity Effect," 79–89.

32. The Cronbach's alpha for the ratings of the male candidate were the following: economic issues, .89; compassion issues, .91; and military/foreign affairs issues,

.93. Cronbach's alphas for ratings of the female candidate were the following: economic issues, .90; compassion issues, .92; and military/foreign affairs issues, .91.

33. The Cronbach's alpha for the ratings of the male candidate were the following: instrumental traits, .79, and warmth/expressiveness traits, .75. The ratings for the female candidate were the following: instrumental traits, .77, and warmth/expressiveness traits, .85.

34. A repeated measure ANOVA revealed a significant issue effect, Wilkes's Λ = .66, $F(2,357)$ = 92.09, $p < .01$, multivariate .2 = .34. Paired sample t-tests revealed that the female candidate was rated as significantly better able to handle economic issues than both compassion issues, $t(358)$ = 2.20, $p < .05$, and military/foreign affairs issues, $t(358)$ = 13.49, $p < .01$, and significantly better able to handle compassion issues than military/foreign affairs issues, $t(358)$ = 11.78, $p < .01$.

35. A repeated measure ANOVA revealed a significant issue effect, Wilkes's Λ = .64, $F(2,357)$ = 99.90, $p < .01$, multivariate .2 = .36. Paired sample t-tests demonstrated that the male candidate was rated as significantly better able to handle economic issues than both military/foreign affairs issues, $t(358)$ = 13.15, $p < .01$, and compassion issues, $t(358)$ = 10.00, $p < .01$, and rated as better able to handle compassion issues than military/foreign affairs issues, $t(358)$ = 7.88, $p < .01$.

36. Paired sample t-tests revealed that the male candidate was rated as significantly better able to handle economic issues, $t(358)$ = 3.03, $p < .01$, and military/foreign affairs, $t(358)$ =2.74 , $p < .01$, and that the female candidate was rated as significantly better able to handle compassion issues, $t(358)$ = -2.47, $p = .014$.

37. Brians, "Women for Women?" 357–75; Dolan, "Is There a 'Gender Affinity Effect' 79–89; Kahn, "Does Gender Make a Difference? 1621195; Rosenthal, "The Role of Gender in Descriptive Representation," 599–611.

38. Dolan, "How the Public Views Women," 41-59; Fridkin, and Kenney, "The Role of Gender Stereotypes," 301,324; Huddy and Terkildsen, "Gender Stereotypes and the Perception," 119–147.

39. Kahn, "Does Gender Make a Difference? 162–195.

40. Rosenthal, "The Role of Gender in Descriptive Representation," 599–611.

41. Dolan, "How the Public Views Women," 41-59; Fridkin, and Kenney, "The Role of Gender Stereotypes," 301–324; Huddy and Terkildsen, "Gender Stereotypes and the Perception," 119–147.

42. King and Matland, "Sex and the Grand Old Party," 595-612; Matland and King, "Women as Candidates," 119–142; McDermott, "Race and Gender Cues," 898–918.

43. Paired sample t-test revealed that the female candidate was rated higher on warmth/expressiveness traits (M = 3.58, SD = .62) than instrumental traits (M = 3.38, SD = .57), $t(358)$ = 5.55, $p < .01$.

44. Alexander and Anderson, "Gender as a Factor," 527–545; Dolan, "How the Public Views Women," 41–59; Fridkin, and Kenney, "The Role of Gender Stereotypes," 301–324; Huddy and Terkildsen, "Gender Stereotypes and the Perception," 119–147.

45. Paired sample t-test revealed that the male candidate was rated significantly higher on instrumental traits (M = 3.46, SD = .59) than on warmth/expressiveness traits (M = 3.37, SD = .57), $t(358)$ = 2.92, $p < .01$.

46. Paired sample t-tests revealed that Egalitarian-Identified women rated the female candidate higher on warmth/expressiveness traits (M = 3.46, SD = .63) than on instrumental traits (M = 3.34, SD = .62), $t(175)$ = 2.40, $p < .05$. Traditional-Identified women also rated the female candidate higher on warmth/expressiveness traits (M = 3.74, SD = .63) than on instrumental traits (M = 3.49, SD = .53), $t(118)$ = 3.73, $p < .00$.

47. Individualist women rated the female candidate higher on warmth/expressiveness traits (M = 3.60, SD = .52) than on instrumental traits (M = 3.28, SD = .53), $t(63)$ = 4.32, $p < .00$. The male candidate was rated higher on instrumental traits (M = 3.46, SD = 61) than on warmth/expressiveness traits (M = 3.25, SD = .46), $t(63)$ = 2.57, $p = .01$.

48. Paired sample t-tests revealed that Egalitarian-Identified women rated the female higher on the warmth/expressiveness category, $t(175)$ = 3.51, $p < .01$, and the male candidate higher on warmth, $t(175)$ = 1.31, $p < .05$, and cautiousness, $t(175)$ = 3.36, $p < .01$.

49. Paired sample t-tests revealed that Egalitarian-Identified women rated the female candidate as coarser $t(175)$ = 1.98, $p < .05$; sterner, $t(175)$ = 3.59, $p < .01$; more aggressive, $t(175)$ = 2.38, $p < .05$; and tougher, $t(175)$ = 2.08, $p < .05$.

50. Traditional-Identified women rated the female candidate higher on warmth/expressiveness, $t(118)$ = 3.95, $p < .01$, and femininity, $t(118)$ = 12.45, $p < .01$, and sternness, $t(118)$ = 1.95, $p < .05$. They rated the male candidate as more masculine, $t(118)$ = 9.21, $p < .01$.

51. Individualist women rated the female candidate higher on the warmth/expressiveness category, $t(63)$ = 5.00, $p < .01$, and on femininity, $t(63)$ = 9.60, $p < .01$. They rated the male candidate higher on the instrumental trait category, $t(65)$ = , $p < .01$ and on masculinity, $t(65)$ = 2.46, $p < .05$.

CHAPTER 8

1. For more information, refer to Tables 1.1 and 1.2 in chapter 1. Information is collected from "The Gender Gap: Voting Choices in Presidential Elections." Center for American Women and Politics, Eagleton Institute of Politics, Rutgers University, 2017, accessed May 1, 2018, http://www.cawp.rutgers.edu/sites /default/files/resources/ggpresvote.pdf; "Party Identification and Presidential Performance Ratings." Center for American Women and Politics, Eagleton Institute of Politics, Rutgers University, 2014, accessed July 19, 2019, http://www.cawp .rutgers.edu/sites/default/files/resources/ggprtyid.pdf .

2. "Gender Differences in Voter Turnout." Center for American Women and Politics, Eagleton Institute of Politics, Rutgers University, 2017, accessed May 4, 2018, http://www.cawp.rutgers.edu/sites/default/files/resources/genderdiff.pdf.

3. "Party Identification Trends 1992–2017." *Pew Research Center*, accessed May 4, 2018, http://www.people-press.org/2018/03/20/party-identification-trends -1992-2017/#gender.

4. "State Results." *CNN Politics*, accessed May 7, 2018, https://www.cnn.com /election/2016/results/states.

5. "A Closer Look at the Gender Gap in Presidential Voting: Top Voting Issues for Men and Women." *Pew Research Center*, accessed May 6, 2016, http:// www.pewresearch.org/fact-tank/2016/07/28/a-closer-look-at-the-gender-gap-in -presidential-voting/ft_16-07-28_gendergap_420px/.

6. Ibid.

7. Clinton, Hillary. "Gun Control and National Security—October 21, 2016." Carrie Chapman Catt Center for Women and Politics Archive of Women's Political Communication, accessed July 19, 2018, https://awpc.cattcenter.iastate .edu/2017/03/21/remarks-in-cincinnati-on-gun-control-and-national-security -oct-31-2016//.

8. "Read Donald Trump's Speech on Trade." *Time*, accessed May 8, 2018, http://time.com/4386335/donald-trump-trade-speech-transcript/.

9. "A Closer Look at the Gender Gap in Presidential Voting: Gender Differences in Views of Trump's and Clinton's Empathy, Judgement." *Pew Research Center*, accessed May 6, 2016, http://www.pewresearch.org/fact-tank/2016/07/28 /a-closer-look-at-the-gender-gap-in-presidential-voting/ft_16-7-29-gender33/.

10. "A Gender Gap in Views of Hillary Clinton, Even among Her Supporters." *Pew Research Center*, accessed May 7, 2018, http://www.pewresearch.org /fact-tank/2016/11/05/a-gender-gap-in-views-of-hillary-clinton-even-among-her -supporters/.

11. Rogers, Katie. "White Women Helped Elect Donald Trump." *New York Times*, November 9, 2016, accessed May 8, 2018, https://www.nytimes.com /2016/12/01/us/politics/white-women-helped-elect-donald-trump.html.

12. Newton-Small, Jay. "Why So Many Women Abandoned Hillary Clinton." *Time*, November 10, 2016, accessed May 8, 2018, http://time.com/4566748 /hillary-clinton-firewall-women/.

13. "Exit Polls." *CNN*, accessed May 7, 2018, https://www.cnn.com/election /2016/results/exit-polls.

Index

Page numbers followed by *t* indicate tables and *f* indicate figures.

About the Author

Kelly L. Winfrey, PhD, is an assistant professor at the Greenlee School of Journalism and Communication and coordinator of research and outreach at the Carrie Chapman Catt Center for Women and Politics at Iowa State University. Her research focuses on the content and effect of political campaign messaging. She has published several academic journal articles and book chapters related to women as voters and as candidates.